# INDUSTRIAL SECURITY MANAGEMENT

# INDUSTRIAL SECURITY MANAGEMENT

**Colonel (Dr.) R P Sharma**
Director
Distance Learning Education
Indian Institute of Modern Management
(Pune)

Publishing Globally
**NEW AGE INTERNATIONAL (P) LIMITED, PUBLISHERS**
New Delhi • Bangalore • Chennai • Cochin • Guwahati
Hyderabad • Kolkata • Lucknow • Mumbai
Visit us at www.newagepublishers.com

Published by New Age International (P) Ltd., Publishers
First Edition: 2004
**Reprint:** 2013



**BRANCHES**

- **Bangalore** 37/10, 8th Cross (Near Hanuman Temple), Azad Nagar, Chamarajpet Bangalore-560 018, Tel.: (080) 26756823, Telefax: 26756820 **E-mail: bangalore@newagepublishers.com**
- **Chennai** 26, Damodaran Street, T. Nagar, Chennai-600 017, Tel.: (044) 24353401 Telefax: 24351463, **E-mail: chennai@newagepublishers.com**
- **Cochin** CC-39/1016, Carrier Station Road, Ernakulam South, Cochin-682 016 Tel.: (0484) 2377004, Telefax: 4051303 **E-mail: cochin@newagepublishers.com**
- **Guwahati** Hemsen Complex, Mohd. Shah Road, Paltan Bazar, Near Starline Hotel Guwahati-781 008, Tel.: (0361) 2513881, Telefax: 2543669 **E-mail: guwahati@newagepublishers.com**
- **Hyderabad** 105, 1st Floor, Madhiray Kaveri Tower, 3-2-19, Azam Jahi Road Nimboliadda, Hyderabad-500 027, Tel.: (040) 24652456 Telefax: 24652457, **E-mail: hyderabad@newagepublishers.com**
- **Kolkata** RDB Chambers (Formerly Lotus Cinema) 106A, 1st Floor S.N. Banerjee Road, Kolkata-700 014, Tel.: (033) 22273773 Telefax: 22275247, **E-mail: kolkata@newagepublishers.com**
- **Lucknow** 16-A, Jopling Road, Lucknow-226 001, Tel.: (0522) 2209578, 4045297 Telefax: 2204098, **E-mail: lucknow@newagepublishers.com**
- **Mumbai** 142C, Victor House, Ground Floor, N.M. Joshi Marg, Lower Parel Mumbai-400 013, Tel.: (022) 24927869, Telefax: 24915415 **E-mail: mumbai@newagepublishers.com**
- **New Delhi** 22, Golden House, Daryaganj, New Delhi-110 002 Tel.: (011) 23262368, 23262370, Telefax: 43551305 **E-mail: sales@newagepublishers.com**

**ISBN: 978-81-224-1519-3**

**₹ 199.00**

**C-12-10-6638**

Printed in India at Mohanlal Printers, Delhi.
Typeset at Le-Studio, Delhi.

**PUBLISHING FOR ONE WORLD**
**NEW AGE INTERNATIONAL (P) LIMITED, PUBLISHERS**
7/30 A, Daryaganj, New Delhi - 110002
Visit us at **www.newagepublishers.com**

# Preface

Due to the increasing terrorist activities in and around our country, which has severely effected our all segments of living in peace and harmony, has created a constant threat to all personnel and materials of our society.

It was a long felt need among the Industrial and other commercial Organizations, to acquire a book containing various facets of modern Industrial and Specialized Security Management. During the last two decades our Management, Scholars and GURUS have undertaken indepth studies of almost all disciplines of Business Management. But unfortunately, the arena of Industrial security and especially the safety of personnel remained untouched, with the result the Industrial security was only confined to the Main Entrance and Exit of the Factory or Office Gates.

With the rapid globalization of industries and introduction of numerous Electronic Gadgets into the vast field of security (both in Internal and External Systems), it has become very essential to change our entire strategy and thought process in relation to existing safety and specialized security required at various Industrial Houses, Airports, Hotels, Banks and Hospitals, etc. Security and safety of commercial premises can't be left at the mercy of unlawful elements who on number of occasions have attempted to hold Industries, innocent society and even whole nation at ransom.

The dastardly incident of 11 September 2001 in New York, Washington and Piltsberg saw the world in a state of stunned disbelief at the most audacious act of terrorism ever committed in the history. In a devilishly brilliant plan designed for unimaginable destruction, the terrorists hijacked four planes and used three of these as suicide bombers into America's most prominent and almost invincible Twin Towers and Pentagon Headquarters within a span of 60 minutes. In order to safeguard our aviation industry and ensure safe air travel, it is absolutely essential that a sincere and concerted effort is urgently needed to boost the existing lipservice in the name of airport security. The unimaginable attack on our Parliament House at New Delhi on

13 December 2001 and ghastly shoot-out at Akshardham Temple in Ahmedabad on 24 October 2002 are very fresh incidents which itself speak about suitability and effectiveness of existing system of our security and safety of VIPS and general public. We must include all available modern electronic gadgets, adopt latest strategies, global concepts and carryout detail co-ordination in organizing our entire Security and safety Management.

An endeavour has been made through the book in the form of a concerted efforts to highlight and suggest various measures for all sizes of commercial/ corporate houses and various organizations to reorganize the Industrial security and safety setup in their respective premises. I have no doubt, this will change the entire concept, thought process, effectiveness of prevailing Security Management and will prove as a tremendous motivating force for achieving their cherished and desired goals by countering unlawful elements belonging to various terrorist outfits in a most effective manner.

Pune — Colonel (Dr) R.P. Sharma, (Retd.)
September 2003 — Ph.D.

# Contents

# 1

# Violence: Historical Background

## INTRODUCTION

Historically and culturally, India has been known as a land of non-violence. We have a vast storehouse of culture and ethnic affinity which has sustained our multireligious, multiracial and multilinguistic society since times immemorial. The Saints, the Gurus, all the religious heads have always preached non-violence. In recent times, this was strengthened by Mahatma Gandhi's philosophical teachings. We won our independence mainly through non-violent means. As a secular state, comprising different casts, creeds and religions tied together by a singular cultural heritage, we have now arrived at the threshold of mistrust among each other.

### The Ubiquity of Violence

'Violence' is as old as the world. In cosmogonies, mythologies and legends, it is presented as something linked with the beginning of the history, always attendant upon the deeds of the heroes and innovators. It is noteworthy that violence, which is so much a subject of hot discussion today, had never been taken as a theme for the meditation of great thinkers of, neither the Western nor Eastern, before the nineteenth century. It had to wait for the modern society to dwell on to it. If we succeed in perceiving the reasons for its emergence and its present upsurge, then we will gain more insight into its true nature. Also, it might enable us to take an objective view of the violence that surrounds the society and to assess the threat it poses to our entire nation in order to seek appropriate and timely remedies. The phenomenon of violence, of late, seems to have gone deep rooted into our society and it is increasing fast with each passing day. We must realize, unless we restore and rebuild amity and national solidarity it will not only impede the growth of our national development but will also threaten the very existence of our secular state image globally.

The founders of our constitution of India had kept the Indian heritage in their mind while framing it. The preamble to the constitution describes India as a sovereign, socialist, secular Democratic Republic and secures to its all citizens liberty of thought expression, belief, faith and worship. Articles 25 to 30, in particular, guarantee to everyone the right to freedom of religion freedom of conscience and the right to freely profess, practice and propagate religion. With all these in hand, our society commenced her march towards progress with a noble background and democratic futuristic outlook.

## Genesis and Growth of Violence in Various States

The recent fury of violence in Srinagar Valley, Gujarat, Assam, Punjab and Maharashtra, etc. has brought the country into an analytical focus with the interaction between religion and politics. This unholy alliance is, of course, related directly to the century old colonial heritage in all facts of life, particularly so in the realm of ideology. This analogy is closely linked with our social values. These are deeply complicated with multiple faces. The continuation of senseless and gruesome violence in J&K and Gujarat has shaken the entire nation and has invited worldwide attention. However, these developments are not totally isolated from the events taking place in other parts of country. It is strongly felt and has been amply proved that fundamentalist's conspiracy is the main force acting behind these events in India by way of fanning extremist violence in especially Srinagar Valley and in other states.

Mohammed Ali Jinnah, The leader of the Muslim League, placed the demand for a separate state for the Muslims on the ground that the Indian Muslim Constituted a separate nation and therefore, must have a separate country. The same theory of separate state for Kashmiri Muslims is being advocated by spreading state wide violence and unrest in Kashmir by religious fundamentalists and political leaders with vested interests.

# 2

# Violence in Society

## THE PROBLEM—ITS ORIGIN AND IMPORTANCE

Various scholars and a number of eminent journalists have probed deep enough into the venomous ocean of extremism, the background, causes, action, reactions and connected prevention measures have accounted for voluminous theories in varied disciplines of militancy. As per 'Encyclopedia Britannica' the extremism for a layman can be defined as, 'the systematic use of terror (such as kidnapping, killing and bombing, etc.) as a means of forcing some political objectives. In the same context it can be safely presumed that violence, denoting intimidation by threat, unlawful exercise of physical force or intensity of force, efforts and feeling, etc. following the similar path in society as that of terrorism. When violence engulfs the whole society, involving largescale movements by particular groups of people professing similar ideology, it gets converted into senseless and mass violence.

Of all the unrealized hopes for the twentieth century the failure to contain mass violence, much less to eradicate it, has been among the saddest. The score of years of the century have witnessed manifestations of violence in every field and the sad killings of the countless people by militant violence in Srinagar Valley, Assam, Bihar and Andhra Pradesh, etc. caused a river of blood and tears by innocent affected kith and kin. Throughout history such violence had been regarded as the most terrible experience dividing communities with avoidable rifts, even separating families with heart bleeding wounds. However, this understanding is being taken at low key, in some portions of the society by handful of interested people.

With the changing social values and a mass awakening caused by the improved media, the relationship between the society and our defence, police and other paramilitary forces have ushered into a new era. For all these law enforcing personnel maintenance of morale is a very strong phenomenon in countering the militancy and other antisocial elements. Leadership at all level must strive to ensure that demoralization does not creep into the welfare measures of subordinates. We must safeguard against the breaches of security at various places and take all precautionary measures to overcome the subversive plans of the extremists.

## PATTERN OF VIOLENCE

The pattern of present violence in various states particularly Srinagar Valley is based on a confused mix of region, religion, economy and political motivation which is beyond the controlled imagination of people with vested interest. The visible contours of violence are deeply penetrating into our society in various parts of the country may be North East Frontiers, Assam South, Gujarat and last but not the least among all Kashmiri Muslim youths. In these region most of the people involved in executing violence are drawn mainly from economically backward and uneducated low castes. Their economic and social frustration has been duly exploited by religious and political fundamentalists for their own purpose and benefits.

While analyzing the pattern of violence, one must keep in mind the vast definition—as per New Oxford Encyclopedic Dictionary is which, denotes "intimidation by the threat, unlawful exercise of physical force and or intensity of force, efforts and feelings, etc".

While studying pattern of violence we must see how mass media has established a very firm base in our modern society, with the result almost every member of the society has managed an easy access to all forms of audio/ video news broadcast and newspapers, etc. Above all, the detail reporting of violence by various newspapers has often been counter productive. Besides that the glorifying of all sorts of crime and violence in films have been instigating younger generation for experimenting one, even may be as mere adventure. Such incidents of violence in our society, have been on increase in UP, Assam, West Bengal, Andhra Pradesh, Maharashtra and J&K.

The advocates of violence are motivated by short and long term objectives, their effort is to create a general disorder by adopting mass violence and create a fear psychosis in the society. This act at times invites a backlash, e.g. post Godhra violence in Gujarat which might lead to complete alienation of one group and hence seem to fulfill their long term goal. The weapon of terror is being used to intimidate people from all walks of life to move along with their purpose of separatism by shaking fait in state administration and discrediting the functional competence of state machinery. Pattern of violence, as prevalent in our society, can broadly be classified into various categories of socio-economic class conflicts, religious, communal and politically motivated.

## RELIGIOUS AND COMMUNAL PATTERN

The mass violence, which has engulfed number of states with its ugly pattern has been leaving adequate indicators that its two broad bases are religion and communal hatred towards other people in the society. The uneducated youth belonging to rural areas, who is further cornered with the problem of unemployment, is an easy prey for the fanatic religious preachers. The seed of hatred with explicit religious overtones are sown in their mind, as innocent people of rural background are not capable of visualizing the dangerous game of vested interests. The complete motivation training has major ideological contents which are founded in the bed rock of religious fanaticism.

The mass violence, erupting through religious and communal hatred, spreads in the form of arson, looting of personnel and public property and murders of innocent people. Recently, the main pattern followed by extremist is mainly the killing of innocent persons including women and children in buses, trains and in other busy localities. The extremists probably have innovated a workable pattern of operation in small and separate group and gangs including suicide bombers. These small group have assigned separate mission by their controlling Headquarters. This modus operandi provides them with additional precision, high mobility and desired maneuverability for executing their allotted tasks. The area of operational responsibility assigned to a group or gang is not delineated by any particular region in the state but at times crosses both state and national boundaries.

The level of indoctrination of these extremists had reached an unimagined peak under the unchallenged self-style leadership of Head of various terrorist groups. Stephen Segaller, in his writing, 'Invisible Armies-Terrorism in the 1990s' has stated, "In the heart of every terrorist action, there is a cause, a political goal, a perceived injustice or denial of liberty that is as concrete to the activist as any Prime Minister's notion of justice or freedom, no political rhetoric can disguise this and no opponent of terrorism should forget this?" The initial objective is what ex-Britain's Prime Minister Margaret Thatcher said, "The oxygen of publicity" for the cause. This is followed by an extreme escalation in demands and an attempt to terrorise the local peace loving population into covert support within the community for fear of retaliation. The next stage is fund raising, through extortion, bank robberies and foreign resources. One international terrorist expert says, 'the existence of this wider theoretical community often allows terrorists a sense of legitimacy that they are taking up the cudgels on behalf of others whom opportunity or lack of courage prevents from doing so'. The subsequent stage is the setting up a parallel administration to settle local disputes, dispense justice and collect taxes. This is followed by random, indiscriminate killings to pressurize the state enemy into some sort of compromise.

## POLITICAL VIOLENCE

After having analyzed the pattern of religious and communal violence, let us devote some time to the study of political violence. In our society we have seen that policemen, employers, shopkeepers and indeed even few security forces personnel on duty engage in some sort of violence. The fundamental suggestion, which has a considerable history. Is not Security Forces or policemen use more than the force allowed by their legal powers? Or that the state engages in war and will use its defence forces against the enemy or revolution. Political violence enables the man who sets the bomb to reply to those who condemn him that they too, engage in violence, perhaps the violence which most of us might describe as unfair, victimization or degradation.

Whatever sympathies one may have with political intentions in the various field of controversy, one may decline to take up the recommended usage or to be bounded by the intended prohibition. If one sets out to find a clear and unimpending pattern of political violence in society it might be pretty exhaustive to explore the base, its causes and operational environment including its propagators.

An act of violence, we may briefly say, is a use of considerable or destroying force against people or things, a use of force that offends against a norm. This is not to presuppose, obviously, that in one's final verdict an act of violence must go wrong. There is not much to choose between this several quoted by eminent writers from various reputed sources as the 'Oxford English Dictionary'. "There an act of violence is one of the physical force, inflicting injury or damage on persons or property". It will be as well to have inmind some extent or magnitude of political violence. While studying it one will have to bear in mind and what follows is roughly the level of violence with which we have become familiar in various part of Indian States. To put the matter differently, if no more, precisely every member of the society will have in mind campaign of violence but not violence at the level of civil war. Nor, of course shall we be concerned with war between nations, which does not fall under the definition of political violence.

Finally, by way of preliminaries, it may be worth pointing out that more will be in questions than exactly the violence which has been most common during the past decade. There can be violence directed to other ends than those with which we are most familiar. We shall be concerned with political violence generally which is to say both actual and possible violence.

The pattern of political violence, initially, is planned in the urban areas by misguide and frustrated educated youth. But the city violence can't assume any decisive role, as it is subordinate to the fundamental struggle being executed in the country side. It has from the military point of view a strategic value: it immobilizes thousands of state soldiers in unrewarding task of protection of personnel and property. No government can protect everything and everyone at every where and constantly. The extremists can strike at anyone any where at any time. Such uncontrolled violence makes every incident seems like an exception to the rules that ought to apply. At times statecraft combines moral political and financial considerations in a complicated game compromise and the operations of compromise allow terrorists to feel that they have a chance creating through their armed propaganda and violent persuasion.

Most governments prefer to explain mass violence or extremism backwards, taking the carnage and destruction as evidence of psychopathic tendencies. Instead, they should regard violent perpetrator's act as a logical step, even if one that inspires revulsion, towards tangible political gains. But all that is of no use unless the political will to curb mass violence exist in the government machinery. Neither can the government afford to abandon the political option, nor the extremist should unduly exert pressure on the state for if logical demands in the garb of violence. During 1984 an international seminar was conducted in Canada. Pointed out: "If the terrorist survive the security response to their use of random violence, they will begin to enjoy a grandiose sense of their power, believing themselves to be the enemies and equal of the state. "The battle against international terrorism has shown that the prevention of political violence is of the greatest psychological value. That means the existence of a streamlined and sophisticated intelligence system to counter the mess violence in society. As Jean Pierre Bourdier of the anti-terrorist French Intelligence brigade says, it is not by putting a guard in front of the door that you are going to stop the bomber from letting off his bomb. The thing is to infiltrate the terrorist's new work and to stop the terrorist before he plants his bomb.

Any democracy, by its very definition poses its own restrictions on the battle against political violence. The challenge to a democracy is to find effective measures without an acceptable diminution of civil liberty, or as FBI's William

Webster puts it, "Without creating the Orwellian police state that civil libertarians have warned about". Nevertheless in the scenario of political violence any democratic government by retaining faith in its established democratic institutions, even at the cost of failing to extinguish terrorism altogether, the state reinforces public confidence in its system of government and publicity asserts its moral and practical superiority.

The glaring example of pattern of political violence in Punjab was the statement and counter statements issued by the Chief Minister S.S. Barnala and Mr J.F. Riberiro. Both of them had claimed that innocent killings and terrorism was at low ebb during their tenure. In fact, centre was trying to appease the farmer lobby in Punjab to isolate the extremists whose cause gets a natural boost during periods of calamity.

## DEMOCRATIC VIOLENCE

If we look at contemporary writing on political violence in the hope of finding cogent argument, either for or against it, and if we are not too disposed to take aside, we are unlikely to be satisfied. This pessimism certainly does not derive only from the writings looked at the first two pattern of violence. There is also something else which cut across some of these pattern of violence. It will be valuable and considered essential in any effective argumentation, to consider how democratic violence is related to other two pattern of violence.

Many of these who condemn violence do so on the ground that it is undemocratic. Many of its apologists are in some higher reasons for what they accept, implicitly or explicitly, to be undemocratic. The relationship between some violence and the arguments for democracy, will then enter into a characterization of one important type of political violence. It is worthwhile to clarify that violence does render system less democratic and create confusion and uncertainty in the society. We all believe that democracy and violence somehow conflict. It is important, however, to know exactly, where they do and where do not conflict or always conflict.

A lesser reason for clarifying the proposition about the democratic violence is to establish the weakness of unreflective and extravagant claims to the effect that acts of violence themselves destroy democracy. In an analytic view it causes deep scar on the society's economic status than on the democratic system prevailing in the society. It is also unreflective, incidentally, to succumb to the generalization that political violence always poses a significant threat to the growth and continuation of the society and government. The supposition here is that violence, however, it may conflict at some moment with this or that part of the system always carries the significant threat of an unpredictable sequence of event ending in the destruction of the system. Collapses of democracies have as often been brought about by their own passivities as by democratic violence.

# 3

# Industrial Security—General

India, after gaining independence in 1947, has been progressing by leaps and bounds in the field of industrial growth. It is mainly due to foresight and vision of late Shri Jawaharlal Nehru, the first Prime Minister, who was able to predict that any nation which dreams of economic and social growth must have sound planning of its industries. Today, as a result of that great leader's vision, India occupies a prominent and respectable place among the developing countries of the world. It is an established fact that a nation is recognized as per its industrial growth and related production which in turn caters for the requirements of own people besides producing surpluses. At the time of setting up an organization the industrialist take care of various areas of management and try to recruit the best trained personnel in various disciplines of Production, Finance, Sales and Marketing, HRD and Labour, etc.

Lately, it has been noticed that the general awareness regarding need for security has occupied a place for concern in the mind of corporate world. However, "Industrial Security" is yet to be regarded as one of main Management Functions". Although it is well known that most of the developed countries in the world are continuously trying for improvement in order to counter the new challenges to security management. As per the available definition in the Industrial Disputes Act, the "Industry" has been defined in generic sense as:

- All manufacturing units
- Agriculture farms
- All commercial organizations
- Other miscellaneous units, i.e. colleges, schools, hospitals, etc.

As per the dictionary the word "Security" is derived from the French word 'cura' means care. In the similar scenario, if we analyze, industrial security means taking care of all personnel, documents and movable/immovable assets in an industry. In the larger term Industrial security must provide complete safeguard from all kinds of hazards, losses and threats, be it internal or from external sources. Considering the above mentioned definitions, industrial security may be well defined as "All actions and or measures adopted to ensure the fullest possible protection for an Industrial Organization" which may arise from any one or more of the following.

- Likely damage, destruction and or other crimes.
- Industrial espionage and sabotage.
- Subversion.
- Miscellaneous risks and threats to lives and property.

If we glance towards the functioning of the small industries it is amply clear that the basic danger arise from thefts, robberies criminal tresspassing, pilferages,fraud and fire, etc. however, in the middle and large segments more danger and problems arise out of strikes, agitations, riots, industrial espionage and other law and order situations. A timely appreciation and correct vision of the potential threats and dangers on the part of alert management is bound to result in a greater realization of the need for an effective industrial security requirements.

In the present society, for industries it is practically not possible to depend fully on local and other public utility authorities for their various timely assistance. Non-availability of these services like police can be easily attributed to their daily increasing commitments with VIP security, maintenance of law and order and other essential duties arising out of fast changing social values. Therefore, for management it becomes imperative to rely on their own security resources to ensure smooth functioning of their industries. Basically, from Industrial point of view the security can be considered in four basic categories.

- Preventive security
- Protective security
- Detective security
- Punitive security.

Sometimes due to lack of experience some management consider that Industrial security encompasses only control of entry and exit of personnel and material (including vehicular movement) at the main gate/gates. In fact, it is a great mistake because of it at times management have to pay a heavy price in terms of losses and or damages. This concept of Industrial security is totally incorrect in the modern technical and most competitive market. Senior corporates and experienced Industrialist realize that modern concept of industrial security has vastly changed from main gate to production lines, HRD, accounts and finance, material stores, Information Technology and including Research and development, etc. It will be out of place if we don't include aspects of labour problems and industrial relations into the vast arena of industrial management.

During the course of planning of industrial security, the director/chief security officer or security officer as the case may be, must ensure that the input level of security resources must be commensurate with the anticipated or real threats and security hazards faced by the organization. Economy of efforts should always take priority with Head of security while planning resources and devices.

Keeping in view all the above factors relating to industrial security management an endeavour have been made in the following chapters to provide, at various levels, the basic and an adequate information for an organization or an individual in-charge of industrial security. The information given includes all the advanced modern devices being pressed into the security service and their best use so that industrial security can provide their share in achieving laid down goals by an industrial organization. It must be always remembered that industrial security basically starts from the perimeter and gates and travels deep right into the core of an industry.

# 4

# Perspective of Security and Safety in Society

When we glance through the shaping of modern history and struggle of a human being from Stone Age into present modern society, the '*security*' has always walked hand in hand with the human being. During the early stage a man used to cover his cave with the help of a huge stone to guard himself from wild animals. Later with the help of wooden logs and bamboos he learned to live with his family at an elevated platform which gave him a sense of security against his rivals. He used ladders to climb into his residence and kept wild animals away by lighting fire at night. As the time passed man used hidden places and caves, etc. to keep his treasures and other valuable belongings. The first known recorded law body called "Hammurabic Code" was established in 1700 BC. It provided legal guidelines for trade, commerce, agriculture and various other professions.

As the history goes the Greeks took the lead by establishing a professional security force which was responsible to protect personnel and property. Caesar Augustus, the emperor of ancient Rome, established the first centralized security force called "The Praetorian Guards" consequently it lead to emergence of urban cohorts which were widely used to maintain the urban security systems.

## EMERGENCE OF INDUSTRIAL SECURITY GROWTH UPTILL EIGHTEENTH CENTURY

In the early days when people had feudal system of government, they were staying in the various groups of their own community. As per their separate locations of villages and towns their community laws were responsible for the entire security. From here the concept of municipal police department was introduced. The William, Duke of Normandy introduced various methods of law reforms and other rules of law enforcing agencies, in 1285 an important system of confinement, presently called curfew and night patrolling was introduced for guarding important entry and exit points at valuable property. England took the lead and in 1500 AD a variety of Police Force and agencies were organized.

Then, came an era of industrial revolution, which posed various security problems. Large number of people from rural areas started moving out towards urban areas in search of better security and means of living. But due to lack of education and technical expertise people started adopting various types of crimes against personnel and property. This situation gave birth to the usage of various security means for preventing theft, robberies, rapes, assault and murders. Number of paid, unpaid and volunteers were used for night and day security watchmen and constables. In 1636 in the city of Boston (USA) a regular night guard system was adopted later it was in the New York city during 1658 and in Philadelphia. It was introduced in 1700.

Slowly, the concept of business company run or owned by one or more family crept in. Here the basic security measures were adopted which were, e.g. proper locks, doors, compound wall and fencing, etc. As these were considered adequate in addition to the physical attendance of the family members. At that point of time it was felt that because of trust and mutual confidence the existing measures were sufficient for preventing theft and losses.

## AN ERA OF NINETEENTH AND TWENTIETH CENTURIES

An outright need for better security services was felt in the growing and better civilized society. During 1822, the Home Secretary of UK, Sir Robert Peel introduced the "Peelian Reforms". The very aim of Peelian Reforms was to replace various security agencies into a Unified Organization to be known as a "Metropolitan Police", Sir Robert Peel also laid down detailed guidelines for functioning of the Police Force in a better and more effectively organized body. It will be heartening to note that first electric burglar alarm was introduced by Edwin Holmes in 1858. Later the idea of a central alarm station was also introduced by Edwin Holmes which became quite popular among industries. As the pace of industrial growth was rising in, 1872, the automatic alarm signaling device was developed by Edwin Holmes, this device had capacity to respond to any breaks in the electric circuit. Similar types of devices with better modification are presently in more use. This was the year, when another development of electric vault protection system took place.

After the nineteenth century, the rapid growth of industries and fast technological developments felt the vast changes in urban society. Influx of people from all strata started flocking at industrial towns. This gave steep rise to various crimes and lawlessness in the society. In USA, during 1909, William J. Burns Inc. established the first private detective agency. During World War I in 1914, the Railway Police was formed to ensure safe transportation of material and personnel. Then came a need of a much better security agency after World War I, USA, in 1924 established and formed "The Federal Bureau of Investigation". After World War II there was a big mushrooming of security agencies in USA, during 1950 Wackenhut Cooperation introduced one of the largest Contract guards and Investigation agency.

During 1960's worldwide a steep rise was noticed in drug related crimes including assault, murder, sabotage and even espionage. With this high rate of crimes, numerous security agencies took birth and latest electronic devices and gadgetry were developed and pressed into industrial security which one can easily trace in the modern security provisions for industries. With the advent of integrated circuits, chips technology, laser sensing and above all computers have opened a pandora box in the field of electronic security devices. Use of Close Circuit TV (CCTV) and other computer controlled devices have provided tremendous technical assistance to all industrial security operators for managing a most efficient and cost effective industrial security.

## GROWTH IN INDIA—A VIEW POINT

By and large in most of the Indian industrial houses after World War II and almost up till 1960's the concept of industrial security in India was delightfully vague. The security measures were considered to be over, when management could see a watch and ward security guard at the main gate of an organization. The basic idea was to appoint a chowkidar or guard who could keep an eye on personnel and material's entry and exit point for the safety and loss prevention. Management could never visualize that besides guarding at the main gate, there were so many other avenues in an organization where security needs were also urgent and important. However, with the passage of time as the industrial management became more analytic in their approach and attained rationale thought process, they moved beyond the main gate into the factory premises, they have come out from the primitive form to more realistic approach towards industrial security. As a matter of fact, now, the security in an organization extends to material procurement, production lines, store and warehouse, outward movements and HRD activities including labour union and industrial relations.

If we glance towards the public and private sectors, it will be seen that in 1965 there were only 15 industrial houses, which had security organizations. In 1971, there were 775 industries which had security facilities. Rapid growth of our industrial houses, both public and private sectors, have necessitated the vast requirements of industrial security. The growing demand have created the numerous reputed security organizations around the country which are providing some of the best adjudged security system as per the world standards. It may be mentioned here that the security giant force called 'Central Industrial Security Force' (CISF), which provide security of a very high order to all public sector undertakings, was given President's assent on 2nd December 1968. The CISF was brought into service as a disciplined, motivated and dedicated force on 10th March 1969 by a notification issued under Clause 3 of Section 1 of the Act. But as on date one can mention with proud that more than 10,000 private security organizations are successfully operating and approximately 500 Public sectors are being provided security by the Central Industrial Security Force (CISF).

## CONCEPT OF INDUSTRIAL SECURITY

In generic terms, when we talk of security, certain ideas are formed in our mind and one starts planning for a safety circle or a safe environment. Therefore, when we define 'security' it can be imagined as—actions or measures taken to create a state of safe environment for protection of personnel and material from various perceived threats and dangers by using manpower, material and machinery. Security can be felt when one feels safe, whether you are in own home and use door bolt at night, you may be driving a two wheeler by putting on a helmet in order to protect against any accident while taking a ride in a boat or may be having a swim on a sea shore, the use of life jacket gives a sense of safety.

## IMPORTANCE OF INDUSTRIAL AND PERSONNEL SECURITY

Security, whether in personnel life or a step further when we glance through industries, the security plays a very significant and scientific role when it is called Industrial Security. Although the main role of any industry is to ensure that production is increasing every month, every quarter or at least every year. With the same analogy, if the management's primary task is to ensure quantity and quality of production, the corresponding task will be to provide safety and security to personnel and material. This action will prove as great assistance in the overall growth of organization. In any industry whether large, medium or small, the production and growth are directly related to the economic growth of the country. Small and medium industries equally play the predominant role towards the growth of large size organizations.

It is a known fact that any country's development directly depends on the progress of its industrial growth. The type and size of produced materials of all kinds are equally important for a country. The defence equipment's, arms and ammunition, automobile, cement and building material and even consumer goods, etc. have their own role to play at the national level. Thus, we can visualize that industrial security plays almost a similar role as defence forces for a country to guard against external threats and danger at our borders, a Police and Para Military Force provide safety and security to society and security against dangers, threats and crimes by ensuring law and orders. Industrial security with no legal authority from either state or centre provides the safety and sense of security to all personnel and material in an organization and assists directly in the overall growth of an industry. The importance of industrial security in an organization is similar to an important part of machinery which can improve the efficiency or ruin the complete performance of it. Management must regard the components of industrial security in the same manner as of production, sales and marketing, accounts and HRD, etc.

The aspects of recruitment, selection and judicious employment should be given a fair deal to boost their morale and motivate them to give their best for the organization. It must be understood that industrial security's role of is two folds—firstly, it serves as an important organ in the overall industrial growth without getting the industries involved in miscellaneous types of interference posing as hurdles in the progress, secondly, economic growth provides a nation better society and well developed all round institutions for the uplift of society and citizens. It is a firm belief that strikes, labour problems and lockout generally take place where an organization is not producing well and not able to look after the welfare of its personnel. Sometimes it is argued among corporate world, that money and other resources spent on industrial security could be saved by utilizing facilities of general insurance companies and already existing Fire Brigade, etc. to confront any threat/danger. But if one analyze the whole scenario by reviewing in detail, it stands out that there is no alternative for an efficient and cost effective industrial security. Hence, here it can be logically concluded that judicious employment of industrial security service is most important for the growth of industry and indirectly even for the nation.

# 5

# Progressive Path of Commercial and Personnel Security

During the last two decades there have been a sudden spurt in industrial crimes, which has forced the corporate world in the industries to pay more attention to this aspect of security. Growing tendency of espionage, sabotage and fast rising terrorism coupled with latest technologies, equipments and scientifically developed gadgetry, which have provided new dimension to the modern educated criminals. In such a scenario it is very prudent that industries security services modernize themselves for being almost at par to counter the challenges faced by them. Now there is always a question mark as far as availability of resources are concerned in the countries who 'Have' and others "Who Have Not". Therefore, there is always an unbridged gap even in the technology and its related resources at the disposal of industries to be used for security. Nevertheless, if management has to face modern criminal techniques, it is never too late to adopt better, effective and an efficient pattern of security services in the industry to ensure rapid growth as per plan.

## SECURITY AND SAFETY SETUP IN AN ORGANIZATION

Having studied in detail the industrial setup of our country, it is not correct to visualize a set pattern of commercial security in all the industries. Generally the security organization will vary as per the size and functioning of an industry. However, under normal pattern of functioning the security organization should consist of security manager/officer or in a large organization a director of security or chief security officer could be the head of industrial security. The suggested organization should be as under.

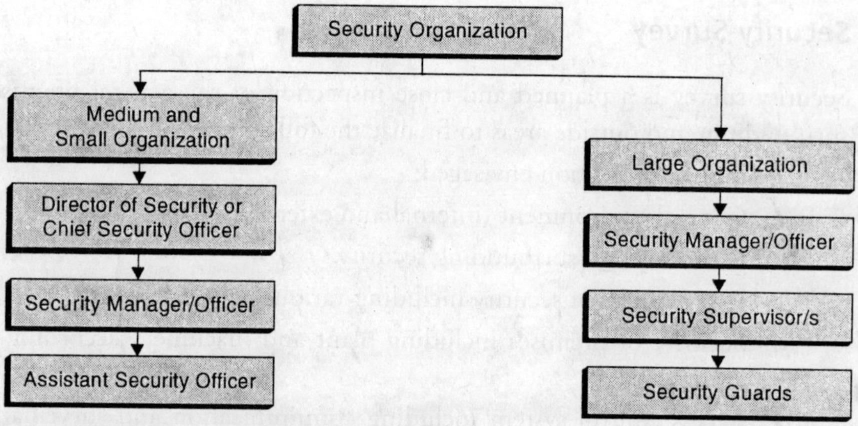


*Note*: More than one security Manager/Officer will only be employed if department is headed by a Director or chief security officer otherwise only one Security Manager/Officer will suffice for efficient functioning.

FIG. 5.1 CHART SHOWING A SECURITY ORGANIZATION

Generally, the security does not operate as a separate department in the industries. It is normally forming a part of personnel or administration department. The Security Manager/Officer is directly responsible to Personnel or Administration Manager. But only in exception it is found that Personnel or Administration Manager is fully qualified in modern technology and scientific gadgetry to ensure proper use of security resources. Management must be careful in selection of such managerial staff so that in long run they should prove as an asset and not a hurdle in forming the efficient organization and functioning of an industrial security system. Security organization in an industry can be visualized as under:

- Strength of staff and its functioning pattern.
- Recruitment and related policy.
- Training.
- Aspects of public relation.
- Duties and functions of various staff.
- Functioning of the security system.

## STRENGTH OF STAFF AND THEIR FUNCTIONS

In order to arrive at the reasonable strength of security staff in an organization, it is imperative that a comprehensive security survey is conducted to ascertain the strength of security staff.

## Security Survey

Security survey is a planned and close inspection of the general premises, surroundings and outside areas to finalize the following:

The type of protection envisaged:

(a) General environment (internal and external)
(b) Perimeter and surrounding security.
(c) Night aspect of security including various lighting.
(d) Security of premises including plant and machinery according to availability.
(e) Access control system including communication and surveillance system.
(f) Fire precautions and emergency plans.

### *Strength of Security Personnel*

Having studied the type of protection needed the next step in security survey will be to work out minimum strength of the force for an efficient and an effective security organization.

### *Approximate Financial Involvement*

Having decided on the strength of the force which will be required one should now work out financial aspect of the whole security services. It should include the number of personnel, all equipment's, gadgetry and vehicles, etc.

While carrying out the security survey the security manager/officer must keep in mind the following:

- The location and size of the plant.
- The strength of the work force.
- Nature of industrial production in the plant.
- General crime trend in the area/state.

### *Survey of Plant's Personnel*

The Security Manager/Officer should carry out detail enquiries in the following manner.

(a) The personnel working in the factory concern, particularly the security personnel which may include the fire-fighting squad as well. He should know the strength of the security section and whether this strength is adequate to meet the security requirements.

(b) Whether the security staff and other persons on key posts have been screened and their characters verified or not. If not, step should be taken to do the same. For this purpose the security officer may interrogate the security staff and during the interrogation may observe the expression on their faces and should note down an instance of dishonesty coming to notice against any member of the security staff and

(c) Whether the security staff have been trained or not, if not, they should be given training in security duties to be performed within the limits of law, and

(d) Whether the security officer can suggest the replacement of unsuitable persons with suitable ones.

(e) Due to lack of proper education in law, the workers have started indiscreetly indulging in agitations or unlawful acts and it is, therefore, that the security officer, while carrying out survey on personnel, should make enquiries about the nature, charácter and potentiality of its leaders, whether they are affiliated to a major political party or whether they have resorted to strikes have served notice of a strike or threatened to serve such a notice, or whether the head of the factory is in a position to get information about the activities of the undesirable personnel or about "What is going to take place"? And whether there are any orders existing regarding the duties of the security supervisors and guards.

## *Survey of Building and Premises of Plant/Factory*

This is an important aspect of security survey. The security Manager/Officer must work out minute details of complete premises and various entry/exit points keeping in view the following.

(a) Any holes or openings in a wall including tunnels, pipes, sewage streams, drains. He should then suggest a remedy for closing/reducing or grilling all ends of such openings. If an opening cannot be closed, or a broken wall cannot be repaired, it should be watched, and

(b) The height or outer wall whether it can be scaled over or if there is any electric pole or sewage pipe near the wall to enable the thief to climb and jump into the factory or whether a truck or car can be parked near the wall to act as a stair case for the thief. He should then suggest a remedy of providing barbed wires over the wall or glass pieces to be studded in the cement or in the mud on the wall.

(c) The arrangement for projecting light either outside the wall or inside the wall. If there is no such arrangement he should suggest the same so that any person coming towards the factory at night time may be noticed by the watchman on duty.

(d) Any grass hedges near the perimeter wall where the material can be hidden by any worker before stealing. He should then get the grass cut, get the area cleaned.

(e) The alarm system whether it is there or not and if it is not there he should suggest the necessity of having one in case of fire or air raid, etc.

(f) The gates if there are too many so as to suggest later the unimportant gates should be closed which will save expenses over the security guards.

## Security Survey of Products and Materials

At the time of security survey it must be kept in mind that most of the time products or materials is very tempting and personnel with doubtful integrity may be involved in theft and pilferage. Some of the important points to consider are:

(a) Whether there is a system of identity cards, gate passes or permit for the purpose of checking incoming or outgoing materials. If there is no such system he should introduce or suggest the introduction of the same as per the needs of the factory.

(b) Whether night patrolling is being done and also whether the same is being supervised properly or whether there is any check by means of punch clock if not suggestions on these points should be given.

(c) Whether the existing security guards are always on the same post or they rotate or change from point to point and whether there is a permanent record of such rotation. If not, such a system may be introduced depending on the availability of the security staff.

(d) Whether the searches of employees are being carried out in routine or as surprise checks, if not, such a scheme should be kept in mind to introduce the same diplomatically at opportune time. Employees may not like this idea, such a standing order can be issued according to the *Standing Order Act*.

(e) Whether the security staff is a conversant with the methods of searching, if not they should be given training whether the tool boxes, tiffin, carriers, cars of engineers/officers, etc. are searched at the gates by the security staff so that suitable suggestions should be given to the administration afterwards. If the women employees are in employment, a women security guards may be appointed and trained to search women employees.

*Note*: Experience has indicated that most of the employees at lower level are afraid to commit theft but the foremen or engineers with doubtful integrity can commit the theft.

(f) Whether there is a perfect system or inventory control in the industry, if not then its importance should be stressed.

(g) Whether the method of storage of cash and valuable material is satisfactory, if not, suitable measures should be suggested accordingly.

## Strength

After completion of the industries security survey the security officer should be able to decide on the strength of the force to be employed. The main factors to be consider are:

(a) Number of sentry/guard locations.

(b) Need for mobile patrols whether on foot or vehicle based.

(c) Requirements for vigilance or any intelligence activities, if yes, then specially trained staff to be recruited/arranged.

(d) Adequate reserves.

The total strength of security personnel must be taken into account by catering leave of personnel, checking staff for incoming and outgoing vehicles, loading and unloading of materials, relief for lunch and dinner during first and second shift. Adequate planning for number of reserves should always be kept in mind.

## Pattern of Security Force

As discussed earlier the pattern of functioning of a security force is generally that the security officer directly reports to General Manager or Personnel Manager or Administration Manager. It will not be correct to assume any rigidity in this matter. It is for the management to decide whether security will be a separate department or will function with personnel/administration.

Depending on the strength of the industrial security staff it is always advisable that the security officer is assisted by requisite number of Assistant

Security Officer, who in turn will be operating with the help of Jemadars/ Havildars acting as Security Supervisor. Under these supervisors all the guards and sentries will function in laid down shift of the organization. Every shift must have an Assistant Security Officer or a Security Supervisor on duty to ensure smooth functioning of the entire security system. Security Officer should always be available either on phone or by personal contact. Employing Assistant Security Officer and security supervisor provides a sort of motivation and incentive towards getting higher promotion for security guard personnel.

It is quite likely that small and medium size industries may not have their own security department/personnel as their permanent employees. These company may hire security personnel from some local agencies. Even then, it will be prudent to emphasize for the same security set up in order to have an efficient security services. However, if due to some reasons the agency is not able to provide the detailed set up, then a suitable officer from personnel/ administration department be tasked to supervise the functioning of hired security staff. Proper and timely checks should be undertaken by the company officer who may act as an effective liaison officer between security agency and the industry.

## Recruitment of Security Staff

As one enters into an organization, right from the main entrance the presence of the security staff must be felt. The security staff will consist of:

1. Security Officer
2. Assistant Security Officer
3. Security Supervisor.
4. Security Guards.

### *1. Security Officer*

In a security setup the importance of a security officer can't be over emphasized. He is the main link between the security organization of the company and all other industrial and public relations. He will always play an important role in the overall image of public relations of the company. Security Officer will be the first officer of the company to meet any incoming dignitary or business customer. The first meeting impression will always be everlasting for any visitor or business representative. Therefore, it is essential that following points are taken care of while selecting a security officer.

*(i) Qualification*: The person must be well qualified from the industry standards besides academic qualifications, legal qualifications will be an additional advantage.

*(ii) Personality and Appearance*: A smart and well-built person will always command respect from his subordinates. He should possess pleasing personality and good appearance. He will always be acting as company's most important representative in the field of industrial and public relation. Management and all other employees including his own security staff will have a close watch on his activities.

*(iii) Professional Capability*: In a nutshell the security officer should be a competent and capable person to carry out his entrusted tasks with full efficiency. He should be capable to organize a well knit team into a result oriented security force.

*(iv) Attitude and Behaviour*: A security officer should possess a positive and optimistic attitude. His behaviour, towards company's employees and outsider visiting company must be courteous, polite, positive and firm. An honest person with high integrity will always prove an asset to the organization. Behaviour towards company's employees should always be soft, polite and must be clear conveyor of company's goodwill and mission. He must convey the feelings that he is the well wisher and a caring person of their welfare. He must always operate within the policies and orders of the management.

*(v) Communication Skills*: He must possess the good communication skills, should be able to communicate well in English, Hindi and the local language of the area. A capable man who can convey his viewpoint politely, softly but firmly will always be liked by everyone. He should use proper communication skills as per the occasion with his seniors, colleagues and subordinates without conveying any misinformation.

*(vi) Cooperation*: The person should be so well mannered that every officer in the company must offer him appropriate cooperation whenever and wherever it is required. In the same way he should be an ever-willing person to offer his cooperation in the field of security, crime prevention and investigation, etc. Employees and his subordinates should feel frank and open to discuss their problems with him developing from company.

*(vii) Turnout*: A security officer should always be smartly and well turned out. A well dressed officer is always a point of interest and motivation for others. His attire must be attractive so that insiders and outsiders should be

forced to look at him for good dress and general turn out. Smart dress with good fittings will always be a source of pride for security's staff.

### 2. Assistant Security Officer

All the qualifications, as required by a security officer, should be applicable to an Assistant Security Officer. Because in due course of time he will be able to take over the duties of a full fledged security officer.

### 3. Security Supervisor

*(i) Education*: Person selected should be adequately qualified academically, and should be qualified on some recognized diploma/course in industrial security. It is always preferable that an ex-defence services JCO or equivalent rank, from para military forces and police forces, etc. will be able to do the task in a better way. The reason being that personnel from defence services, para military and police, etc. will be better disciplined, motivated and with high character and integrity. A person with all these qualities and traits will fit well in the security set up of any industry.

*(ii) Personality and Appearance*: Security supervisors must bear a good and smart appearance. He should be having good physique so that all security guards working under him takes motivation from him. A person with well behaved attitude will always be able to perform well.

*(iii) Professional Knowledge*: Must posses adequate professional competence.

*(iv) Turnout*: Lots of emphasis should be laid on turn out. Smartly put on uniform with a good personality will be source of motivation for security guards.

*(v) Positive Approach and Communication*: A person with positive approach and optimistic thinking can solve any problem during a crisis management, e.g. labour unrest, riots and cases of arson or normal fire. Security supervisor should possess cool temperament and with good communication skill. He should be able to carry his team of security guards with full faith and confidence, subordinate must understand him well as their not only senior but well wisher also.

### 4. Security Guards

Security guards must be so selected that they should be able to convey good impression on all staff of factory and on all the visitors to company's premises. He should be able to read and write well in English, Hindi and knowledge of local language is certainly preferable. His general appearance, physique and communication skills must be good. Therefore, it is always preferable to select ex-servicemen, paramilitary forces Jawan and police constables, etc. They will be better disciplined, motivated and dedicated to job with high character and integrity. They should always be polite and treat every visitor and staff in a courteous manner. They must have full loyalty towards the organization in the event of strike and labour unrest, etc.

## Organization of Training

### *General*

The training of entire security staff should be planned as per the requirements of industrial products and its geographical location. Although ex-defence Para Military and Police personnel are trained for security duties but still it may be possible that they could not get adequate exposure for industrial security duties.

For Security Officers and Assistant Security Officers, diploma course in Industrial Security Management from a reputed institution should be considered adequate. An earlier experience in similar concern will be an additional qualification. Security Officer must be provided with any special programme concerning the industry. Every industry by virtue of their product, being of a particular nature and location will have some critical areas where security officer has to pay special attention in planing security training. It is advisable that proper "Refresher Course" is planned at a suitable interval for Security Officer and Assistant Security Officer.

The training of supervisors and security guards must be planned right at the time of entry. A good concentrated dose with all aspects of industrial security should be provided in the form of theoretical training for adequate duration. A four to six weeks training capsule by any security agency or by company's security officer should be sufficient. After the theory part, a practical training on various posts or points will give him adequate exposure for practical training. Training programmes for security guards should be conducted at suitable intervals, so that it serves as refresher for them. Training programmes must contain all problems of security nature from each department and a copy must be forwarded to the respective heads of department. It will inculcate a sense of confidence among all management cadres about the importance of security in the industry. It is always advisable to conduct on irregular intervals various mock up exercises and drills to judge the efficiency and capabilities of security staff. After that proper debriefing and summing up should be conducted by security officer or chief security officer as the case may be.

## Aims and Objectives

### *Aim*

The management in any industry always try to create a trouble free environment without any labour unrest, theft and pilferage, etc. thereby ensuring that human resources, material and machinery of the company can produce optimum quantity and achieve laid down growth targets. In the same context it can be safely presumed that aim of industrial security "Is to develop a safe and trouble free industrial environment in order to prevent any theft, pilferage, sabotage and lobour unrest, etc. thereby assisting industry in its economic growth".

### *Objectives*

As discussed earlier the industrial security must be able to play a very positive and progressive role in the overall growth of an industry. At no stage the management should consider the security setup as a negative force or a hurdle in the endeavour of attaining its setout targets and goals. It should project such an image of itself and the parent organization that fulfillment of its initial and final objectives are complete. In view of the foregoing the "objectives" of the industrial security can be énumerated as per succeeding paras.

### *Cohesiveness*

Right from the start whether security is from the parent company in the form of permanent employees or it has been hired through a security agency, all personnel must consider themselves as a part and parcel of the company like other departments. Their behaviour, attitude towards work, dedication to assigned duties and integrity must be unquestioned beyond any doubt. Their acts of duties should be an indicative of oneness and the whole team must perform with the only objective in mind, i.e. absolute sense of belonging. They must always project their entire charter of duties as a single cohesive team of the industry. The sense of cohesiveness will make an unforgettable place in the mind of management and other individual staff. These all will undoubtedly prove that industrial security is a major booster in the overall growth of the industry.

### *Preventive Security*

As it is rightly stated that "Prevention is better than cure" it is very much applicable to the industrial security. The management and head of security must work out various contingencies, keeping in view the industrial relations, impact and attitude of labour union with the industry, state of labour welfare, chances of theft, sabotage and espionage, etc. must be thought off and adequate preventive measures planned accordingly. One who learns from his own mistakes cannot compete and who learns from others mistakes wins the competition and is called a successful leader. Security officer and supervisors including guards must keep their eyes and ears open carefully watch activities of all suspected staff and visitors. Proper and timely liaison with civil police and labour office will always prove fruitful in gaining important information.

### *Planning with Foresight and Vision*

Management and head of security must always plan and perform with adequate foresight and positive vision. Future plans and strategies must be chalked out by keeping in view the overall strategies of the organization. The security plans must always fit well into the corporate plans. Proper foresight and vision must always form part of security officer's action plan.

### *Cost Effective and Efficient*

Management in all the industries will always endeavour to achieve better results of their annual growth and economic development. Therefore, all resources planning in the industry has to be by keeping a proper check and balances on the financial input and final output of sales. Similarly, the security staff and gadgetry must be so selected and procured that industry can attain maximum efficiency with bare minimum financial expenditure. Therefore, security officer must be able to advise management on the best quantity and quality with proper cost effective planning.

## Classifications of Security Services

The requirements of security services in all the industries is vital and its importance cannot be over emphasized. Irrespective of size and type of product, each industry requires adequate security setup to safeguard their personnel and property. Basically there are two categories of security services normally used in industries these are:

(a) Proprietary services.

(b) Contracted or hired services.

## Proprietary Services

Large business houses in public and private sectors preferably have their own security setup. Complete staff is on their permanent pay roll and all their actions are governed by the management. Their recruitments are governed by the management. Their, recruitment, training and all other activities are directed by their own security officer as per company guidelines issued from time to time.

## Contracted or Hired Services

Medium and small size industrial houses generally prefer to either use the services of an agent or hire out the security staff as per their requirement. These private security agencies are doing a good business all over the world and especially in developing countries like India. These agencies, in exceptional cases, follow proper rules and regulations in hiring retired personnel from defence services. Paramilitary and Police services. There are no proper training infrastructure and also do not follow legal norms in laying down proper service terms and conditions. They do not pay actual salary as laid down by state governments for unskilled, semiskilled and skilled labours. These agencies take undue advantage of employment and rehabilitation problems faced by ex-defence and paramilitary personnel.

### *Advantages of Proprietary Services*

1. Complete security staff has full knowledge of company's strategies, plans and final objectives, thereby better cohesiveness.
2. Preference can be given to well trained and qualified ex-defence, paramilitary and police officers and other ranks.
3. Adequate command and control can be exercised by company's officers/executives.
4. After recruitment their training can be suitably planned and undertaken within the overall company's training schedule.
5. Due to permanent employment their motivation, morale and dedication to company's growth will always be high and reward worthy.
6. A feeling of comradeship and better sense of belonging among all staff.

### *Disadvantages of Proprietary Services*

1. Management will be bound by legal terms and industrial laws being permanent employees.

2. All welfare measures like housing, medical and LTA, etc. will have to be provided.
3. More administrative backup needed for keeping records of PF, Gratuity, Pension, etc. as per rules.
4. It is not cost effective and leads to greater financial burden in the long run.
5. Trade union contacts and its impacts on functioning cannot be ruled out.

*Advantages of Contract/Hired Services*

1. Selection liabilities is of the agency.
2. Deployment can be flexible.
3. Training obligation not on company.
4. Bargaining on financial terms and conditions.
5. No trade unions involvement.
6. Overall cost effective.
7. No responsibility for welfare measures.
8. Indisciplined and absentees can be charged with no legal implications.
9. Command and control can be exercised by company's security manager/officer.
10. No service liabilities.

*Disadvantages of contract/hired services*

1. Lack of cohesiveness and sense of belonging.
2. No job evaluation and effective growth for the staff.
3. Proper training as per company's requirements is not there.
4. Selection of personnel cannot be adequate as proper salary is not given.
5. Lack of morale and motivation to job and loyalty to company.
6. Smart turnout and alertness cannot be expected.
7. There will be very little continuity in job, as agency keeps shifting their personnel due to absence, leave and sickeness, etc.

## Code of Conduct

Every organization has some ethics and code of conduct for their employees, in order to project an image of their industry to outsiders and inculcate an environment of staff welfare and harmony among themselves. Similarly, any security setup in an industry must operate under the preview of a certain code of conduct which will mould them into a dedicated and motivated force. The main points of code of conduct can be enumerated as under:

1. Be punctual on duty or at any other place wherever presence is needed to carry out a task.
2. Always smart turn out with good uniform speaks itself about functional ability of a person.
3. Understand your duty well—"What To Do", "Where To Do", and "How To Do"—whenever in doubt, clarify with your seniors.
4. Every act on duty should be to protect and prevent theft, crime, sabotage and riots, etc. for the welfare of personnel and material of the company.
5. Avoid personal friendship, prejudices and animosities from mixing with official matters.
6. Ensure that an important secret and top-secret information is not leaked to any unauthorized person.
7. Security officer and supervisors must keep themselves well informed with the latest scientific developments.
8. Always keep good relations with local law enforcing agencies.
9. Be polite but firm while conversing with a person or answering a telephone call.
10. Never lose your temper even if other person does so. Be courteous and avoid foul language.
11. Try and develop a habit of good listener, you may extract sometime valuable information from a talkative person.
12. Be short and precise in your conversation.
13. Avoid "We Versus Them" attitude.
14. Do not believe a stranger on the face value and his turnout. All these are quite deceptive in business.
15. Do not forget to report to your seniors at the earliest opportunity about any information that may be of some use for the organization.
16. Never rely too much on your memory, wherever possible make a note of all points, you hear or notice.
17. Never leave your place of duty unless you are properly relieved or ordered by your seniors to leave.

# 6

# Security Management in Commercial Organizations

In the modern times Industrial Security is a fast progressing function which is being recognized by the management in the industrial world. The importance of Industrial Security Management is further enhanced since ever increasing challenges are posed by various threats in one form or other. There is therefore, a need to chalk out all aspects of security management involving an Industry. The general impression, that Industrial Security is only confined to main gate for checking of personnel and vehicular movement, hold no ground in modern competitive environment. In fact security can be classified as under:

1. Security of Personnel.
2. Security of Information, office documents and Information Technology.
3. Security of material, buildings, plants and machinery.

## Security of Personnel

One of the most vital functions of the Industrial Security is to carry out, within the overall corporate planning the preventive security of all personnel whether employees or not. The personnel security will include internal and external security of all people who are in one way or the other connected with the Industry. In most of the Industries the security Department is regulated by the General Manager or Manager of the Personnel or Administration Department. Therefore, it will be under one of these departments that entire security set up will carry out various functions. While carrying out the personnel security tasks, basically it will amount to carrying out two jobs as under:

1. System of Identification/Personnel Identity.

2. Time office functions and its coordination with security set up.

## System of Personnel Identification

The major task, of security organization in any Industry is to recognize all the personnel before they are allowed entry into the premises. Therefore, Personnel or Administration Department, depending upon the management policy, must issue valid identity cards or any other valid document for his/her identification. All personnel including permanent, temporary employees, contractors or casual labours and all other categories must be in their possession of a valid identification document for seeking entry into the premises. In case of absence of such system it may be possible that an unauthorized person can get into the premises with wrong intentions. Basically, there is a strict need for introducing an identification document for the following categories of personnel.

1. All employees whether permanent or temporary.
2. Contractor's and casual employees.
3. Badlis (Replacement of temporary nature)
4. Visitors.

Management, in all the Industries must ensure that proper identification document is issued to all the above mentioned categories of personnel. This will facilitate the system of entry into the premises with adequate checks by security staff.

## Employees Identification

In the security identification, no one is to be believed or taken for granted on his/her face value. Every employee whether permanent or temporary must be issued with an identification document. The best way these days is to adopt the procedure of issuing a personnel identity card with a photograph. The identity card must contain the following details:

1. Full name of the company (whether printed or embossed).
2. Employees name.
3. Residential address. (not obligatory)
4. Date of birth of employee's, height, colour of eyes and hair and a visible identification mark on the outer part of the body.
5. Location of company.

6. Signature of the employee.
7. Signature and date of issuing authority.
8. Photograph (pasted or embossed).

It is seen that in most of the company's only 'attendance cards' are used. These cards are punched by the time machine at the time of arrival and departure by each employee. But this system is not considered very satisfactory as its basic aim is to workout the monthly salary of each employee. This card cannot be used as an identity card. Another method, used by the small organizations, is only recognition by the security guard. Small business houses feel that since only few employees are working with them, security guard is able to recognize each employee and thus entry is allowed. As per the security norms it is not valid argument. The strength of the employee is not the guiding norm for the issue of suitable identity cards. An organization should not rely primarily on the recognition power of an ordinary security guard.

These days some of larger size organizations and commercial complexes have adopted the method of issuing anodized aluminum plated identity card. This can be of any colour and size. It can have personal particulars and photograph embossed on the anodized aluminum plate. It is provided with a hook clip or chain which can either be put on the employee's apparel or chain worn around the neck and identity card hangs out on outer apparel. This is a very easy system of recognition and can be stored nicely.

Temporary employees can be issued with an identity card with a different colour paper or even without a photograph. These can be issued for a certain period i.e. 3 months or 6 months. Further renewal can be done for similar period. Once the employee is 'Confirmed', then a permanent identity card should be issued on returning the earlier card. No entry must be allowed inside the premises without the valid identity cards. This system will generate a sense of consciousness among all the staff.

## Points to Remember for Designing an Identity Card

Management must keep in mind the following important points while designing an identity card:

1. The background should be so selected or printed with Company's name that copying may be difficult.
2. The paper or anodized material should be hard and water/fire proof.
3. It should have enough space for a front view easily recognisable photograph of the employee.

4. Issuing authority must always sign and stamped signature should not be used.
5. All identity cards must have a serial number and company's stamp at the time of issue.
6. It should be tamper-proof.

## Record of Identity Cards

Personnel or Administration department must maintain a proper identity card issue register. This must be checked by the department head every month or at least every quarter. This register must contain the following columns.

1. Serial No.
2. Date of issue.
3. Name in full.
4. Date of Birth.
5. Residential address (could be optional)
6. Identity card serial number.
7. Department of employee.
8. Signature of the individual.
9. Signature of the issuing authority.

The security officer must brief in detail all the security staff as to what all essential information to be checked at the main gate or elsewhere. The important points are as under:

1. Clearly visible serial number of identity card.
2. Company's seal or stamp should be half on the card and half on the photograph of the individual.
3. All the columns are properly typed/written.
4. The signature of the individual and issuing authority should be used in ink. The signature should not be stamped.
5. In case of an unknown person the personal particulars e.g. colour of hair, colour of eyes and identification mark should be carefully checked.

## System for Casual Employees

All casual employees who are coming to the organization must have proper identification system. A register should contain the personal particulars of casual employees. At the time of seeking entry into the factory or office premises an identification 'Token' with proper serial number must be issued to him. The same token must be returned to security staff at the time of leaving the premises. A proper record must be kept of these tokens. Token must have company's name and its serial number.

## Contractor's Employees and Labourers

Most of the time in the Industries some contract works are undertaken. Contractor bring their own labour for the contracted task. For security reasons proper identification is very essential for those personnel. Security officer must maintain a 'Contract-Labours Register' with all relevant information as under:

1. Serial No.
2. Date
3. Contractor's name and address.
4. Total number of labourers (male and female)
5. Nature of tasks and location, etc.
6. Signature of contractor.

Besides the above information each labour or contractor's employee must be issued with a proper security slip or 'Token' with company's name, serial number and could be letter "C" to denote contractor's employees. Preferably, colour of permit or token should be different than that of permit or token issued to casual labours. "Surprise Checks" by security officer/supervisor must be carried out to ensure that all these work force do not move around in factory premises, where they are not suppose to go. At times contractors insist on issuing bulk tokens/permit to him for the use of his work force in the premises. This practice must be discouraged. Every person must be issued security permit/token on daily basis at the time of entry and returned at the end of the day. Security must ensure that all token's are kept and properly accounted for in the security office/time office.

## System for Badlis/Replacement

In fact, this system of temporary replacements/Badlis is not very much in use, because of its inherent technical and administrative de merits. However, in case it is taken into use then proper security Permit/Token must be devised for issue. Proper record of these personnel should also be maintained.

## System for Visitors

There are quite a number of people who pay visits to industry in business connection, personal meetings and for other miscellaneous tasks. Security staff must be trained to handle all visitors to the organization in a very polite, courteous but firm behaviour. The conduct of security staff with visitors will always give an everlasting impression about the industry and its management. At the same time no visitor must be given undue liberty to loiter around in the factory premises, as he may try to acquire some technical information which he is not suppose to be aware of. Generally, a visitor must be conducted in an organization as under:

1. On arrival, the visitor should be escorted to the visitor's room and security supervisor on duty should enquire about the Manager/Officer to whom he wishes to meet.
2. The security staff must take him to the "Reception Counter" the receptionist will ask the concerned Manager/Officer whether he/she will like to meet the concerned visitor.
3. Visitor should be requested to enter his/her particulars in the visitor's Register, to be kept either at security Room/Time Office.
4. Once Manager/Officer, to be visited, gives his/her consent to meet the visitor. Security staff must properly brief the visitor about the office location. In case of any doubt, he should be escorted up to the concerned Officer/Manager. In an organization where entry or area is 'RESTRICTED' from security point of view, then invariably all visitors will be escorted.
5. Before leaving Reception, a visitor's Pass must be prepared and handed over to him/her. This pass must be returned at the issuing place before leaving the premises.
6. Visitor must be requested to get the signature of the officer visited alongwith "Time of Departure" from the office. This should be properly checked at the security office to ensure that no other place in the factory was visited by him/her due to security risk.
7. Visitor's time of departure must be correctly entered in the visitor's Register to counter-check from the visitor's Pass, in case need be.
8. If there is any visitor for some employee working on the shop floor, the visitor should not be sent to shop floor or workshop. The concerned employee, if the need arises, should be called to visitor's room.

Visitor's Register is an important document which must be properly maintained at the security office near the main entry/exit. The specimen of 'Identity Card', visitor's pass and visitor's register" are given at the end of this chapter.

### *Exit Pass*

Whenever an employee wants a short leave during working hours of shift/ office an 'Exit Pass' will be issued by the officer. I/C of the shift or department. This exit pass will contain employee's name, designation, department, duration of leave and likely time of return on duty. Employee will hand over this exit pass at the main gate to security guard for further records.

**Specimen of Identity Card**

**Name of Company** . . . . . . . . . . **Serial No.** . . . . . . . . . . . . . . . . . . .

Name: ..........................................

Designation: .................................. Department/Section: ..............................

Date of Birth: ..................................

Height: ............ Weight: ............ Colour of Hair: ..................................

Identification Mark: .......................... Colour of Eyes: ..................................

Place: ..........................................

Date of Issue: ................................ Company Seal: ..................................

Signature of Employee Signature of Issuing Authority

FIG. 6.1 FRONT PORTION

**Reverse Portion**
**Identity Card**

Instructions

1. Always carry this card with you.
2. In case of loss, report the matter to issuing authority immediately.
3. Finder is requested to post this card to security officer of the company.

FIG. 6.2 REVERSE-PORTION

**Visitor's Pass**
**Name of the Organisation**

Book No: .................................... Serial No: ................
Date: ................

1. Name of visitor:
2. Name of organisation/firm:
3. Name of officer to be visited:
4. Purpose of visit:
5. Mention if any specific area to be visited:
6. Time of arrival:
7. Time of departure:
8. Signature of officer visited:

Place:

Signature of HR Manager/Security Officer

FIG. 6.3 SPECIMEN OF VISITOR'S PASS

**Exit-pass/Gatepass**
**Name of the Organisation**

Book No: .................................... Serial No: ................
Date: ................

Name of Employee: ............. is permitted to go out on duty/on short leave of absence.

Shift: ................ Time out: .....................

Expected Duration of Duty/Leave: ................

Time of Return: .....................

Signature of officer/
Head of Department

Signature of HR Manager/
Security Officer

FIG. 6.4 SPECIMEN OF EXIT-PASS/GATEPASS

| Sr. No. | Date | Name of visitor | Address of visitor | From which company | Name of officer to be visited | Purpose of visit | Time in | Time out | Signature of visitor | Signature of security supervisor |
|---|---|---|---|---|---|---|---|---|---|---|
| 1 | 2 | 3 | 4 | 5 | 6 | 7 | 8 | 9 | 10 | 11 |

FIG. 6.5 SPECIMENOF COLUMNS IN VISITOR'S REGISTER

## SECURITY OF INFORMATION, DOCUMENTS AND INFORMATION TECHNOLOGY

In the modern competitive industrial world, there is always a keen desire for 'One Up Manship'. This attitude in the corporate world have significantly increased the security aspects of all technical and non-technical information. A decade earlier the main emphasis was laid on security of Information, documents and Information technology, mainly in defence installations, units producing defence material, arms, ammunition and other Research and Development scientific organizations. But now the same importance is given to Private Industrial Houses engaged in chemical Engineering, IT firms, Pharmaceutical Productions and other ancillary units manufacturing small items for defence forces. In both Public and Private sector units there is always an increasing threat of espionage, Industrial Espionage and even sabotages.

### Means of Acquiring Information

Personnel who are involved in breach of security and leakage of information either in Public or Private sectors are adequately trained in various clandastine activities. They can easily judge a person who can be used for passing on valuable information or can act as an agent for arranging a meeting with such person. Their main interest generally are:

1. Defence strategies and planning.
2. Defence Preparedness in terms of equipments and stores and information technology sectors.
3. Leakage of secret nature manufacturing processes.
4. Information on Research and Development in various equipments and other highly competitive consumer goods.
5. Information on Nuclear Technology and space Research Programmes.

In order to acquire the above information from various offices, Research and Development units and other manufacturing installations, the following means are adopted:

1. Becoming friendly with persons who have either access or handling valuable information including files, etc.
2. Gaining an entry into such offices, organizations and units in the garb of employee, vendor or visitor, etc.
3. Operating as Newspaper vendor, auto repair shop or small tea shop next to such important offices/installations.

4. Listening carefully to the careless-conversations among employees and extracting required information.
5. After gaining some information, then using it to bribe the concerned person or blackmailing to extract more information.
6. Posing as influential person in political circles, business world and bureaucratic circles.
7. Arranging valuable gifts and lavish parties for concerned personnel and for their families.

## INDUSTRIAL ESPIONAGE

The word 'Espionage' can be defined as an act of gathering intelligence through clandastine means concerning a nation's security, its planning, preparedness including nuclear and space programmes and its related economic resources. Similarly, when we talk about industrial security espionage, it encompasses an act of gathering technical and financial information pertaining to plant processes, IT know-how and other related department by clandastine means. Industrial espionage, whether in Public or Private sectors, is occupying an important place in corporate sectors. The main sources of leakage of information can be attributed as under.

1. Employees of offices, units and Industries working in sensitive departments and Research and Development.
2. Through files containing secret information about national security, nuclear and space Research Programmes and Economic growth.
3. Personnel who are close associate of Politicians, scientists, and bureaucrats having access to sensitive areas and offices.

For further discussion on security of Information, Documents and Information Technology the Industrial units can be divided into two groups as under:

1. Public Sector Units.
2. Private Sector Units.

## PUBLIC SECTOR UNITS

In Public sector organizations, offices and industries, the importance of security of Information and documents increases many fold. This is because the Public Sector Industries are producing equipments, arms, ammunition and other scientific gadgetry including sophisticated devices for nuclear and space programmes. Some time back the main source of leakage of information was an officer or other employee. But nowadays with the modernization of scientific devices used for bugging and espionage activities, the problem of guarding the valuable information has taken a complex shape. It is becoming almost impossible to detect the source of leakage before the real damage is done. Use of micro-camera in wrist-watches, briefcases and office bags, laser monitoring devices, transmitters in ball pen and wristwatches, etc. has posed the severe threats to the guardian of security in the organizations.

In most of the correspondence received at or originated from public undertakings and Government offices, the following security classification is given as per its importance:

1. Top Secret Documents
2. Secret
3. Confidential
4. Restricted

## Top Secret Documents

This is the highest security classification which can be given to a document/file. This type of documents/files are of very vital nature concerning the organizations or office, etc. Generally, this type of highest security classification pertains to matters related to defence planning, equipments of critical nature, arms and ammunition, information of national and state level security. Other information related to Industrial policy, future growth plans and report on trade unions, etc. could be graded by the originator of the report or letter as *Top Secret.* Handling of *Top Secret* documents should always be done by a responsible officer. It should always be the prerogative of senior management to initiate such correspondence.

## Precautions for Handling Top Secret Correspondence

This Correspondence requires absolute personal attention at the Originator's and Receiver's offices. Main points are as under:

1. *Top Secret* documents must only be typed by selected and of high integrity steno in the presence of an officer who is authorized to know the contents.

2. Each page must be properly numbered serially on top centre just below the security classification which must be typed at the bottom centre of the page.
3. Once the entire correspondence is typed then total number of pages in words e.g. twelve pages only must be typed on the top centre of the first page.
4. Each page must be initiated by the originator of the correspondence.
5. The letter should be sent in two (inner and outer envelopes). Once letter is put into the inner cover it must be closed and sealed in the presence of initiating officer. Inner cover should have the name of the officer to whom it is addressed and his/her designation. The inner cover must be stamped on top and bottom as *Top Secret.* The outer cover will have inner cover and will be closed and bear on top "To Be Opened By Addressee Only", name and address of the recipient. It should also have the Industry's/office seal, letter no. and date and will be signed by the initiating officer.
6. It must be sent with Registered AD or even Insured, and proper record of receipt must be kept.
7. Proper register, of all *Top Secret* correspondence will be maintained in the office and it will be inspected by a responsible officer once a month or quarter.
8. All waste paper concerning *Top Secret* correspondence including Carbon paper and spoiled ribbon must be destroyed by burning and records should be maintained.
9. Correspondence with computers must be copied on a floppy and no records will be left on hard disc. The floppy and its cover should be marked as *Top Secret.*
10. On computer a separate 'password' should be allotted to each *Top Secret* file to avoid its use by any unauthorized person.
11. All *Top Secret* files must be marked with *Red* colour Band or (X) mark for easy identification.
12. All files must have *Top Secret* written with *Red* on top and bottom centre to avoid mixing up with other correspondence.
13. *Top Secret* files, documents, charts, floppies and drawings must always be kept in a separate almirah or box. This container be marked clearly "Remove First In Case of Fire." The duplicate Key No. of this almirah should be written on it.

14. In case *Top Secret* documents are to be delivered to an officer located in the same premises, then the envelop alongwith "Acknowledgement Receipt" should be taken by an officer for delivery.
15. All personnel handling *Top Secret* documents must be re-verified through civil police every year.
16. Under no circumstances *Top Secret* correspondence should be taken to the residence of any officer.
17. It must be ensured that no spare copy of this document/letter are made. All other copies should bear the "*Copy Number*" on each page of the letter. Proper record of all copies to be kept in the relevant register.
18. Document will not be handed over to any officer/manager without a proper receipt.

## Secret Documents

Generally, in Public sector units and offices there are number of documents and letters which are graded as '*Secret*'. These documents contain valuable and sensitive information, which if leaked, can effect the overall functioning of the organization, unit or undertaking. Organizational expansion plan, minutes of an important meeting, memorandum of understandings or notes on collaboration with foreign firms or financial institutions, remodeling of a product, financial grants, loan documents and various vital case studies may be included under this security classification. Since this is next to *Top Secret* classification, adequate system for handling and custody of all documents/files must be carefully devised to avoid any leakage.

## Guidelines for Handling

The instructions for handling safe custody of *Secret* documents are enumerated below:

1. Only nominated Steno should type out all such letters and documents, etc.
2. No extra copies of the documents will be made, only requisite number of copies should be prepared and proper records be maintained.
3. First page of the letter should have "Total pages" records, e.g. a letter containing six pages will have total six pages.

4. *Secret* correspondence must be addressed to an officer/manager by name, Head of the department can nominate a senior manager to handle such correspondence.
5. Correspondence should be only opened by the officer to whom it is addressed. Records of receipt and dispatch including acknowledgement will be kept in the register.
6. All rough papers including draft, waste papers, used carbons, etc. must be disposed off by burning and record of destruction be maintained.
7. *Secret* documents/files should never be left unattended on the office table. It should not be taken to residence for work.
8. In most of the public sector undertakings and government offices, a *Secret* cell is established where all *Top Secret* and *Secret* documents, letters, charts and graphs, etc. are prepared.
9. While preparing the documents with computers a secret password should be allotted to each secret file to avoid access by others. This password should be noted in a register for the use by authorised manager/officer.
10. While using computers the letters can be prepared in 'A' drive for copying all matters on floppy. These floppies must be kept with proper markings under lock and key.
11. In case of dispatch from one department to another or locally to some other unit/office, proper record of dispatch/receipt must be kept. Receiving officer should sign for the letter in dispatch book.

## Confidential Documents

This type of correspondence contains the information which is primarily for the use of few selected or concerned manager/officer. The matter in these documents/letters pertains to important investigation, court of inquiries, annual confidential reports, trade union activities and list of important customers, etc. There is a requirement of careful handling and safe custody of these documents/files. Suggested guidelines are appended below:

1. Typing of these letters/documents must be done by selected stenos only.
2. Record of all typed and prepared copies should be kept in a register.
3. Dispatch of such mail will be done in a sealed single envelope, the name and address of the recipient officer should be properly mentioned on the envelope.

4. Proper records of all dispatch and receipts must be maintained in dispatch book.
5. Such correspondence should be handled by nominated manager/ officer or section officers in government organizations.
6. All files/documents must be kept under the charge of an officer/ section officer under lock and key.

## Restricted Documents

Restricted Documents nature of security classification is given to those letters/ documents which are generally required to be seen by certain levels of even junior officers and supervisors. However, precautions are to be observed that such correspondence do not get into the unauthorized hands and press, etc. Proper records of dispatch and receipts are to be maintained at each office. Each file must contain the highest security classification according to the letters filed in it. For example, if a file has *Secret*, confidential and also restricted letters then file should be classified as *Secret*. Restricted correspondence can be entrusted with senior steno of the department.

## Reviewing of Security Classification

In all the department of an industry and public sector offices, it is the duty of the head of the department to carry out review of all classified documents especially *Top Secret* and *Secret* at regular intervals. The points to be remembered are:

1. Examine the contents of the letters and of the plan, programmes and information, etc. if it has been made public or other industries/ offices have been informed about it, then the classification of the documents can be considered for lowering to secret or confidential, etc.
2. The security classification of the letter/document can be downgraded by the originator only. In case recipient feel that the existing security classification is no more valid, then originator should be asked to do the needful, if found necessary.
3. Once letter of downgrading is received then letter should be downgraded and existing security classification must be put on top and bottom centre of each page of the letter. Relevant entry to this effect should be made in the concerned register.

4. In case originator desires to take back the letter, then it should be returned as per the security classification and record of dispatch should be kept in the register.
5. If the originator informs that letter to be destroyed by burning and destruction certificate forwarded accordingly. Necessary action to be taken by authorized Manager/Officer and records be maintained accordingly. Letter should either be destroyed by burning or put into a shredding machine for total destruction of the document.

## Disposal of Classified Waste Papers

1. It should be ensured by the officer, incharge or designated officer/section officer or superintendent of the office that all waste papers are put into shredder for daily disposal. The caretaker of the office must exercise supervision of disposal.
2. All classified wastepapers must be burnt in the incinerator properly so that no half burnt or badly burnt papers be left.
3. All *Top Secret* correspondence must be destroyed in a incinerator in the presence of a nominated officer and destruction record should be maintained in a register.
4. At no stage any classified wastepaper should be allowed to be destroyed by an ordinary safaiwala or staff members.

## Handing and Taking Over of Classified Documents

1. All classified documents and floppies must be properly handed, taken over between authorized or designated officers. The entries to the effect must be made in the relevant register.
2. *Top Secret* correspondence, files, charts, graphs and floppies, etc. must be properly and physically checked/counted at the time of handing/taking over. The record of handing/taking over must be entered in the relevant register.
3. In case of any shortage and discrepancies in number of papers and connected documents must be immediately reported to the head of the department and originator of the letter.
4. All relevant office seals and stamps classified alongwith documents must also be taken on proper charge while handing/taking over.

## Security and Custody of Keys

Locks and keys are the important security items to safeguard the security and safety of the office, machine room and store room, etc. The following measures must be adopted while handling the keys.

1. It must be ensured that a proper key register is maintained in security guardroom or at the main gate. The deposit and withdrawal of all the keys of offices, stores and other rooms, which are not required to be kept open 24hrs, the keys after locking must be deposited in security office.
2. All withdrawal and deposit must be either supervised by the security officer or supervisor of the concerned shift.
3. All departments must intimate in writing to security officer the particulars of the employee or officer alongwith his specimen signature, who is authorized to collect and deposit the key of concerned office or department.
4. The Key Boards, one for Duplicate Keys and other for Original Keys, must be placed at suitable place in the security office. All key locks must be provided for each key. Name of Office/Department should be written on it over the key hooks inside the key boards.
5. Key of the Duplicate Key Boards should be kept under safe custody of the security officer.
6. Records of all deposits/withdrawal should be entered in the key register.
7. No key should be having any marking of office/department for security reasons.
8. Any loss of key must be immediately reported to the head of department and security officer. The lock of lost key should be opened with the duplicate key and then same lock must not be used for the office to avoid any security risks.
9. Security officer must ensure that after the end of working hours all keys are deposited in the security office. If not, then it must be checked up from the concerned office the reason for delay. Head of the department must ensure that in case of delay due to some urgency of work, security officer is informed well in advance.
10. Security officer or shift supervisor must check up while going around the premises that all offices/stores are properly locked and doors/windows are secured.

### Preventive Measures in Industries/ Offices for an Effective Security

In all the industries and offices whether in Public or Private sectors, it is always an individual through whom only leakage of information takes place. Therefore, it is imperative that any individual with doubtful integrity should be kept under close watch. Special attention should be paid to the following:

1. Person who is in the habit of showing off during conversation with others–fond of loose talking.
2. Undue interest in trade union and political activities, or group rivalries in the industry/office.
3. Fond of staying late in the office with some or other excuse.
4. In the habit of making personal notes from important files/documents found making extra copies of classified letters/documents.
5. Taking undue interest in matters, meetings and conferences, which are not related with work schedule.
6. Fond of reading a particular type or religious literature and showing keen interest in an ideology.
7. Person who has weakness for wine and woman.
8. One who is always keen on earning money by fair or foul means.
9. Who is fond of some type of gambling, may be under heavy debt and in the habit of borrowing money. Presumably living beyond his own means.
10. Habitual of asking frequent leave or may be absenting from office on a fixed day and fixed time.
11. In the habit of putting on costly clothes, extravagance according to his known sources of income.
12. Frequently meeting a particular visitor in a suspicious manner.
13. Security or vigilance officer must arrange re-verification by police of employees showing doubtful behaviour.
14. Personnel from border areas, of the country not having very cordial relations, should be treated carefully. If need requires a separate register could be maintained of all the personnel.

## SECURITY OF INFORMATION IN PRIVATE SECTORS

As far as security of information documents and Information Technology is concerned, there is a major difference only in classification of letters and documents, etc. The security classification used in public sectors and government offices have already been discussed in detail. In private sector units and industries few corporate houses also follow the classification as under:

1. Secret correspondence.
2. Confidential correspondence.
3. Personal (not for press) correspondence.

It is an easy task to lay down rules and regulations for strict enforcement in public undertaking units and government offices. Implementing security of Information thus, becomes easier. But it may not be possible to enforce any such rules or regulations in private industries and offices. Scope of security laws and orders will invariably depend on size of industry, nature of products, its location and size of workspace. It will be the sole prerogative of the management to decide the extent of danger and threats to the security of information and documents. On the basis of threat anticipation, the necessary security measures will be adopted. Basically, private sector's units and industries can pick and choose various preventive measures to guard against any leakage of information.

In the field of security one should always follow the rule of, "Prevention is Better than Cure." In other words adequate precautions taken in early stages will always prove cost effective than the damage caused by the leakage of vital information. It must be remembered by the management that your business adversary is always ready to pay the requisite cost for an appropriate and timely information. It is a well known fact that various agents, engaged in nefarious activities of espionage, sabotage, subversion, extortion, kidnapping and terrorism, have posed a grave threat to the security of our industries and offices. In such scenario the security director and officer of any undertaking, unit and office will have to remain always be alert with his eyes and ears open. They have to employ and make use of all available manpower, scientific devices coupled with foresight and vision to protect and safeguard the information, personnel and valuable technology from falling into the hand of adversaries.

## SECURITY AND SAFETY OF MATERIALS, BUILDINGS, PLANTS AND MACHINERY

This aspect of security, among the industries irrespective of public or private undertakings, plays a very predominant role in the overall security scenario. The basic aim of this aspect is to safeguard, against theft and pilferages including sabotage, all materials (both raw and finished products), immovable and other movable assets of the organizations or Industries. The theft can be categorized broadly under two heads:

1. External thefts.
2. Internal thefts.

Both the above categories will be discussed subsequently in this chapter.

## Security of Material

One primary task of security staff in an industrial organization is to check and prevent all the actions leading towards thefts and pilferages of materials both externally and internally. General belief, that if proper checks of all the personnel at main entry/exit will stop thefts and pilferages, is indeed far from reality although it is one of the preventive measures in the security process. Management and security chief should always think ahead about various ingenious methods which people can adopt to carry out theft and pilferage. Therefore, it must be carefully analyzed that during the process of procurement of materials, which are the places where possibly theft and pilferage can take place.

Once the above areas are identified, whether during external or internal procurements, adequate built in measures can be implemented to plug-in existing loopholes. The security of material encompasses the external and internal thefts and pilferages. In the subsequent para's each stage of material management will be analyzed to provide adequate security measures.

## System of Procurement

Every Industry and office carry out various purchases for procuring raw material and other technical and consumable office goods. This job is normally carried out by purchase or administration department. Besides, the raw material, if the organization operates a canteen or cafeteria then the quantity and number of items increase manifold. During the procurement process various quotations are obtained and the supplier with lowest amount will normally get the supply order. In this entire process the management must keep a close vigil to avoid external and internal misappropriation. Close watch should be kept by security officer on the following aspects:

1. Any leakage or compromise on cost quoted accepting quotations.
2. Accepting commissions for issue of supply orders.

3. Adequate favours in various forms for accepting items, equipments and goods below the Qualitative Requirements (QR).
4. Favours and commissions from main contractor while giving sub-contracts for supply of materials.
5. Instances have been there in government undertakings and offices where only small quantity is supplied or even no supply was undertaken against a valid supply order, only the paper transactions took place and full payment was made. These incidents can only happen when senior officers from Purchase and Finance/Accounts departments are hand in hand.

Management must keep proper and strict vigil on the entire process of procurement to avoid any of the above mentioned incidents.

## Arrival and Receipt of Materials

Once the material arrives at the main gate of an industry, the escort representative of the company will hand over the copy of the chalan to the company security supervisor of the shift. At the gate it may not be possible to check the quantity, quality and correctness of the material. Only a rough check can be carried out by security as per delivery chalan. It will not be possible to unload and check it for correctness.

Unloading of material will be done at the stores, it is here that security staff must closely supervise the entire process. The quantity and containers can be checked for correctness. Any discrepancy from delivery chalan must be noted and security officer/manager of the department should be informed accordingly.

## Inspection and Physical Checks

Once the material delivery is taken as per chalan, then physical proper inspection by the concerned staff must be carried out for quality requirements, proper inspection by the concerned staff must be carried out to ascertain the quality and other technical parameters. Any deficiency should be noted down for quality and quantity. It will be prudent to segregate the substandard items and must be returned to the supplier. This quantity must be mentioned in chalan from the company.

Only the material, which is correct as per required parameters, should be sent to stores for storage.

## Storage of the Material

Following points need specific attention by both store and security officers:

1. The building or storage place should be adequately secured against theft and pilferage.
2. All stores must have adequate protection from inclement weather.
3. Buildings must not have unwanted openings. All windows and ventilators must have security grills to avoid unauthorized entry.
4. At the end of the day all stores, keys must be deposited in security office.
5. All valuable stores as per their size and weight must be stored in proper bins and secured almirahs.
6. Proper bin cards must be maintained for all stores so that correct state and quantity can be found out at any moment.

## Process of Issue of Material

Issue of the material is an important process and adequate security checks must be enforced to avoid any security lapses. Main points are as under:

1. Entry to the stores must be restricted, only concerned staff must be allowed access to the stores premises.
2. Proper requisition slips duly signed by the officer/manager and issue slips of stores must be accounted either manually or on the computer.
3. Once the items and or stores are issued the relevant entry in the cards or in the computer should be carried out for inventory control.
4. Proper issue timings for stores issue must be adhered to specific sanctions must be obtained for any Emergency/Urgent issues.

## Storage of Finished Products

Once the finished products are ready, it should be carefully carried to the proper stores/ware houses. Adequate measures for storage should be taken similar to raw material. It must be ensured that packing or the product itself should not be damaged during handling. Due care to be exercised to prevent interior theft and pilferage.

## Loading and Dispatch of Material/Products

While loading and during dispatch the following points must be observed:

1. Loaded quantity must be properly supervised and correct number must be noted for tallying with chalans.
2. No damage to packing and goods should be caused.
3. After loading and checking is done the vehicle or container should be properly secured to avoid any damage from weather and prevent theft and pilferage.

## Disposal of Scrap

This is an important aspect of the material management. Generally, it is neglected area and therefore, it can attract wrong person to carry out thefts and pilferage. The main points from security angle are as follows:

1. Proper orders must be laid down for all shop floor in this regards.
2. All scraps must be daily collected from all shop floor/machine shops.
3. Adequate scrap yard with proper security surroundings must be earmarked for scrap storage, separate storage compartments must be there storing each type of scrap.
4. Scrap yard must have proper locking arrangements and key should be with store manager or security officer.
5. Loading of scrap must be properly supervised at the time of weighing.
6. Once the vehicle is loaded, the security guard must escort the vehicle to the main gate, care must be taken to see that no other product/ item is put into scrap.

## Security of Buildings and Premises

The security of immovable assets of an organization and office is an important charter of duties for the security staff. It is the entire premises, plant and machinery which must be guarded at all times to avoid any theft and pilferage for the building and other structures following to be emphasized:

1. Proper demarcation of all the buildings and structures to avoid unauthorized occupation.
2. Proper perimeter wall/adequate fencing is constructed to avoid illegal entry.

3. No unwanted growth of trees and shrubs should be allowed near boundary wall. It will prevent any intruder from hiding inside it.
4. Only restricted number of entries to the buildings must be there which should be guarded at all times.
5. No drainage or tunnels are allowed to pass which can help in illegal entry to the premises.
6. Strong gates with proper locking facilities should be fitted at all gates.
7. Adequate lighting should be there during the hour of darkness especially near boundary wall and near plant and machine shops.
8. If need be, in large organizations suitable watch/observation towers with adequate light must be erected for security purposes.
9. Modern devices like CCTV, ultrasonic motion detectors and Intrusion Detection sensors can be provided as per need for better security purposes.

## Security of Plants and Machinery

Following should be emphasized:

1. No unauthorized person should be allowed an access to shop floors/ Machine shop, etc.
2. Photography by an employee/visitor should be prohibited.
3. Proper lighting inside and outside the plant must be arranged.
4. Only visitors with valid pass must be allowed inside the plant/machine shop.
5. Plant and machinery should not be left unattended, in case it is not operating then proper locking system should be followed.
6. Carrying of personal tools/equipments must not be allowed.
7. Any repair by the outside technician must be in the presence of own employee nominated by the manager/supervisor.
8. Valid gate pass must be made for taking any part outside the premises.

Security of personnel, information, documents, movable and immovable assets of an organization and office is not the only duty of few personnel of the security staff. It must be realized that it is the basic responsibility of all managers and employees to keep their eyes and ears open. Any laxity on part of any one can cost very dearly to the reputation and growth of the whole industry.

# 7

# Functions and Parameters of Commercial Security

In an industrial environment, the basic aim of industrial security is to provide an umbrella of protection and safety for personnel and material. The important functions of industrial security are enumerated as under:

## FUNCTIONS OF INDUSTRIAL SECURITY

(a) Maintain law and order in and around the industry and concerned offices.

(b) Measures to prevent theft, pilferage and industrial crimes.

(c) Enforce company's policies, directives and criminal laws.

(d) Adequate access control.

(e) Keep a close watch on personnel with doubtful integrity and if required, investigate their activities.

(f) Promote safety and reporting of any unusual incident e.g. fire, theft and pilferage, etc.

(g) At the time of need assist employees and visitors, provide basic first aid in case of emergency.

### Physical Security Parameters

During the last chapter (CH-IV) we have analyzed in detail all the aspects of security in relation to personnel, information and documents, material, plants and machinery. Now, we will confine our discussion to:

(a) Area security.

(b) Security parameters of building and premises.

(c) Perimeter and exterior protection.
(d) Access control.

### *Area Security*

While planning parameters of area security of an industry, the emphasis must be laid on the following:

(a) Carry out a self-appraisal of all the aspects of security in the entire area.
(b) Familiarize with the overall activities, including production of the organization.
(c) Carry out on paper detailed analysis of major activities in relation to all acts of theft and pilferage, etc.
(d) Later proceed to ground for confirmation and any addition or deletion.
(e) Prepare the complete work chart and drawing of area security.

Physical parameters in area security must include the following:

(a) Assess all the entrances through fencing and perimeter protection.
(b) Direct and indirect effects on buildings and plant shops in relation to area security.
(c) Special protection and security for secret documents and research work places.
(d) Important assets having intrinsic and inherent values.

## Security Parameters of Buildings and Premises

While assessing the security parameters of any immovable asset, following merits need consideration.

(a) Analyze the overall vulnerability from the points of theft, pilferage and espionage, etc.
(b) Plan adequate surrounding security by way of boundary wall, fencing or electronic beam barriers.
(c) An effective access control with gadgets like electronic card and magnetic card system, etc.
(d) An effective and modernized alarm system.
(e) Ensuring restricted entry.

(f) Fire prevention and adequate safety means be arranged in the form of smoke, heat and flame detectors and automatic extinguishers of Halon or $CO_2$ gases.

(g) An efficient and effective communication system.

## Perimeter and Exterior Protection

Adequate protection by means of physical presence of security guards, manned and electronic barriers, proper lighting, guard post, watch towers and mobile patrols supported by modern electronic gadgets will prove great deterrent for any trespasser or intruder. The system of electronic barriers will be discussed in detail while considering use of electronic devices in exterior security. The use of various type of lighting, in the security parameters is considered as one of the best available means. Basically there are five types of security lighting as under:

(a) *Continuos lighting*: Are fixed and permanently fitted light fixtures which are used during the hours of darkness.

(b) *Stand by lighting*: Which are not continuously switched on but are automatic or manually controlled in case of any suspicious activity located.

(c) *Movable lighting*: Rotating or search lights which are manually operated and can be transported from one place to another.

(d) *Entrance/Exit lighting*: Proper light which are used to light up entry/exit points for personnel and vehicles.

(e) *Emergency lighting*: These are normally self-operational in case of failure/shut off of main current.

The most commonly used sources of light in Industries are as under:

1. ***Incandescent***: Normal bulbs are the most commonly used sources of this lighting

   (a) *Advantages*: Low cost, good colour rendition and instant turn On/Off.

   (b) *Disadvantages*: Short life, low efficiency, low lumens per watt and high operating cost due to short life.

2. ***Fluorescent***: Most commonly used in interior lighting in Offices and Industries.

   (a) *Advantages*: Good colour rendition, high proficiency and low operating cost.

   (b) *Disadvantages*: Length of tube and its fixture and relatively short coverage.

3. ***Mercury vapour***: It is a gaseous charge lamp in blue and white colours.
   (a) *Advantages*: More efficient bulbs, longer life and low operating cost.
   (b) ***Disadvantages***: Slow warm up and recovery, some of the gaseous lamps need 2–5 minutes to recover once power shut of.

4. ***Sodium vapour***: It is gaseous discharge lamp which emits golden yellow or white light. These are available in high and low pressures.
   (a) *Advantages*: High efficiency, low operating cost and long life.
   (b) *Disadvantages*: Slow, warm up and recovery for high pressure units. It demands relatively high cost for installation.

## Access Control System

In our country, most of the industries are still dependent upon the good old manned barrier and lock technology of the main entry gate. The gate is normally guarded round the clock by adequate security staff. Although better sophisticated gadgets and electronic equipments have been developed for access control, still some weaknesses are there in mechanical controls. Therefore, the system of security guards and physical control is still considered very efficient, cost effective and flexible in its operational proficiency.

Access control in an organization is very important function of the security. It is the main control room from where all the entry/exit of the personnel and material is checked and properly regulated as per the policies laid down by the management. The security aspects of personnel and materials have already been discussed in chapter four. Here we will only analyze the main aspects of access control, which are as under:

- Checking of identification.
- Co-ordination with time office.
- Searches.
- Control room duties.
- Patrolling.

### *Checking of Identification*

All personnel whether staff, labourers and visitors must be properly checked by the security guard or supervisor of the shift before the entry is allowed into the premises. Proper identity cards or temporary identity cards, token or permit must be scrutinized at the entry gate. Similarly, visitors must be issued valid pass after confirming from the officer to be visited.

*Vehicle's Identification*

All vehicles including private cars and two wheelers must be checked from security point of view. All cars of company managers and officials can be checked as per guidelines laid down by the management. Other vehicles carrying raw material or equipments and finished goods must be thoroughly checked as per Delivery Chalan and if need be, it must be escorted to and from the main gate by a security guard. In case visitor's cars/two wheelers are not allowed inside the premises then it should be directed into the visitor's car/scooter park.

***Coordination with Time Office***

Generally, time office is co-located next to security guard room. The aim of time office is to check the arrival/departure of all the employees of the organization. Number of punching clocks are put near the time office for punching the cards by the employees. In the morning or at the time of shift end when an employee enters the main gate, after proper checks he/she walks into the time office, picks up his/her card from the "Out Rack", puts the same into the punching clock for entering the time of arrival. After punching the card, it is kept into the "In Rack" which means that employee is inside the factory premises. After finishing the duty, the card is collected from the "In Rack", and time out is punched by putting it in the punching clock. Then card is put into the out rack, that indicates that employee is out of the organization. In some big industries the punching clocks are put near the respective departments to monitor the employees time of arrival/departure from the department. Based on this time the time office employee completes the muster roll for each employee. The muster roll copy is forwarded to account branch for working out salary of each person.

Another important aspect of coordination, between time office and security office, is to ensure that, once the card is put into the "In Rack" after punching, an employee does not waste any time in roaming around the other departments. Security officer and other department incharge should not encourage such activities. There can be instances when an employee will punch the card 'on time', but will not reach department for quite some time for such people either security staff or department head should inform the accounts branch, "HR dept" about late coming on duty, so that leave can be shown for such people.

***Searches***

At the main gate entry, depending upon the policy of the management, the kind and type of products, being manufactured, it may be necessary to carry out searches of all the employees. Search can be of outward nature i.e. lunch box, newspapers/magazine and umbrella/raincoats, etc. or the body search in which security staff have to feel with the help of hands that no item is being carried by an employee out of the factory premises by unauthorized means. Following points must be borne in mind by the security staff.

(a) As far as possible a senior person, either security supervisor or assistant security officer must carry out the search.
(b) Search must always be done in the presence of another person/security staff.
(c) Search of a woman employee should be, as far as possible, carried out by a woman security staff or in the presence of another woman employee.
(d) All employees must be made to read management policy about searches and should sign as having read, in the absence of it, some employee can raise a legal objection to it.
(e) If an employee resist for the search, then he/she should not be forced, but the particulars of employee and reasons for not allowing the search should be noted for future action if need be.
(f) Security officer must ensure that all security staff is fully aware of the policies of management.
(g) Security staff must be courteous and polite towards staff at the time of search.
(h) Security officer must differentiate between the routine searches of the employees and the search of a person who is caught while indulging in theft, espionage and pilferage, etc. his search should be thorough in order to find out any hidden arms ammunition and explosive, etc. on his body or person.

*Search of vehicles*

There are no set pattern or instructions for checking/searching the vehicles at the time of entry, exit from the factory. It's the prerogative of the administration/personal department to lay down various search/checking procedures related to their organizations. All vehicles must halt at the main gate, if empty then security staff must check inside the vehicle and also driver's cabin including tool box, if any. If vehicle is loaded, the Delivery Chalan must be checked as thoroughly as possible. If vehicle load is to be unloaded at the stores/someother department, then a security guard must escort the vehicle uptill unloading destination. At the time of going out of factory, proper gate pass and delivery chalan must be checked. Following points need careful checking in a gate pass.

(a) As far as possible it must be on a printed form.
(b) Must bear serial number of the gate pass.
(c) Contents in the vehicle and vehicle number.
(d) Destination.
(e) Ink signature of the officer authorizing gate pass.
(f) Gate pass must be entered into the gate pass register at the end of the day.

***Checking of vehicles supplying material by tanker***

Security staff should be vigilant towards the supply of material by volumetric measurements like petrol, diesel, mineral turpentine and Aviation Gasoline, etc. the supplier or the transporter use many foul means to pilferage the items in following ways:

(a) Having a secret compartment.
(b) By using only one dipstick.
(c) By using one dipstick for each compartment, whereas each compartment has different dipstick.
(d) By using temperature variation to advantage, that is to load the vehicle in the morning when specific gravity is more and unload in the afternoon when specific gravity reduces. The driver can remove the expanded material above dipstick mark before coming to the company.

***Foul means in the supply of material by volume***

Security staff should be careful in checking the materials like sand and manure, etc. supplied by volume. The transporter or supplier unloads a part of the material before coming to the company. The material is then dug-up and loosened so that the volume increases. This will give false dipstick readings. To prevent/check such fraud following measures will be of great value:

(a) The weigh-bridge should function under security department and watchman on duty at weigh-bridge should be frequently changed.
(b) Training regarding weigh-bridge operations and detection of fraud at weigh-bridge should be calibrated periodically.
(c) The vehicle should be escorted from weigh-bridge to stores and dispatch department or *vice versa*.
(d) No material, unless emergency should be allowed after the general shift is over.

(e) Whenever, there is a interplant moment of material, a security guard should escort the vehicle physically. Security department must be provided with the copies of purchase order, scrap contract and transport contract, etc.

(f) In case some crime is detected the concerned supplier should be called by the security officer or head of the concerned department and warned/cautioned. In case of repeated incidence, fine may be imposed or contract be terminated according to terms and conditions.

*Control room duties*

As per the size of the industry and number of employees, there is a need of security control room or guard room. This will be located next to main entrance and manned 24 hours by the security staff or representative of administration/ personal department. The control room will keep a close watch on the following activities.

(a) All personnel and vehicular movements.
(b) Regulating the visitors and visitors register.
(c) Issue/deposit of key and maintenance of key register.
(d) Collection and issue of gate passes.
(e) Collection of exit passes from employees.
(f) Maintenance of fire, unusual incidence and records of fire extinguisher's testing registers.
(g) Records of duty roaster of security staff.

*Patrolling*

It is an essential part of the charters of industrial security. Time bound and at random patrolling can instill a sense of confidence among all departments and employees. Patrols are of two types:

(a) Mobile foot patrol.
(b) Vehicle based patrol.

Patrolling must be organized by the security officer to ensure that no unusual incidence and fire, etc. takes place without the knowledge of security staff. An alert patrol of minimum two guards can serve as eyes and ear of the organization. A timely action to prevent any theft, pilferage and fire, etc. can be of tremendous value in terms of men and material for an industry. Following points must be borne in mind for an effective patrolling whether on foot/ vehicle.

(a) Patrol should be vigilant and always look for an unusual incidence, moment, fire, etc.
(b) In case of any crime detection, fire breakout or other incidence, patrol must immediately inform the shift incharge or security officer.
(c) If any office, shop floor or machine room is found unattended, patrol should inform control room/guard, who will checkup whether its key is deposited or still with some employee. Necessary action to lock it, must be taken to ensure proper security.
(d) In case any person with suspicious nature is found in factory premises, he must be stopped, checked for identification and investigated.
(e) Patrol during night should check all lights in working condition, in case any change is required of bulb or tube, etc. must be done.
(f) All perimeter wall, boundary wall and fencing must be checked for any unauthorized exit point. If any noticed, then action may be taken to repair the same.
(g) In guard room/control room proper register must be maintained for foot/vehicle patrols.

***Use of modern devices in access control***

Although most of the industries are still following the old time tested means of mechanical locks and keys. But with the all round scientific wave of developments in the field of electronics access control, the modern thinkers have switched over to latest electronic devices in access control system. The development in microprocessor technology has lead to the introduction of 'card access control system'. The main difference between the electronic access control system and the conventional locking devices is that, access control not only controls the entry exit but also recognizes the entrant, records his time of entry and also exit through a entry, exit point. Besides, it also alerts the security guard in case of any intrusion. Further, computer controlled access control system can be programmed in more than one ways. It can only allow the entry to the particular personnel, during specific timings and also days. It also provides information whether the entry/exit point is locked, unlocked, closed or open.

For the first time, it was in 1941 when IBM invented the magnetic card system for regulating the entry in any restricted/locked premises. The system has a plastic card embedded with micro magnet points in a particular pattern along with a door opening machine which is able to detect the magnetic points and thus gate opens. This mechanism has been further modified into a better technique involving the use of magnetism, inductance, capacitance, colour, fiber optic, magnetic wire and holography, etc. Now, we will discuss some of the devices which are being used in various offices and industries for access control system.

## Card Reader Device

This system comprises of a plastic card bearing distinct, invisible coded numbers and a card reading mechanism fitted on the entry/exit door, which is capable of reading the coded numbers on the card. Further the card reader is connected to the door opening device through a control box or microprocessor. This system can be operated by programming to allow only specific number of authorized persons between preset duration through a particular entry point. In case it is connected to a computer, it can provide with a print out of the names of individuals who sought access through the entry point. It can also mention the names of the absentees.

In the "Restricted" entry areas where only selected people are permitted, generally the entry point is guarded with a close circuit television camera (CCTV) for the ease of recognition. This system can be further strengthened where a computer can instantaneously compare the photograph on the identity card of the person with the real time photograph already stored in the computer file. In order to prevent the misuse of this card by some unauthorized person a technique known as: "Anti pass back" is used. In this the card reading device is fitted at both entry/exit points. After entering the premises, the employee/visitor cannot use this card for another person. Because if the card records in entry/exit are different then control room is given an alert and so access to another person is denied. In case of theft/loss of the card the code on the card can be altered immediately to deny recognition at the entry point for lost card.

*Optically coded badges*

It is another important electronic device used in access control system. In this system optically coded badges possessing a geometric array of spots are printed on an insert and laminated into the badge. The optical transmission of the spots are detected by the photo detector in the badge reader. The badges are opaque to visible light and transparent to infra red light.

*Magnetic card reader*

These cards are primarily used for personnel and vehicular traffic control. In this system a plastic card contains a series or mini magnets embedded over it in a particular pattern. For access control, when a genuine card is inserted in the card readers slot fitted to the door mechanism it releases the locking device and opens the door. In case of any forged card is inserted the card reader will activate the alarm for alerting the security staff.

*Remote controlled electro mechanical locks*

This system provides a facility where in all movements of personnel and vehicles can be easily controlled from a separate place by using buttons and or switches. In sensitive areas like defence research and development institutes, Space and Research Organizations, Nuclear Installations where key of the main entry point cannot be entrusted to anyone man since identification is needed for every person and each time. Such entry points are controlled from a separate point through electromechanical locks. CCTV cameras carry out actual identification of an individual. This technique is also quite useful for the gates where entry is not frequent and large in number so that it becomes cost effective from the point of security investments.

*Computerized vehicle—access control*

It is an interesting system where vehicle movements can be controlled by computers. In this, gates are fitted with computer controlled card readers which will only open to known vehicles. In case of an unauthorized entry the guard room/security guard will be alerted, at the same time the vehicles photograph will be automatically taken. Besides the vehicle number will be also noted for action.

*Card control turnstiles*

A card operated turnstiles is used to control the entry into sensitive and large organization where physical checking of all personnel is not convenient or possible. In this system a plastic card is encoded with a invisible number, when this card is inserted into the card readers slot, the code number is flashed to the central processor which in turn identifies the validity of the entry. In case of any unauthorized intrusion, the alarm is sounded at the main processing unit for alerting the security guard.

*Electronic coded badge*

There are active and passive electronic badges which carry out unique task in identifying the person. The passive badge is covered with a network of electrically tuned circuits. A sweep radio frequency field is generated and then the frequencies at which the significant energy is observed by the card is detected. If the absorbed frequency corresponds to the tuned circuits with in the reader, then the door lock is activated and it opens. In case of a forged badge the alarm is activated. A single card reader unit can read about ten thousand different frequencies.

The active badge consists of an electronically coded badge and a reader unit. The power is supplied by the reader unit to the badge components by magnetic induction which receives and decodes the credential number transmitted from the badge. In this electronic system, the card may remain in the valet and the unit will read the signatures automatically while the person is passing through the radio frequency field generated by the interrogation unit.

*Attendance and payroll card*

It is a card with dual functions capability. Basically it has been devised to regulate the entry of authorized personnel through the entry point. It is designed to record the time and date of entry of each individual on a print out. It can prove a big help for accounts branch for preparing pay rolls of all employees and overtime, etc. without putting in much efforts.

## Miscellaneous Identification Methods

*Fingerprint and hand geometry*

It has been found with the past experience that finger prints have proved to be one of the most reliable methods of identification along with the hand geometry. Finger prints and hand geometry of two persons are never alike. This wonderful gift from the almighty can be used by the electronic equipments for identification. These can be stored in the data file of the computer. At the main gate while seeking entry the individual puts his palm on the top of the reading unit. The electronic reader system identifies the fingerprints and hand geometry of the individual. Based on the acceptance or rejection of both the things, the entry is granted otherwise refused to the individual.

*Electronic signatures*

The system contains a pressure sensitive pen and a micro computer that is capable of comparing the signatures of an individual with the same which are digitally stored in the computer file. The micro computer measures the pressure of the pen as the function of time to identify the signature.

*Speech verification*

It is now commonly used system to recognize an individual. The system operates on a principle of repeating a four (4) words phrase selected at random by a computer from a file consisting of 32 phrases constructed from 16 monosyllable words. The repeated phrase is processed and compared with the data already stored in the computer file, once it is compared and recognized then command goes further and door will open. This system is considered to be very effective and reliable, thus being used in sensitive organizations and corporate houses.

### Use of Computers in Access Control

Computer, if adequately operated and well programmed can carry out almost every task with perfection and excellence. It is capable of handling any number of people through entry point by regulating their entry at pre-specified place, time, date and for number of days. All the particulars in respect of each individual i.e. photo, palm and fingerprints and signature, etc. are stored in a file inside the computer which can be used for recognition and identification. By sitting in the control room, the operator can find out whether door is closed, open, locked or unlocked.

#### *Monitoring of patrol*

Computers can monitor effectively the location of each patrol. The patrol on duty, are required to punch their cards in the monitoring booths located at specific places inside the premises or nearing the perimeter/boundary wall. All patrolling programs including their routes and time, guard duty roster are fed into the computer files. Guards and patrols are instructed to punch their security card in the monitoring booths during their patrolling at a preset time schedule. If a patrol fails to punch its card, at a preset time, the alarm is sounded and the lapse, if any, can be traced.

### Use of Sensors and Detectors in Access Control System

X-ray Screening Machine: This system operates with an advanced technology which enables to have a clear picture of the object with minimum use of x-ray doses. It is generally used in sensitive, high risk areas and at International Airports for screening the briefcases, suitcases and other baggages. The system has a linear X-ray sensor to view the expected baggage/items in slices as it moves through a narrow beam of X-ray. The slices are converted directly from X-ray to video signals and the picture of object is displayed on the TV monitor. The system does not use any camera. Wires as thin and as fine as of 34 gauge can be detected inside a suitcase. The system is capable of screening more than 1200 baggages in an hour.

## DOOR METAL DETECTORS

This system is very frequently used during VVIP's visits, important conferences and seminar, etc. It is used to trace/detect a ferrous as well as non-ferrous metals carried by an individual. The detector is in the form of a door which can be erected any where without any detail preparations. It consists of a search coil and control module housed on an archway. It is used where large number of personnel are expected and frisking everyone may hamper the normal activity. The detector have a preprogrammed sensitivity levels which can be preset to "Low, Medium or High" levels. Low sensitivity level is used for detection of large objects like grenade and metallic bombs, etc. Medium level is used to detect small fire arms and 'High' sensitivity level is meant for detecting small metallic objects like coins, etc. Control and audio visual alarms are fixed on top of the rear side of archway. The system occupies a very small piece of ground measuring about 5.52 meters. The passage clearance is about 610 mm × 710mm × 1950mm. It requires nearly 10 minutes for installation.

## Hand Held Metal Detector

This system also detects ferrous and non-ferrous metals i.e. including gold, silver and mercury, etc. It can operate in any environment with temperature varying from 14 degrees centigrades to 15 degrees centigrades and with humidity about 95 per cent. It is used as a hand scanner for regulating a sensitive entry point. It weighs about 500gms and operates on the similar principle of door metal detector. It has also three (3) sensitivity levels which can be chosen by the operator as per the requirements.

## Letter Bomb Detectors

This system is mainly used in the areas where terrorist threat exists. It is capable of screening hundreds of letter in one minute. As soon as metal or similar object is detected inside an envelope/package audio signals are generated as alarm. Letter containing any metal either in the electrical circuits or in the detonator can easily be detected.

## Baggage Explosive Detector

This type of detector consists of a vertical unit which incorporates a series of extractors which uses sample air from and around the body of the individual while passing through the system. It is known that all explosives emit some vapours which are typical of the chemical used in the explosives. If the air contains even minute traces of the explosive vapour the alarm is sounded. It's fitted over the baggage conveyor and brushes the bag/suitcases with large sampling heads they pass over it. The sampling heads extract air from the baggage and process it to determine/detect the explosive vapour. It can also be operated in conjunction with the x-ray screening system.

## Personnel Explosive Detector

These types of detectors are used to detect whether an individual is carrying any explosive. This system operates on a similar principle as that of a baggage explosive detector. when a person passes through the detector, the vertical unit incorporates a series of extractor which examine samples of air from and around the body of an individual passing through the system. Since all explosives emit some vapours similar to the chemical used in the explosives. If the air contains even minute traces of the explosive vapour the detector will raise audio alarm. The unit also comprises of a remote control system which regulates the entry of the personnel through the entry point.

### *Laser Alarm Devices for Point Protection*

This system is basically used to screen objects in high risk areas like safe and almirahs housing *Top Secret* and highly sensitive documents R and D documents in connection with missiles ammunition, nuclear equipments and space programmes, etc. This device operates on battery and thus not dependent on domestic electric supply. If any person tries to manipulate the container or tries to carry away the box/almirah, etc. the system will activate the alarm as soon as the laser beam is interrupted. If anyone is moving in front or behind the box/almirah and secured object, etc. the system does not activate the alarm.

### *Infra-red Thermal Viewer*

This system is capable of displaying the thermal view of the scene during day, night, through smoke and dust, etc. It's highly sensitive and operates on the principle of detection of thermal energy which is emitted by all objects. However, there is always a temperature difference between infra red energy radiated by the human body and the surrounding objects. This device scans the infra red emissions through a window. A reflecting prism converts the infra red radiations into electrical impulses. Thus it provides a two dimensional picture as in case of telescope and the pictures can also be photographed. The system provides a field of view which is 18 degrees vertical and 7.5 degree horizontal. The dimensions are 15.2 × 20.3 × 22.9cms and has an approximate weight of 3.3 kgs.

### *Infra-red night vision devices*

These devices are generally used by defence and para military forces during night for discharging their night duties in peace times and also during operations. When the device is "Switched On" it floods the observer's front view with invisible infra red energy. When the operator looks into the eye-piece of the device, the area under coverage is clearly visible. The mechanism of the device converts the area under coverage into a visual display on the eye-piece, the maximum range of the night vision device is about 500 meters. It is mainly used for night surveillance by patrols and by an artillery Observation Post Officers to direct the artillery fire onto the enemy targets.

### *Laser devices for identifications and surveillance*

These days laser devices are quite frequently used for identifications and surveillance purposes in order to locate a person or an object. It operates by generating a narrow beam of infra red light which is 15cms in diameter at the range of 100 meters. It can be used up till a maximum range of 500meters. The narrow beam is extremely effective in pinpointing a person or an object. The beam has a great psychological effect when it strikes someone. It can cause immobilization to an individual for sometime and thus situation can be exploited by the security staff. The measurements of the devices are 350 mm × 100 mm and weight is approximately one kilogram.

We have seen how the access control system should operate to avoid any theft, pilferage and espionage, etc. in an organization. The golden rule of the industrial security to be followed is that "No one is to be believed on the face value" security staff must verify the person and politely enquire whom and why he/she is paying a visit to the industry or office. A little security is worse than not having any security. Where there is no security at all, management can well appreciate the risk and plan accordingly with adequate measures. But where there is only a token evidence of security management may undergo a grave risk for which no provision is made.

# 8

# Induction of Modern Equipments in Industrial and Corporate Security

The challenges involving high risks in terms of both men and machine, are increasing in a big ratio among the industries. The loss of products due to theft and pilferages, or quantitative losses resulting in less growth and above all the ever-mounting pressure from political leadership and trade unions for their personnel and selfish gains enhance technical and tactical problems for management at various levels. The glaring example of Bharat Aluminum Company Ltd (BALCO) is quite fresh in our mind causing tremendous avoidable financial losses to the employer and employees. The unending problems of industries in the state of Bihar, Assam and Meghalaya, etc. can provide us with volumes of difficulties arising out of ULFA, naxalities and other frustrated groups movements. All these group's people are a great challenge to the industrial security management in the modern scenario. The old method and techniques of security managements are undergoing a fast changing operational tactics coupled with modern equipments to boost up the overall image of industrial security.

In an industry, basically all aspects of security are covered in two broad categories as under:

- Interior Security
- Exterior Security

In chapter four, we have already covered all the aspects of security involving personnel, information, documents, building, plant and machinery. Therefore, it will not be prudent to repeat any thing relating to those aspects. However, now we will critically analyze all the usages of modern equipments in interior and exterior security systems in an organization.

## MODERN DEVICES IN INTERIOR SECURITY SYSTEM

In any industry it is not the end of security functions once an individual is identified at the main entry point. In the real terms the security of an industry starts after the entry gate. The management and chief of security must not lose the sight of it, but should evolve an almost foolproof security set up which can withstand the tricks and techniques of people who are bent upon to breech it in one or other manner.

During the succeeding paras we will critically analyze some of the important modern equipments, presently available in the markets, which if deployed, can enhance the interior security set up. These are:

### Electromagnetic Contact Devices

They are as follows:

1. *Magnetic contact switches*: Magnetic switches are the simplest devices used in industrial security. The system is activated on direct physical action. There may be two circuit conditions of the switch i.e. "open" or "closed". In open circuit, the switch is installed in such a way that when the door is opened, the magnetic field also moves and the switch opens to create alarm. In closed circuit condition the magnetic contact switches work as sensors. The switch is mounted on the door frame and the activating magnet fixed on the door. When the door is closed and the system switched "on" two magnets come in contact with each other and become the part of the complete loop which provides continuous circuit for the flow of current and establishes "no alarm" condition. As soon as the magnet contacts are separated due to opening of doors, the electrical loop is broken and the flow of current is stopped.
2. *Mechanical switches*: Mechanical switches are operated through spring loaded plungers. They are either push button types or lever actuators. Push button switches are mounted on the hinge side of the door, cabinet cover or windows in such a way that any attempt to force open shall make the switch contacts active and initiate the alarm. This device is cheaper and have a simple mechanism, when the door is in "closed" position, the device is completely concealed and invisible. In push button type, the door should open enough to "switch on" the circuit. In order to remove this drawback, lever type switches are used. The lever opens as soon as the door is forced open by the intruder and the alarm conditions are created. Mechanical

switches are used in low level security areas, they can be defeated through thin pieces of plastic, insulation tapes or any other skilled operation by the intruder.

3. *Recessed magnetic switches*: The mode of functioning of recessed magnetic switches are similar to those of surface mounted magnetic switches. The switch unit is concealed within the door frame and the magnet unit in the door which makes it more protected against tampering. These switches should be used only on wooden doors or doors made up of non-magnetic materials which should open inside, because proximity of another magnet or ferrous material may defeat the system. If the door is made up of magnetic material, it will short-circuit the magnetic field of the magnet unit. In case the door opens out, the magnet in the frame cannot be placed properly for correct alignment. These switches are far superior in quality than the mechanical switches.
4. *Balanced magnet switches*: The system consists of a switch assembly mounted on the door frame. The switch assembly contains a 3 positions read switch and a small adjustable magnet known as *Balancing Magnet*. Both components are placed side by side. Another magnet which is called *Balancing Magnet* is mounted on the door in such a way that when the door is closed, its position comes exactly below the switch assembly. When the system is switched "ON" the read switch is held in the centre by two interacting magnetic fields of the balancing magnet and the balancing magnet maintains "no alarm" condition. When the door is forced open, the balancing magnet moves away from the magnetic switch and the primary magnetic field generated by the magnet disappears. This causes disturbance in the stable magnetic field which was keeping the read switch in the centre "no alarm" position. In the absence of primary magnetic field, the magnetic flux of the balancing magnet displaces the read switch from "no alarm" position and the alarm system is activated. During installations and adjustment of switches the critical position of the switch where the opening of door shall initiate the alarm should be adjusted through the balancing magnet of the switch assembly. The adjustment should be made in such a way that even a little opening of the door initiates the alarm. This system has better efficiency than the magnetic or mechanical switches but it can be defeated if the door is penetrated by the intruder and not opened, as usually done.

5. *Window foils*: Window foils are used to protect window glass or walls against forcible penetration. This foil is a metallic conductive tape made up of a thin alloy which has very little tensile strength. It is pasted around the periphery of the window glass in the form of a loop. A coating of varnish is applied over the foil to insulate it electrically and protect it against splitting, ageing, temperature variation and moisture. The foil used for the protection of walls should be concealed with the help of wall paper on plywood paneling.

   Two terminals of the foil are connected to the control units. In "ON" condition, continuous current flows through the loop and "no alarm" condition is maintained. In case the window glass cracks or breaks, the current in the foil is interrupted and alarm initiated.

   This system can be defeated by electrically shorting the two ends of the foil tape. Foils are no longer the popular device but are still in use in low-risk areas.

6. *Trip wire*: Trip wire alarm system consists of a spring which is attached to a terminal block and a thin wire 10–20 feet long which fits into a ball shaped contact point. The wire is laid across the vulnerable approach at the height of about 12 to 18 inches above the ground, so that an intruder is bound to walk into the wire. When bumped, stretched or retracted, the spring loaded wire is pulled out of the ball, opening the circuit and actuating the alarm. The wire is supervised to prevent failure due to cutting or snapping. Sometimes, one end of the wire is connected to a cup containing phosphorous compound, which is ignited through a spring loaded plunger, emitting bright flame for 30–40 seconds to deter the intruder and to attract the attention of security guards. This device is used to provide protection to vulnerable approaches, corridors or hallways. A trip wire switch is used for actuating the alarm.

7. *Pressure mats*: Pressure mats are used for protecting vulnerable approaches, entry points or specific places. One type of mat consists of series of parallel ribbon switches constructed from two strips of metals in the form of a ribbon separated by a insulating material. Another type has two layers of coper wiremesh separated by a soft sponge rubber insulation with large cavities in it. Two wire leads are taken out from each mesh and connected to the control unit and enunciator. The whole mat is then sealed in a rubber jacket. When an intruder steps over it, the copper mesh comes in contact with and closes the electrical circuit for alarm.

Pressure mats are also used for perimeter protection. The sensors are buried underground inside the perimeter fence at likely approaches. The mat should always be concealed under carpet, tiles or other floor coverings. Mats can also be tailor made for specific places. Mats are generally used in low security risk areas but in several circumstances these can be used in high security areas along with other devices.

## Electromechanical Alarm Systems

Electromechanically alarm systems are activated by the physical action of an intruder, such as the cutting of the wire, opening the door, stepping on pressure sensitive devices, etc. Even today, conventional electromechanical devices like mechanical magnetic door switches, magnetic contact switch, window foils, floor mats, sensitive microphone, burried sensors and traps are widely used for industrial security. These devices are normally used to provide protection at specific points, individual openings or narrow passages. However, these systems do not detect intrusion in open space or large areas. On intrusion, the system may actuate a siren, flicker, buzzer or transmit a message to a desired location such as the security or police control room.

### *Characteristics of a Conventional Alarm System*

An alarm system is considered to be effective when it has the following characteristics:

- High degree of efficiency i.e. instantaneous response to the intrusion or contact.
- It should not create obstructions in the smooth functioning of the undertaking.
- It should not be defeated or made disfunctional easily by the intruder
- It should be economical and easy to maintain.
- It should not develop frequent mechanical defects.
- It should not trigger off frequent false alarms.

1. *The sensor*: Sensor is device that detects or senses any change in the status of stable surrounding conditions, mechanically or electrically. Like sensory organs of the human beings, it senses intrusion by a feeling of touch (contact switches, pressure mats, taut wire), sound (vibration, audio detectors) or sight (radio or electromagnetic waves).

All electromechanical sensors are normally switches, activated external force that changes the switch position from "OFF" to "ON" and activates the alarm system. Working of sensors in the electromechanical alarm system is confined to closing a contact between two pieces or displacing a component from on position to another which causes changes in the electrical circuit condition and initiates the alarm. However, these sensors cannot differentiate between an authorized or unauthorized entry. Its components are as under.

2. *Control unit and signal communication path*: As soon as the sensor is activated, it generates electrical pulses which travel to the control unit through a conductor, normally a copper wire. Communications path may also be a telephone line, domestic power line, shared channel or radio circuit. The function of the control unit is like the human brain. It receives signal from the sensor, processes in a logical manner and decides appropriate action. Finally, it activates the local annuciators or transmits signal to a remote servicing station for necessary action. A single control unit may handle a number of alarm circuits and also perform some other functions simultaneously like opening and closing of doors.
3. *The annuciators*: The annuciator receives electrical signals from the control unit through the communication path and announces the alarm or alerts the guards. The annuciator could be a bell, flashing light, siren, buzzer or telephone. A single sensor needs only one annuciator. In some cases a number of annuciators located at different places may be connected to a single sensor. One sensor may activate different annunciators simultaneously like siren at the security control, flashing bulb in the police control room and also convey a recorded message to the hospital or fire station, etc.

When a large number sensors are involved, the annunciator panel is used instead of a single unit. A single panel may have multiple sets of status indicator lights. In such cases the whole set up is divided into zones and the status of each demarcated zone is constantly displayed on the panel. Any change is immediately displayed on the panel and identified by the operator. Coloured bulbs are used to display different locations and status. Light emitting diode (LED) units are used for numerical indication, communicated by the digital dialers and multiplex systems. Illustrated display are the common features in the modern control rooms for quick identification of the troubled spot and response by the security staff.

## Structural Vibration Detectors

Structural vibration detectors are used on walls, floors and ceiling of the buildings. It senses low frequency energy or vibration produced by mechanical chopping, swing or drilling. All such attempts cause the physical barrier to vibrate and generate specific band of frequencies. Lower frequencies with high amplitude travel several feet away from the point of impact of instrument used by the intruder and actuate the transducers secured to the barrier. When a hole is made in the wall buy drilling/hammering vibration waves travel from the point of impact to the transducer which is secured to the wall. The control unit which is connected to the transducer senses the vibration and actuates the alarm.

1. *Piezoelectric transducer*: Two types of transducers are used for converting mechanical energy into electrical energy namely piezo-electric transducer and mechanical switches. In case of piezo-electric transducer the mechanical energy created due to vibration is converted into electrical pulses proportional to the magnitude of the vibration and fed to the signal processor for deciding alarm criteria. From there the signal is sent to the annunciator units. To reduce false alarms due to accidental impacts, the system uses "adjustable pulse count technique." The pulse count circuits are present to count specific numbers of pulses with specific magnitude to initiate alarm.
2. *Mechanical contact switch*: In mechanical contact switches, a small weight (seismic mass) which responds to vibration is used. The mass bounces vertically on external stimuli and opens the contact switch for initiating alarm.

   These detectors are used for the protection of walls against penetration. The transducers should be fully secured to the structure for efficient performance. They should be deployed in such a way that the whole surface area of the wall is secured.

## Capacitance Alarm System

Capacitance devices are generally used for the protection of metal, safes, and cabinets. It works on the principle of invisible radio frequency capacitance field created around the object which is to be protected. Like other electronic capacitors, the object itself act as one of the plates of the capacitor. The second plate is an electrical reference ground plane under and around the protected safe or the cabinet. The objects must be insulated from the ground, on ground the object acts like a dielectric medium. Any intruder approaching the object creates disturbance in the object capacitance to ground field which is detected by the signal processor and alarm conditions are created.

When the system is in 'ON' position of the object becomes electrically charged to a potential which creates an electro-static field between the metal object and the reference ground. When an intruder approaches within the capacitance field of the object, electrical conductivity of his body causes change in the stable capacitance field and activates the alarm. The sensitivity level of the system is kept low to avoid false alarms. Detection area of the system is only upto a radius of 4 to 5 feet from the object.

These detectors are used to protect safes, cabinets, paintings or valuable art objects in the museum or art galleries. Insulating material should be of plastic or non-hydroscopic material. Moisture is a hazard for the dielectric medium; hence wooden blocks should never be used.

## Ultrasonic Detector

The ultrasonic system works on the principle of detection of ultrasonic waves (Inaudible to human ears). Ultrasound waves are generated by a transmitter which floods the protected zone. These waves are reflected from the surrounding objects like walls, doors, floors, fittings, furniture, etc. and received back by a receiver. In 'no alarm' condition reflected waves have the same frequency as the transmitted waves; hence an equilibrium is maintained. Any intrusion in the protected zone disturbs the frequency equilibrium and shifts the frequency of the reflected waves which is instantaneously detected by the signal processing unit and the alarm is created.

1. ***Doppler effect***: Ultrasonic motion detectors follow the phenomenon of doppler effect. "Doppler Effect" is the apparent change in the frequency of a sound or radio wave when reflected or originated from a moving object (an intruder). The system operates between the frequency range of 20 kHz (Kilohertz) to 40 kHz. Acoustic (sound) waves above 19 kHz are inaudible to human ears and therefore, called "Ultrasonic waves".

   (i) *Advantages*: Since ultrasonic waves cannot penetrate through physical barriers like walls, doors and windows, all energy is reflected back in the protected zone and fills it completely. In other words, there are no "dead spots' left. Reflected waves envelope those corners also which are left by the direct transmitted waves.

(ii) *Area coverage*: Area coverage of the system depends upon the configuration and installation of the transreceivers. A single transreceiver mounted on the wall at the height of about 6 feet may cover an area of $30' \times 20' \times 12'$. When a transreceiver is mounted on the ceiling of a room it produces a cone-shaped 3 dimensional energy pattern covering an area of about 30 feet diameter. Systems with the coverage range of about 70 feet area are also available in the market. Miniature detectors are used in small rooms. Such devices have the size of 8.5 cm × 5 cm × 4.5 cm and they operate on 12 volts DC power supply.

(iii) *Application*: Ultrasonic motion detectors are used to provide protection in the interior of the building like rooms, halls, stores and art galleries, etc. The system is adversely affected by strong air, thermal air current, humidity, hissing noise, vibration, ringing sound and all these produce false alarm.

Various signal processing techniques are used like; filtering energies with frequencies above and below the signals with frequencies characteristic of a moving intruder, sensing fluctuating strange frequencies and automatically adjusting the alarm threshold to a higher level, ignoring signals which do not represent the net change in range which is the characteristic signal of intrusion and the use of compensation circuits.

## Passive Infra-red Motion Detector

1. ***Principle of operation***: Infra-red is a silent, invisible and transmittable energy emitted by all objects having temperature more than-273 degrees centigrade (absolute zero). It also warms the surface on which it falls. Any device capable of detecting the change in temperature can sense the infra-red energy. The infra-red spectrum ranges between visible red light (about 0.75 m and shortest microwave about 1,000 m). However, the common detection range is between 8–14 microns. Typical characteristics of the infra-red wave, are utilized in the infra-red motion detector for detecting intrusion in the protected zone because the human body also radiates infra-red energy. The device detects the body heat of thermal energy at the frequencies corresponding to the body temperature of 98 degrees Fahrenheit.

2. ***Merits of passive IR system***:

(a) It does not require visible light (as in case of CCTV system) for its operation.

(b) It does not require any transmission of signals like microwave or ultrasonic systems.

(c) It is neutral and harmless.

(d) It is unrelated to noise as in case of audio-detectors.

3. *Types of passive infra-red systems*

There are three types of sensors:

(a) Pyroelectric

(b) Thermister bolometer

(c) Thermopile sensor

In pyroelectric device (ceramic or plastic), a change in the temperature of the surrounding areas causes electric current to flow into the device and cause change of polarization, which initiates the alarm. At constant temperature of the element, no current flows and equilibrium is maintained.

Thermister bolometer devices respond to the entire wave length of the infra-red spectrum i.e. from longest infra-red to shortest ultraviolet region. In this device infra-red energy falling on the sensor raises the surface temperature of the sensor and changes the resistance of the sensitive (semi-conductor oxide) material used in the sensor. The change in the resistance activates the alarm. The signal processor of the system can differentiate between thermal variations of the environment like changing of air temperature and change due to intrusion.

Thermopile sensors have a pair of thermoelectric junction of dissimilar metals. Out of two, one is shielded from radiation and the other blackened to absorb more radiation. When radiation from the surrounding atmosphere falls on the junction it causes difference in temperature and production of electromagnetic force. The detector monitors electromagnetic force and initiates the alarm.

4. *Demerits of passive infra-red system*: This system has some limitations. It is vulnerable to false alarm due to interception by flying insects, birds or domestic animals. While doing selection and arranging installation, these limitations should be given due considerations. Since the device is sensitive to heat it should be kept away from the working machineries or systems producing heat. It should not be mounted near radiators, thermal pipes or heaters.

### *Applications*

(a) Infra-red devices are used for providing protection in high security zones; inside the rooms, halls or long corridors, retail stores, etc. Depending upon the type of coverage required, the system may have single or multiple beam configurations.

It may be interesting to note that during the Vietnam war passive infra-red device was used to detect enemy encampments from a reconnaissance plane.

(b) With the help of fresnel lens and modified elements the field of view of the device can be enhanced to 30′ × 30′ × 7′ and upto a distance from 150′ × 300′

## Microwave Detectors

The ultrasonic system generates sound waves or acoustic energy in the frequency range or 20,000 hertz to 40,000 hertz per second which fills the protected zone. Some of the energy is reflected back to the receiver from the surrounding objects like walls, ceiling, floor, furniture and fixtures, etc. when any intruder moves into the protected zone he causes changes in the frequency of the reflected energy due to "doppler effect". The shift in the frequency of the reflected sound waves is registered by the receiver and the control unit actuates the alarm.

The microwave system generates electromagnetic energy, greater than 10 million cycles per second instead of sound energy as in the case of ultrasonic system. These frequencies are 100 thousand times greater than the frequencies shown on the dial of a domestic radio receiver. Electromagnetic waves in the microwave band ('X' band) are generated by a transmitter and beamed into the protected zone. Some of the transmitted energy is absorbed by the surrounding objects like wall, furniture, door, etc. and the rest is reflected back from these objects. The reflected waves are picked up by the microwave receiver and a stable "no alarm" condition is maintained. When intrusion takes place in the protected zone, the stable status is disturbed and the reflected waves have no longer the same frequency. This shift in the frequency of reflected waves is noticed by the receiver and the processor unit which activates the alarm.

### *Coverage Pattern and System Configuration*

The shape and pattern of the transmitted energy and its characteristics decide the application and utility of the system. The pattern depends upon the antenna configuration which can be designed for different uses. Microwave antenna generating omni-directional and directional patterns of energy lobes are available. The pattern of radiated energy may be circular do-nut-shaped, elliptical or hemisphere.

A quaterwave monopole antenna, mounted on metal disc ground plane generates omnidirectional do-nut shaped wave pattern about 60' in diameter. Directional teardrop shaped pattern are generated by dual or single wave guide horns. In 'no alarm" condition, the frequency of the transmitted energy is equal to the frequency of reflected signals. Any movement in the protected zone causes shift in the frequency of the reflected signals and initiates alarm. In this pattern the teardrop shaped energy pattern can be directed to the area of protection and focussed away from the source of system hazards to reduce false alarms. The size of the energy lobes may be 15′ × 20′ or 40′ × 50′. Broad patterns are used for the protection of large areas while the narrow pattern is used for protecting lanes and narrow corridors. Detectors using dual horns use two separate wave guides, one for transmission and one for reception.

### *Precautions While Handling*

While using microwave devices some precautions are necessary:

(i) Directional antenna should never be pointed towards exterior walls specially when the wall is facing a common vehicular road, because the system picks up the movement of metallic vehicles on the road far away from the protected zone and create false alarm. Microwave energy is more attenuated by building materials like bricks, doors, wooden windows and sheet rock but are reflected by glass and steel bodies.

(ii) The angle at which the transmitted energy strikes the wall or object determines the amount of energy that will penetrate the object or shall be attenuated by it.

(iii) The amount of absorption depends upon the nature density and distance of the object from the transmitter.

(iv) Microwave energy reflected from the surrounding metallic object may result in the concentration of energy in the protected zone and help in eliminating "dead spots".

(v) Vibration of the surface on which the unit is mounted may cause false alarm, passing trains or working compressors may cause vibration of the base on which the transreceiver is installed and initiate false alarm.

(vi) Proximity of a fluorescent lamp shall activate false alarm due to on-off ionization cycle of the lamp.

(vii) Metallic objects should be removed from the coverage zone because metals reflect the energy like the mirror reflecting light. Steel cabinets, tables, etc. may be placed in a suitable position to avoid causing false alarm.

(viii) Microwave energy pointing towards the rotating objects like door, fan blades, etc. also shifts the frequency of the reflected energy.

(ix) Microwave detectors should be mounted high near the ceiling of the area to be protected in such a way that the transmitted energy pattern is directed in the desired direction but away from the metallic objects or doors, etc.

### *Advantages*

The microwave system has many advantages over other active volumetric detection systems:

(a) It is immune to the change of temperature, humidity, air current.

(b) It is immune to the high frequency noise of sirens, ringing bells, etc.

(c) It can be preset to ignore frequency shifts due to movement of insects and domestic animals. These qualities keep the rate of false alarm to minimum.

(d) The system is equally effective in open areas as well as long hallways or corridor.

## Audio Detection System

The audio detection system works on the principle of converting sound energy into electrical impulses which are ampllified and fed to the annunciator i.e. a loud speaker. It can also be connected to a recording mechanism for continuous recording of events.

### *Principle of Working*

Cracking noises due to intruder 'section generate audio signals which are picked up by the detector and sent to the signal processor which decides the alarm criteria. The system is normally tuned to pick up sound frequencies between 1,500 and 6,000 Hz. and ignores frequency below 1500Hz and above 6000 Hz. In this way unwanted external noises which are not in the preset frequency detection ranges eliminated. This measure reduces nuisance alarms. The frequency range covers more or less all noise frequencies generated due to movement or action of the intruder.

### *Advantages and Application*

Audio receivers may be programmed to pick up only those frequencies, which are created due to the intruders movements. The system can be connected to a remote control place, may be 30 kms away, where a person on duty continuously listens to the noise created in the protected area also records the sound for appropriate action. In the audio system even the conversations between the intruders can be monitored and recorded. Remote listening facility enables security guards to identify false alarms to a large extent; whereas in other systems it is not possible for the guard sitting in a remote location to differentiate between a true and a false system.

The existing public address system networks in the concerned building can be converted into audio detection devices after the working hours without the burden of additional cost.

## CLOSE CIRCUIT TELEVISION (CCTV) SYSTEM IN INDUSTRIAL AND CORPORATE SECURITY

Close circuits television (CCTV) system has been regarded as one of the most important sources in all types of security. In Industrial Security Management, whether it is exterior or interior security requirements, the CCTV occupies a predominant position. It is considered to be a perfect, reliable and dependable security source which can provide real time information about all events and actions taking place at any place and time. It is capable of displaying a complete picture of the area under surveillance on a monitor located in the control room. The CCTV is meant for providing audio and video information from a particular location through a close circuit.

The complete system of CCTV consists of a camera installed at a specific location to keep/view the area under surveillance, coaxial cable for transmission of audio and video signals, a monitor and power supply for operation.

### *Operating Principle*

The camera converts the optical picture into electrical signals, which are transmitted to the monitor through the coaxial cable. The monitor converts the electric signals into a picture. Speech can also be transmitted along with the pictures if so desired.

### System Configuration

1. *Single camera with multiple monitors*: CCTV systems are available in various configurations. Normally, a single camera is attached to 3 monitors which may be allocated to different places. Video signals from the camera are transmitted to three monitors through a distribution amplifier so that identical and clear pictures are reproduced on all screens. This configuration is adopted when a sensitive area is desired to be viewed by different persons. The distance between the CCTV camera and monitors may be ranging from a few meters to kilometers.
2. *Single monitor with multiple camera*: This configuration involves a single monitor connected to number of TV cameras. The number may be upto 6 depending on the area to be covered and the ability of the control room to take follow up action at various spots. Too many screens may cause confusion and fatigue to the viewer in the control room. To avoid this factor, several cameras may be "sequenced" into a single screen on time sharing basis. This camera configuration also inter-connects intrusion detection devices with individual monitors.

### Application and Uses

The CCTV system is used for continued surveillance of the following:

(a) Perimeter fencing.
(b) Isolated and vulnerable areas.
(c) Loading/unloading places/locations.
(d) Entry/Exit Gates.
(e) Sensitive working places.
(f) Stores/Warehouses.
(g) Museums.
(h) Banks.
(i) Air ports.
(j) Railway stations.
(k) Hospitals.
(l) Hotels.

Cameras should be installed at vulnerable places after analyzing the requirements.

### *Choice of Equipment*

It is the prerogative of the management on the advice of the Head of the Security to choose the most suitable CCTV system for the organization. Selection of a particular hardware, with its inbuilt merits and demerits should be an important task in this direction. However, some of the important factors as mentioned below, must be borne in mind.

(a) Define the areas to be kept under surveillance.

(b) Size of the object/area to be viewed.

(c) Distance between object and the camera location.

(d) Types of surveillance whether of moving or stationary objects.

(e) Extent of light intensity in the area.

(f) Extent of details and clarity required in the system.

Different types of cameras, lenses and monitors are required in each different case. For surveillance purpose, clarity of the picture is important and for clarity "horizontal resolution" is the key factor which is measured by the maximum number of individual picture elements that can be distinguished in a single horizontal scan lines. The image on a TV monitor is composed of hundreds of horizontal lines. The average home TV receiver has a minimum of 380 horizontal lines but CCTV monitor have more such lines for clarity and details. A zoom system may have 1,000 lines. With increasing resolutions lines the cost of the camera also goes up. In such places like loading points, etc. where only movement is to be monitored, there is no need of purchasing a costly high resolution camera. In general, five types of cameras are used.

(i) *Vidicon Tube*: It is the most popular and cheap tube used for indoor as well as outdoor application. It is effective under fairly bright light conditions.

(ii) *Newvicon Tube*: This type of camera is used in poor light conditions in parking places, and warehouses, etc.

(iii) *Silicon Diode Tube*: This type of camera is used under artificial lights like mercury tube lights, bulbs, etc.

(iv) *Intensified Target Tube*: This type of camera is used in dark nights. These cameras are very expensive but invaluable in extremely sensitive locations.

### *Components of the System*

A CCTV camera is fitted with the following facilities which can be controlled from a remote location i.e. a control room or any other desired place.

(a) *Pan*: Pan is the facility to move the camera in horizontal axis. With the help of a remote switch the camera can be rotated upto 300 degrees in horizontal plain. The speed of rotation is about 6 degrees per second.

(b) *Tilt*: Tilt is the mechanism to move the camera up or down upto 90 degrees with the help of a remote switch. The speed of the movement is about 10 degrees per second.

(c) *Zoom*: In zoom system a distant image can be brought closer on the monitor for minute observation. For this purpose the camera lens used is of multiple focal length. Like other facilities zooming can be controlled from a remote place/switch. A 300 mm telephoto lens can zoom up to 1 km.

### *Weather Proof Housing*

In a situation where CCTV camera is to be installed in open weather then it should be housed in a temperature and weather proof housing, at a sufficient height to protect against climatic conditions like, rain, dust, snow, for wider coverage.

### *Recording Facility*

One of the biggest advantages of the CCTV system is the audio and video recording facilities. Video tape recorder (VTR) can be connected to the monitor for continuous or selective recording of events which can be used for future references or evidence purposes. There is no use of continuous recording, which may be huge waste and very costly. Nowadays 10–30 minutes repeating cassettes are used. The tape repeats the circuit after every 30 minutes and erases the previous recordings. VTR systems are available with date and superimposing capabilities which are used when the video tape is to be produced in the court as evidence.

### *Monitors*

Different CCTV monitors are used for different uses. In a single monitor multiple camera configuration a 19″ – 24″ monitor is normally used. In some cases one monitor is used with each camera. However, this configuration increases the number of monitors on the control panel. As per the experience, not more than 10 screens can be scanned effectively by a single viewer, hence 9″ monitors should be used in these cases. In order to minimize fatigue, monitors should be installed in a console slightly below the eye level of the viewer and angled in a manner to keep the scanning range to the minimum. All monitors should be fitted in a curved configuration in front of the viewer so that all are at an equal distance from the eye of the viewer. Monitor screens should be placed in a systematic manner to avoid confusion. It should also be fitted with filters to prevent glare in the eyes of the viewer. Experiments have proved that women are much suitable for this assignment than men.

### *Application in industrial security*

CCTV is the most effective security system for use with security organizations. It can be used in all security functionings and may be hooked up with other devices also. However, its adoption in developing countries is rather slow due to the higher costs as compared to the other systems.

## MODERN DEVICES IN EXTERIOR SECURITY SYSTEM

In all the industries, it is not only the interior security system which matters, but management of exterior security system is equally important. It is the prime concern of the chief of the security to be more vigilant about exterior set up. Generally, all the treats and other unlawful activities starts in case there is laxity in the exterior security set up. To counter all possible threats, there are number of electronic and mechanical devices which if incorporated, in the regular security set up, the overall functional capabilities of industrial sccurity will be enhanced to a greater extent.

In the succeeding paragraphs we will study most of the modern devices which are currently in use by developing countries.

### Electromagnetic Interference

Exterior intrusion systems are highly vulnerable to electromagnetic interference from high power transmission lines, radar, power plants, etc. electromagnetic shield and power line filtering, fielding should be adopted in cases where such hazards exist. There are two types of electromagnetic interference, one is radiated and the other conducted. Radiated interference occurs when radiated energy comes in direct contact with electronic equipment, power and signal lines. Conducted interference are induced on the power line by electrical equipment and lightening, etc. In such cases large electromagnetic field is induced by lightening which causes false alarm.

(i) *Tuning of the equipment*: Sensitivity of the equipment should be adjusted to an optimum level laid down by the manufacturer. This aspect should be checked periodically. Increasing the sensitivity level more than the operational requirement will increase the rate of false alarms and decreasing the sensitivity level below a preset level shall decrease the efficiency of the system. Therefore, the ideal tuning must be ensured by constant checks.

(ii) *Design of the equipment*: While selecting and designing the system critical threat analysis is important. An expert should conduct detailed survey of the area. The survey should include complete perimeter, the ground outside as well as inside, vegetation's exterior ground around the building, topography and the proximity of any source of electromagnetic interference. Designer should have the plan that shows the perimeter fence building position, floor plan and other details which may be important for design consideration. The type of the perimeter (wall or fence) washouts, height, likely approaches, weather conditions are the other factors which affect the choice of the equipment.

## Electromechanical Transducers

Electromechanical transducers change mechanical energy into electrical signals. Two configuration of these transducers are available i.e. closed or open switch type. These switches open momentarily on vibrations of this fence created by forced actions of the intruder and generate electrical pulses. These pulses are analyzed by the signal processor and the alarm criteria decided. The numbers of pulses are proportionate to the induced vibration.

The first type uses a mechanical inertia switch consisting of a single or double metal seismic mass that rest on two multiple contact rods or triple electrical contacts in normal conditions. The moveable mass reacts to the vibrations created due to intruder's actions and determines the 'alarm' condition by opening or closing of circuit. The frequency of opening or closing of the switch is proportionate to the actions of the intruder. The mass moves vertically on vibration and when it is lifted up it produces opens–circuit pulses. The other type of switch is mercury switch which consist of a glass vial containing mercury and two electrical contacts immersed in it. In "no alarm" condition, the switch is closed. In case of forced action by the intruder on the fence, the vibration generated reach the vial and displaces the mercury, thus opening the electrical circuits at short intervals, which in turn generates short electrical pulses proportionate to the intruder's action. The signal is sent to the processor for analyzing and intiating the alarm.

I. ***Equipment installation***: Electromechanical switches are installed on the fence post. Each sensor is connected in series along the fence with a common cable. Switches can be arranged to create "Zones" for easy maintenance and effective detection. In order to keep the nuisance alarm to the minimum level the fence fabric should be tight and fence posts well anchored to avoid vibrations due to wind. Sensors should be housed in sealed and tamper proof boxes.

II. ***Precautions***:
   (a) The post should be well anchored to avoid vibrations.
   (b) Vegetation, trees or other objects should be cleared from the fence to avoid rattling.
   (c) Extend the bottom of the fence to sufficient depth underneath the ground to avoid tunneling efforts by criminals or saboteurs.
   (d) The fence fabric should be tight and well secured.

## Piezoelectric Transducers

Piezoelectric transducers convert mechanical vibration into electric energy in the form of analog signals which vary proportionally to the amplitude and frequency of the mechanically induced vibrations on the fence due to intruders action. The device uses a thin film of quartz material, silicon dioxide which is specially grounded to respond to the particular vibration frequencies generated on the fence and produce electrical signals which are proportional to the induced stress. A signal processor is used to analyze the signals and decide the alarm criteria. The system may react to winds more than 30 kilometer per hour and initiate the false alarm.

Piezoelectric transducers can be mounted on the fence fabric or posts 30 feet apart in a configuration required for a particular situation. A moderately dense configuration is more effective because vibration waves caused on the fence fabric due to intruder's action do not have to travel long distance to reach the transducer. Piezoelectric transducers are connected in parallel (electrically) to the signal processor. Shielded cables are used to prevent unwanted induced signals. "Pulse counting technique" and band pass filters are used to minimize false alarms. The fence fabric should be very tight, well secured and free from vegetation.

(i) *Precautions*:

(a) Increased density of sensors will increase the ambient background noise.

(b) High velocity wind, more than 20–25 mph may induce false alarms.

(c) The cable should be shielded properly.

## Geophone Sensors

A geophone transducer consists of a tubular seismic mass wound with a coil of fine wire and a cylindrical permanent magnet. The permanent magnet is fixed to the geophone housing while seismic mass suspended in spring balance around the magnet. When external force is supplied on the fence by the intruder, it creates mechanical vibration which displaces the permanent magnet from its position toward the seismic mass. As soon as the magnet comes closer to the mass, the coil of the mass cuts the magnetic field of the magnet and induces electromagnetic force in the coil. The magnitude of the induced analog signal is proportional to the magnitude and frequency of the external stimuli. Consequently, electrical signals are published by the coil and transmitted to the signal processors for analysis and establishing alarm criteria.

Geophone transducers are mounted in the centre of the fence fabric about 20 feet apart. They are mounted in such a way that the axis of vibration is in vertical direction. This arrangement reduces the false alarm due to wind, the axis of which is always in horizontal direction. The density and number of geophones to be fixed depends upon the area of protection and the security hazards.

The fence posts should be well anchored and fence fabric should be kept tight. Sensor cable should be shielded properly and protected against any kind of tampering.

## Electrets Cable Transducers

Electrets cable transducer is a sensitive coaxial cable. The centre portion of the cable is a conductor covered by a low loss dielectric material to carry a permanent electrostatic charge. On top of these two, there is a another cover of woven wire. The whole assembly is enclosed in a weather resistant jacket. Mechanical vibrations generated on the fence due to intruder's activities induce distortion in the coaxial cable and in turn it generates analog signals proportional to the mechanical stress on the fence. These signals are analyzed in the signal processing unit and alarm criteria determined by the system. For installation of the device, the cable should be secured to the chain link fence in the middle of the fabric with plastic chords.

The transducer can be equipped with a listening device which can differentiate between the noises created by wind, rain and sound generated by the forced operations of the intruder. Electric cable sensors are available in varying length between 300 to 1000 feet. Indicators can also be fitted on the control panel for pinpointing the location of intrusion. The signal processor should be housed in a weatherproof box with electromagnetic shielding.

## Electric Field Sensor

Electric field sensors work on the principle of detection of charge in the electrostatic field between two parallel conductors due to intrusion of a foreign body. Two conductors are installed parallel to each other. One is known as "Field Wire" and the other as "Sense Wire". Omnidirectional electric field is generated through AC current in the field wire. The sensing wire picks up the electric field generated by the field wire. In "no-alarm" condition, the signal processor monitors the stable electric field between two wires. Any intrusion within the energy pattern changes the induced electrical signal and initiates the alarm.

This system is mostly used for fence protection. It can be programmed to reject high frequency signals generated by high velocity wind and other disturbances and low frequencies generated due to impact of animals on the fence. The sensing wire may be tuned to react only to frequencies generated due to intruder's movements. The wires must be erected under high tension to reject higher frequencies. The signal processor of the system has a self-adjusting circuit which automatically adjusts the detector sensitivity to compensate for the metallic objects moved closer to the sensor. This property enables the system to provide protection to metallic bodies like cars, etc. placed within its sensitivity zone.

## Buried Line Sensors and Stress/Magnetic Line Sensors

Buried line sensor is a transducer cable buried under the ground at a depth of about 6″ to 14″ under the soil. The sensor cable can detect both magnetic as well as seismic stimuli. Magnetic detectors sense magnetic flux of ferrous metals carried by the intruder like weapons, belt buckle, etc. while seismic detectors react to the foot-steps of the intruder walking over the ground. The cable transducer consists of a magnetic material wound with a pair of sense coil winding, wrapped with a stainless steel jacket and covered with an outer plastic jacket. The sense coils are connected together in a manner to conceal far frield seismic and magnetic disturbances.

An intruder crossing over the cable induces stress on the ferromagnetic core material and after magnetic flux that generates a voltage in the sensewinding overlay around the coil. Any intruder carrying ferrous materials disturbs the earth magnetic field and alters the coil magnetic flux. At the end, voltage is generated in the sense winding. Voltage in both cases are analyzed by the signal processor for initiating the alarm.

Sensor cables are used for perimeter protection. The standard length available is upto 600 feet. It can also be used inside the perimeter as the 2[nd] line of defence.

## Invisible Barrier Detectors

Invisible beam barriers are created by generating a narrow beam of invisible energy across the zone of protection. A transmitter is used to produce the energy across the zone of protection and a receiver is placed opposite to the transmitter to receive the signals. Transmitters and receivers are placed in the line of sight and properly aligned. Mis-alignment may reduce the efficiency. The beam pattern is affected by the vegetation and broken patches, hence the ground between the transmitter and receiver should be leveled and made free from the growth to prevent nuisance alarm.

The system works on the principle that intrusion through the beam temporarily blocks the energy which disturbs the equilibrium of the 'no alarm' status and the alarm is activated. There are basically two types of active barrier detectors. One is the microwave and the other is infra-red. Both generate beams in their respective bands of frequency spectrum. In case of microwave detectors, intrusion causes distortion in the energy pattern or causes shifts in the microwave energy multipath signals. These variations are detected by the signal processor for initiating alarm.

Infra-red detectors are installed in columns across the protected zone, in the line of sight and with proper alignment. They generate multipath beam patterns of modulated infra-red energy. On intrusion, the frequency of the beam received by the receiver undergoes a shift which is sensed by a device known as the signal processor for creating the alarm.

## Photo Electric Beam Barrier

### *(i) Operating Principle*

Photoelectric detector uses a light beam across the protected zone for detection. Any interruption in the beam due to intruder's action is registered by the system and alarm is sounded. The system consist of a transmitter which uses Gallium Arsenide LED (Light Emitting Diodes) to generate invisible "red" light in the infra-red region of the frequency spectrum i.e. 0.9 mm wavelength. This light is modulated to change the intensity of the light source to 1000 times per second. The transmitted light beam is monitored by a receiver placed opposite to the transmitter in the line of sight across the protected zone. The receiver uses a photoelectric cell for detection and converts light energy into electrical signals, thereafter, the signals are amplified, detected and processed for deciding alarm criteria.

Photoelectric beam is modulated to reduce false alarm and to make the system more effective because modulated waves are not affected by sunlight or any other steady light source. In some cases mirrors are used to extend the coverage and the pattern of the light beams. In this way a signal transmitter can be used to provide coverage to large areas by putting mirrors at different corners to reflect the incident beam. In "no alarm" condition the transmitted light beam is continuously received by the receiver and stable "no alarm" status is maintained. On intrusion a major portion of the light beam is blocked and the alarm situation is created. Breakage of light beam even for a fraction of second initiates the alarm.

### *(ii) Pattern of Coverage*

The typical coverage pattern of a photoelectric beam is 152.4m long, 7.6m thick beam aiming at 180 degrees horizontal and 46 degrees vertical angle. The beam has 9400 Angstrom pulsed energy at 1000 pulses per second. Use of mirrors reduces the range and the intensity of the beam due to refraction and scattering of the light energy. Smoke, dust, birds and animals are the potential hazards for the system.

Photoelectric sensors are used across the vulnerable approaches, doors, windows and galleries, etc. for sending early warning alarm signals.

## Laser Beam Barrier

### *Working Principle*

Laser beams are used for permeter protection. LASER is an acronym for "Light Amplification by Stimulated Emission of Radiation". The system uses a semiconductor gallium arsenide crystal for producing laser beam. When stimulated by focused light waves, the gallium arsenide crystal amplifies and concentrates the waves into a very intense narrow beam. Laser only operates when the stimulation process predominates over the absorption process throughout the laser medium. The stimulation process starts when the atom becomes excited by absorbing a photon of light and gaining the energy. For continued reaction, more and more atoms should be put in the excited state for predominated emission action. In this condition, the distribution of energy level is upside down. This distribution pattern is called "inverted population" produced by a process called pumping. Within the broad wave length band of laser which covers the entire optical region i.e. from 0.1 m to 100 m gallium arsenide can be made to almost any specific frequency.

The laser wavelength is determined by the energy separation of the conduction and the wave bond of the crystals. When laser diode operates in infra-red wavelength, two semi-conductors such as Indium Arsenide and Indium Phosphide are combined to make alloy and laser diode, which radiates at the wavelength of 0.9 micron to 3 micron.

The major difference between the laser system and the infra-red system is in the light source. Laser beams are very sharp and can travel to long distances without distortion. When used for perimeter protection it can create an invisible barrier of about 10,000 feet.

## Active Infra-red Detectors

The "active infra-red system" transmits infra-red energy from a transmitter across the protected zone, which is received by a receiver and analyzed by the signal processor for initiating alarm. The frequency is just below red colour invisible light spectrum. That is why infra-red energy is invisible to naked eyes.

## Working Principle

The transmitter uses solid state infra-red source, gallium arsenide light emitting diode for producing infra-red energy and the receiver uses a photoelectric cell which receives the transmitted energy and reacts to the intrusions in the protected zone. The light source is modulated and pulsed to a specific frequency to avoid compromise and reduce false alarm and the light is changed in the form of beam through lens and transmitted towards the receiver, placed across the protected zone. A collecting lens in the receiver focuses the radiant energy into a photoelectric cell which changes the radiant energy into electrical signals proportional to the transmitted energy. Alarm is initiated when the blockage of the beam is 90 per cent for 75 milliseconds. This system reduces the chance of false alarm due to intrusion by insects and birds.

### *Application*

Infra-red barriers are used as second zone of perimeter protection. They have high detection probabilities while crawling, jumping or running across the protected zone.

## Microwave Beam Barrier

Microwave detectors are used as beam barriers in external application. Microwave energy in the frequency range of about 10,525-megahertz is produced in the transmitter by using Gun Diodes. A corresponding receiver is placed across the zone of protection in the line of sight of the transmitter. Depending upon the antenna size and its configuration, a narrow beam of microwave energy is transmitted to the receiver. When an intruder passes through the beam the receiver detects the loss of signals and distortion in energy pattern and initiates the alarm when a preset alarm criterion is achieved. Blocking of the beam by the intruder while walking, running or jumping at the rate between 0.15 and 5 meters per second initiates the alarm.

Generally, the frequency used by the exterior microwave detector is 10,525+25 MHz and the field strength is limited to about 250 millivolts per meter at the range of 30 meters. The range and energy pattern depends upon the antenna configuration. Larger reflectors produce more sharp and narrow beam and have longer range. The maximum range of coverage is between 200:150 length.

Antenna configuration used are: slotted arrays, waveguide horns, stripline array and parabolic dish. Since the antenna of the transmitter and receiver are identical and the field of acceptance of the receiver is also identical to the transmitted detection pattern, the energy pattern between the transmitter and receiver is always symmetrical.

## Use of Optical Fiber for Various Security Systems

### *Working Principle*

Optical fibers are the devices which incorporate the advance technology of optical communication. The fibers are the small filament of glass having diameter of about 0.2 mm. The fiber is highly polished from inside. Light wave in the frequency of 1 m (micrometer) to 30 m are pulse coded and transmitted through the glass. At the other end these pulses are decoded and used for alarm purposes. Optical fibers are used in different configurations like fence, tapes, grills, panels, etc.

### *Advantages*

Fiber optic devices have many advantages over other systems like the following:

(i) It is immune to climate and weather condition.
(ii) It is not affected by electromagnetic disturbances.
(iii) It can be used as free standing barrier in the open.
(iv) It can be used as under water barrier.
(v) It is used in fire risk areas like LPG and petroleum industries.
(vi) It is anti-corrosive.
(vii) Maintenance is easy.

Some of the fiber optic device, which are extensively used by modern security organizations are the following.

## Fiber Optic Alarm Grills

In this device optical fibers are used in the form of grills. The optical fiber is made up of extremely thin glass through which pulsed light signals are transmitted and decoded at the other end. In case of break of the fiber the alarm is created. The grills are manufactured from extruded glass reinforced plastic tubes which are highly resistant to corrosion. The grills are fastened to the fiber optics in such a way that a connector can be located at each corner of the grill.

The matrix is connected to the control unit through the fiber optic unit. Any effort to break the grill results in the initiation of the alarm. This device can be used in industries which are using it as exterior as well as interior barrier.

## Fiber Optic Panels

Fiber optic panels are the woven net of fiber optics ultrasonically welded and secured at each cross-over joint with high impact security fixing. The basic material used for making the panels are the inorganic materials consisting of a matrix of hydraulic cement and fine aggregates reinforced with alkali resistant glass fiber. The panel has two components; a carrier panel and cover plate, between which is laid a continuous run of optimesh. The fiber optic panels are used primarily as the under water alarm barrier. It can also be used to provide a false alarm for a building protection system. The panels can be either integrated into the fabric of the building or fitted on the outside surface of the existing structure.

## Fiber Optic Fence

Fiber optic fence is made up of barbed swaged steel tape containing the glass fiber. Any attempt to cut or break the fence initiates the alarm. This device is mostly used for exterior protection. It can be made free-standing or supported on the wall. The barbed tape is available in the form of straight wire or concertina. Straight wire can be used on outriggers fitted over the perimeter wall or ordinary fence. The concertina can be used as a temporary first line barrier or effective second line of defence.

### *Requirement and Choice of the Equipment*

It is very essential that management is properly advised by the chief of security about the requirements and choice of the equipments. It will be imperative to keep in mind the limitations of the equipment alongwith the organizational need and overall cost effectiveness of the entire setup. It should be well understood that basic source of security setup is the men behind the equipment. Therefore, the equipments selected for the interior and exterior security set-up must be such so that it is closely co-ordinated into the existing set-up to enhance the modern and technical capabilities in order to fit in as a well knit team for achieving the management goals.

# 9
# Industrial Crime Management

The basic tasks, which are assigned to the head of the industrial security and its security organization, are to plan and ensure prevention of industrial crimes in an organization. An industrial crime is a civil offence which in the legal language can be defined as under.

## CRIME

"Crime is an act which, because it effects injurious society as a whole or a member of it, infringes some law enacted to prevent such injury and thereby attracts the punishment prescribed by the law for such infringement."

The above definition of crime brings out that any act, which is injurious to the society or its members, will attract punishment as prescribed by the law. Similarly, any crime committed by an employee or visitor, etc. Which causes any damage to a person, material or information of an organization/ office must be prevented. It is an important function of the security in-charge to keep his eyes and ears open to foresee an incoming act of crime.

In an industrial organization, basically there are three types of crimes as under:

- Crimes/offences against industrial and commercial information.
- Crimes/offences against personnel.
- Crimes/offences against property.

### Crimes/Offences Against Industrial and Commercial Information

Management of security of information, related to an industry/office has already been discussed in detail in earlier chapter. Here the discussion will be restricted to various aspects of crimes against industrial and commercial information. In the corporate world it is an unending race to prove its excellence in providing a better product/service to its consumers/clients. The challenges are so high and difficult that every industry/organization tries to attain "one up manship" by using fair or foul means to any extent. The rising rate of industrial and commercial crimes is very alarming. It is primarily for the large corporate houses a serious cause of concern where they have to adopt strict and comprehensive preventive measures to safeguard against such crimes.

### *Common Sources of Crimes*

Security staff must be very vigilant in their daily routines, since many agency keep collecting important industrial and commercial information under the garb of " Economic Market Research". These agencies compile and analyze these collected sensitive datas regarding business rivals, bulk of these information is collected, and compiled from the following:

- Prospectus of organization.
- Brochures of annual general meetings, etc. Containing annual reports including balance sheets.
- Trade journals/magazines.
- Directories.
- Details of expenditure on research and development, marketing and business developments.

### *Dangerous Activities for Informational Crimes*

In any industrial organization one has to keep a close vigil on some frequent but dangerous activities related with industrial information. Some of the common hazards which may open the flood gates of valuable information are enumerated in succeeding paras.

### *Change of Employment by Senior Managers*

These days in the corporate world, daily, one can read in the newspaper, frequent change of employment is becoming a high tech fashion. Senior professionals including technocrats keep changing their employer for better pay and perks. It is quite likely that these people may have free access to company's vital and closely guarded information which in case he/she joins a rival group can pose a severe threat. The loyalty of such employees can't be trusted beyond main gate. On joining the new organization, the person may reveal either full or part of the sensitive information.

### *Frustrated Employee*

An employee who has reached his/her ceiling may not hesitate to divulge a sensitive information which during his/her service tenure, might have acquired in the organization. The loyalty of such persons is very fragile and can be moulded for some personnel gains in one or other form.

### *Business Consultants*

Almost all business consultants are providing their services to many industrial houses/office organizations in one or other fields. During the course of their advisory services they collect various information/data from the company for compiling their reports. It is quite likely that during the course of their service contract, some vital information may be leaked out to another rival group/company. Although legal and ethical compulsions are binding on them to keep the organizational secrets as **SECRET**. But in the changing social value's world there are many people who can be bought for various prices. Therefore, management must exercise due caution in selecting consultants.

### *Business Publications and Journals*

Various business publications, magazines and journals keep publishing vital professional and technical information, which if compiled carefully over a period can give lots of sensitive data for interested parties/groups. Management and security officer must be very careful to divulge any sensitive information for survey and economic research, etc.

### *Technical Collaboration and Joint Ventures*

These days number of technical collaborations and joint ventures are formed by large business houses. The technical collaboration can be proved as a double edged weapon in collecting vital information for individual company's interest. Once the information is extracted then in number of cases the collaboration or joint venture does not materialize. In such cases the technical head and management must be fully alert and vigilant.

## Offences Against Personnel

In an industry, we have seen that mostly offences are against personnel and property. The common offences against personnel are as follows:

**Table 9.1**

| Offence | Indian Penal Code (IPC) Sections (S) |
|---|---|
| 1. Unlawful Assembly | IPC S 141, 143, 144 |
| 2. Riots | IPC S 146, 147,149 |
| 3. Assault | IPC S 351, 353 |
| 4. Affray | IPC S 159,160 |
| 5. Hurt and grievous hurt | IPC S 319, 321, 323, 324, 325, 327, |
| | IPC S 329, 332, 333, 337, 338, |
| 6. Wrongful restraint, wrongful confinement | IPC S 339, 341, 342, |
| 7. Murder | IPC S 300, 302, 304-A, 307, 309 |
| 8. Culpable Homicide not amounting to murder | IPC S 304 |
| 9. Molestation | IPC S 354 |
| 10. Rape and unnatural offence | IPC S 376, 377 |
| 11. Official secret Act ( spying for any purposes ) prejudicial to the safety or interest of the state | Indian Official Secret Act 1923 |
| 12. Bribery | PC S 161 to 165 |
| 1. **Obstruction** | |
| (i) Obstructing public servant when suppressing riots. | IPC S 152 |
| (ii) To any public way or line of navigation | IPC S 283 |
| 2. **Kidnapping** | |
| (i) For murder | IPC S 364 |
| (ii) For secret and wrongful confinement | IPC S 365 |
| (iii) To subject a person to grievous hurt | IPC S 367 |
| (iv) Keeping a kidnapped person under confinement or concealment. | IPC S 368 |
| 3. **Harbouring** | |
| (i) Of an escaped offender | IPC S 216 |
| (ii) Of a deserter from Army, Navy and Airforce. | IPC S 136 |
| (iii) Of hired persons for unlawful assembly or rioting. | IPC S 157 |
| (iv) Of dacoits or robbers | IPC S 216–A |
| (v) Of spies | Indian Official Secret Act 1923 sec 10 |
| 4. **Criminal** | |
| (i) Breach of trust | IPC S 406 |
| (ii) Breach of trust by clerk or servant | IPC S 408 |

5. **Dacoity**
   (i) Preparation or attempt — IPC S 395, 397, 398, 399
   (ii) With murder — IPC S 396
6. **Disobedience**
   (i) Of lawful order of public servant Causing obstruction, annoyance, etc. — IPC S 188
7. **Explosives**
   (i) Causing explosion likely to endanger life or property — Explosives Substance Act 1908 Sec 3
   (ii) Making or in possession of explosive substance under suspicious circumstances. — Explosive Substance Act 1908 Sec 5
   (iii) Persons committing dangerous offences relating to explosives. — Explosive Act 1884 Sec 12
8. **Suicide**
   (i) Attempt to commit — IPC S 309
   (ii) Abetting commission of — IPC S 306
9. **Worship**
   (i) Injuring or defiling a place of — IPC S 295
   (ii) Maliciously insulting any religion or religious belief. — IPC S 295–A.

## Offences Against Persons

### *1. Unlawful Assembly*

*Sections 141,142* and *143* deal with this offence. Unlawful assembly is defined in *Section 141* of the I.P.C.

The definition is given below:

An assembly of five or more persons is designated as "Unlawful Assembly", if the common object of the persons composing that assembly is:

1. To overawe by criminal force, or show of criminal force, the Central or any State Government or Parliament or the Legislature of any state or any public servant in the exercise of the lawful power such public servant.
2. To resist the execution of any law or of any legal process.
3. To commit any mischief or criminal trespass or other offence.
4. By means of criminal force or show of criminal force to any person to take or obtain possession of any property or to deprive any person of the enjoyment of a right of way or of the use of water or other

incorporeal right of which he is in possession or enjoyment or to enforce any right or supposed right.

5. By means of criminal force or show of criminal force to compel any person to do what he is not legally bound to do or to omit to do what he is legally entitled to do.

The main ingredients of the above offence are: (a) five or more (b) common object (c) to resist the execution of the law or legal sources (d) by using criminal force. The most important ingredience are five or more and common intention and to resist the execution of law by using criminal force. *Section 142* mentioned above being a member of unlawful assembly, *Section 143* is the Penal Section.

### *2. Riots*

*Sections 146 to 149* deal with the offence of riots. Rioting is defined as follows:

Whenever force or violence is used by an unlawful assembly, or by any member thereof in prosecution of the common object of such assembly every member of such assembly is guilty of the offence of rioting. *Section 147* is the Penal Section for the offence of rioting, *Section 148* deals with rioting armed with deadly weapon.

### *3. Assault*

*Section 351* of the I.P.C defines as:

Whoever makes any gesture, or any preparation intending or knowing it to be likely that such gesture or preparation will cause any person present to apprehend that he who makes that gesture or preparation is about to use criminal force to that person is said to commit an assault.

*Explanation*: Mere words do not amount to an assault. But the word which a person uses may give to his gestures or preparations such a meaning as may make those gestures or preparations amount to an assault.

This is a very common offence which occurs in industries particularly where rival unions are functioning. Hence, security officer should know what exactly an "Assault" means.

*Section 352* is the Penal Section stating the punishment for such an offence. *Section 353* is also an important section since it deals with assault or use of criminal force to deter public servant from discharge of his duty.

### *4. Affray*

*Section 159* defines affray. When two or more persons by fighting in a public place disturb the public peace, they are said to commit an " Affray". Two main ingredience of this offence are:

(i) Two or more persons must fight
(ii) They must fight in a public place
(iii) They must disturb the public peace

### *5. Hurt and Grievous Hurt*

*Section 319* of the I.P.C. defines hurt. The definition is given below:

Whoever causes bodily pain, disease or infirmity to any person is said to cause hurt. This is simple hurt, and *Section 323* makes it a non-cognizable offence, *Section 325* defines "Grievous Hurt". The following kinds of hurt only are designed as "Grievous Hurt":

1. Emasculation
2. Permanent privation of the sight of either eye.
3. Permanent privation of the hearing of either ear.
4. Privation of any member or joint.
5. Destruction of permanent impairing or the powers of any member or joint.
6. Permanent disfiguration of the head or face.
7. Fracture or dislocation of a bone or tooth.
8. Any hurt which endangers which causes the sufferer to be during the space of twenty days in severe bodily pain, or unable to follow his ordinary pursuits.

What is important to remember is the difference between a "Simple Hurt" and the "Grievous Hurt". The former is a non-cognizable offence whereas the latter is a cognizable offence.

*Section 323* is the Penal Section for "Simple Hurt "whereas *Section 325* is the Penal Section for voluntary causing grievous hurt.

There are a number of other sections connected with hurts upto *Section 338* I.P.C. but it is not necessary for the Security Officer to learn them by heart. A reference could be made to the book on I.P.C.

## 6. Wrongful Restraint

*Section 339* defines wrongful restraint. Whoever voluntarily obstructs any person so as to prevent that person from proceeding in any direction in which that person has a right to proceed, is said wrongfully to restrain that person.

***Explanation***: The obstruction of a private way over land or water which a person in good faith believes himself to have lawful right to obstruct is not an offence within the meaning of this section.

### *Wrongful confinement*

*Section 340* defines this offence whoever wrongfully restrains any person in such a manner as to prevent that person from proceeding beyond certain circumscribing limits is said wrongfully to confine, that person. *Sections 341, 342* are Penal Sections for the above offence.

The above two offences are important in view of the present labour situation. There are several instances where the officers are "Gheraoed" inside and outside the premises while coming in or going out to any other place. This amounts to wrongful restraint. If an officer is sitting in his cabin and the cabin is surrounded by the workers so that he is unable to come out of the cabin. The workers surrounding the cabin have committed an offence of wrongful confinement. The Security Officer should study these sections carefully along with its ingredients, as he may be called upon to deal with such situations.

## 7. Murder

This is one of the most heinous offences and it is defined in *Section 300.*

It is necessary to know the details about this offence as this is of rare occurrence in industries. *Section 302* and *Section 304* are Penal Sections for the offences of murder and culpable homicide. Whenever a person causes death due to grave and sudden provocation it amounts to a culpable homicide and not murder. *Section 300 and 304* are Penal Sections for the above offences.

## 8. Molestation

*Section 354* defines Molestation.

Whoever assaults or uses criminal force to any woman intending to outrage or knowing it to be likely that., he will thereby outrage her modesty, shall be punished with imprisonment of either description for term which may extend to two years or with fine or with both.

### *9. Rape, Unnatural Offence*

*Section 376 and 377* are Penal Sections for the above offences. Since these offences are of very rare occurrence in industries, we are not discussing the details or the ingredients of these offences.

Every industry should have a small library pertaining to books on security as also important books of law such as I.P.C. Criminal Procedure Code and Evidence Act, that these will serve as reference books to security officer as also Administration/Personnel/Labour officers who exercise control over security.

## Offences Against Property

It has been generally found that in the industries or any manufacturing unit offences against property in general and offences relating to mainly theft and pilferage in particular are of quite common nature. The cases of theft and pilferage are two important kind of industrial crimes which a security officer or his staff is confronted with during and outside working hours. Other crimes related to property are not very common and only in rare cases i.e. during strikes riots and lockout, etc. there could be some incident of such other severe nature.

Based on the experience the security officer and management must be aware of various industrial crimes/offences related to property. Those are enumerated as under:

Table 9.2

| *Offence* | *Indian Penal Code (IPC) Sections (S)* |
|---|---|
| (i) Theft | IPC S 378,379,380,381 |
| (ii) Extortion | IPC S 383,384 |
| (iii) Robbery | IPC S 392 |
| 1. **Burglary** | IPC S 454, 457 |
| 2. **Criminals** | |
| (i) Breach of Trust | IPC S 405,406,408,409 |
| (ii) Misappropriation of Property | IPC S 403 |
| (iii) Receiving/Purchasing of stolen property | IPC S 411,413,414 |
| (iv) Arson | IPC S 436 |
| 3. **Cheating** | |
| (i) By personation | IPC S 419 |
| (ii) By including delivery of property | IPC S 420 |

| | |
|---|---|
| 4. **Purchase, sales, possession in contravention of orders** | Essential Commodities Act 1975 Sec. 7 |
| (i) Criminal conspiracy | IPC S 120-B |
| 6. **Forest offences** | Indian Forest Act 1917 Sec 64. |
| 7. **Mischief** | |
| (i) By fire | IPC S 435 |
| (ii) By fire to a dwelling House | IPC S 436 |
| (iii) By killing, poisoning of animals of Rs 10/- or upwards | IPC S 428–429 |
| 8. **Motor vehicles** | |
| (i) Driving recklessly or dangerously on a public road/way | Motor Vehicle Act 1939 Sec 116 |
| (ii) Rash or negligent driving in a public way to endanger human life | IPC Sec 279 |
| 9. **Railways** | |
| (i) Drunkenness by a railway servant on duty. | Indian Railways Act 1890, Sec 100 |
| (ii) Entering compartment reserved for families/ladies. | Indian Railways Act Sec 119 |
| (iii) Damage or destruction of certain railway properties | Indian Railways Act Sec 126-A |
| (iv) Maliciously hurting or attempting to hurt persons travelling by railways | Indian Railways Act Sec 127. |
| 10. **Criminal Trespassing** | IPC Sec 411,417. |
| 11. **House Breaking** | IPC Sec 448,445,454,457,461. |
| 12. **Falsification of Accounts** | IPC Sec 477-A |

## INDIAN PENAL CODE (IPC)

In order to handle all the industrial crimes speedily and within the legal limits it is imperative that security head must have adequate knowledge about Indian Penal Code (IPC). This code primarily covers and define a large number of offences particularly against personnel and property. IPC also gives out details of punishment for each offence. In the subsequent paras one can make out the comprehension of important offences and their ingredients which form the act of that particular offence.

It is worth while to know that IPC contains a total of almost 510 sections, which define various offences, ingredients and also extent of punishment prescribed for each offence under laws, if the charges are established and the person is convicted by a valid court of law. Some of the Sections are of peculiar importance as these do not deal with any offence but legally define various word/phrases used under IPC.

*Section 33*

Defines the word "Act" which denotes as well as a series of acts as single act. The word omission denotes as well a series of omission as a single omission.

*Section 34*

Deals with acts done by several persons in furtherance of a common intention. This section is defined as when a criminal act is done by several persons in furtherance of the common intention of all, each one of such person is liable for that act in the same manner as if it were done by him alone.

*Section 38*

Deals with persons concerned in criminal act may be guilty of different offences. This is defined as when several persons are engaged or concerned in the commission of a criminal act, they may be guilty of different offences by means of that act.

*Section 53*

The punishments to which the offenders are liable under provision of this code are:

1. Death
2. Imprisonment for life
3. Imprisonment, which is of two descriptions, names;
   (a) Rigorous-that is, with hard labour.
   (b) Simple.
4. Forfeiture of property.
5. Fine.

*Sections 96 to 106*

Deal with what is called "Right of Private Defence". According to these sections every citizen has got certain rights in respect of the defence of the body as well as property. The body of property may be his own or of some one else. The important sections among them is *Section 100* which clearly states, the Right of Private Defence of the body extends to the voluntary causing of death of any other harm to the assailant if the offence which occasions the exercise of this right by any of the following:

(a) If the assault causes fear of death.

(b) If the assault causes fear of grievous hurt.

(c) If the assault is for committing rape.

(d) If the assault is for committing an unnatural sexual offence.

(e) If the assault is for kidnapping or abducting.

(f) If the assault is for wrongfully confining a person.

According to *Section 101*, the right of private defence of body does not extend to causing of death if the assault on body is not an act of the nature specified is the above sections i.e. *sSection 100*.

*Section 103* states that the right of private defence of property extends to the voluntary causing of death or of any other harm to the offender, if the offence about to be committed is robbery of house breaking by night or mischief by fire on a building used as a human dwelling or a place for the custody of property or an offence of theft, mischief or house trespass, likely to cause death or grievous hurt.

*Section 104* states that in cases other than above, there is no right to cause death. Any other harm could be caused if necessary.

According to *Section 106*, if in the exercise of the right of private defence against an assault which reasonably causes the fear of death the defender be so situated that he cannot effectively exercise that right without risk of harm to an innocent person, his right of private defence extends to the running of that risk.

*Section 107* of this code explains what is meant by the Abetment of a thing. This section is defind as:

A person abets the doing of a thing who:

1. Instigates any person to do that thing or
2. Engages with one or more another person or persons in any conspiracy for the doing of that thing. If an act or illegal omission takes place in pursuance of that conspiracy, and in order to the doing of that thing or
3. Intentionally aids, by any acts or illegal omission, the doing of that thing.

***Explanation***: A person who, by wilful misrepresentation, or by wilful concealment of a material fact which is bound to disclose voluntarily causes or procures of attempts to cause of procure, a thing to be done is said to instigate the doing of that thing. It would thus be seen that by abetting the commission of an offence, the person who abets is also liable for punishment of the offence as an abettor.

*Section 120 A* and *120 B* of this code deal with acts of criminal conspiracy. We are not much concerned with these sections but it may happen that in an industry a fraud may be committed by a number of white-collared employees by making a conspiracy. In such cases which must invariably be referred to the local police, the above two sections would be applied along with the relevant sections of offence. We are giving below the definitions of the above mentioned two Sections.

*Section 120 A*

When two or more persons agree to do or cause to be done.

(a) An illegal act or

(b) An act which is not illegal by illegal means, such as agreement is designated a criminal conspiracy.

Provided that no agreement except an agreement to commit an offence shall amount to a criminal conspiracy, unless some act besides the agreement is done by one or more parties to such agreement is pursuance thereof.

*Explanation*: It is immaterial wheather the illegal act is the ultimate object of such agreement or is merely incidental to that object.

*Theft*

Out of these offences the one of common occurrence in all industries big or small is the offence of theft. *Section 378* defines theft as follows:

Whoever, intending to take dishonestly any moveable property out of the possession of any person, without that person's consent, move of that property in order to such taking, is said to commit theft.

In order to constitute theft, five factors are essential:

(a) Dishonest intention to take property.

(b) The property must be moveable.

(c) It should be taken out of the possession of another person.

(d) It should be taken without the consent of that person.

(e) There must be some moving of the property in order to accomplish the taking of it.

In industries this is the most common crime where company's property is stolen from the company's premises without the knowledge of any official. If the property is removed from the open area the penal section is 379, whereas if the theft is committed from any building, tent or vessel which building tent or vessel is used as a human dwelling then *Section 380* which means theft from a house comes into play. *Section 381* deals with theft by clerk or servant of property in possession of the master.

We have dealt in details in prevention of theft and pilferage in the earlier chapter. As the maxim goes "Prevention is better than cure" it is much easier to prevent the commission of theft from the industries by adopting various measures mentioned in that chapter. A security officer must be thoroughly conversant with these measures since mostly his duty will be preventing theft and pilferage from the industries and inspite of these measures if thefts take place, his next duty is detection and investigation of theft.

*Extortion*: This category of crime is not of common occurrence but it is worthwhile to know the distinction between theft and extortion.

### *Robbery*

It should be remembered that theft and robbery are not synonymous terms. *Section 390* defines robbery, as in all robbery cases there is either theft or extortion.

Theft is robbery if in order to the committing of the theft or in committing the theft is carrying away or attempting to carry away properly obtained by the theft, the offender for that end voluntarily causes or attempts to cause to any person death or hurt or wrongful restraint or fear of instant death or of instant hurt or of instant wrongful restraint.

It would thus be seen that the commission of the offences of robbery, the person committing the offence uses force, causes hurt or causes wrongful restraint. If these conditions are satisfying the theft becomes a robbery. *Section 392* is a Penal Section mentioning the punishment for robbery. Since this offence is not common in industries we need not go into other details.

### *Criminal misappropriation of property*

Criminal misappropriation of the property is defined in *Section 403* as follows:

Whoever dishonestly misappropriates of converts to his own use any moveable property shall be punished with imprisonment of either description for a term which may extend to two years or with fine or with both.

As this offence is not of common nature in industries, there is no need to elaborate on this point.

### *Criminal breach of trust*

*Sections 405 to 409* of the I. P. C. deal with this type of offences. *Section 405* defines criminal breach of trust as follows:

Whoever being in any manner entrusted with property or with any domain over property dishonestly, misappropriates or converts to his own use that property or dishonestly uses or dispose of that property in violation of any direction of law prescribing the mode in which such trust is to be discharged or of any legal contract expressed or implied which he has made touching the discharge of such trust or willfully suffers any other person commits criminal breach of trust.

This type of offence is not of common occurrence in industries hence, there is no need to elaborate on this. *Section 406* is the Penal Section and *Section 408* deals with Criminal Breach of Trust by clerk or servant, whereas *Section 409* deals with Criminal Breach of Trust by public servant or by banker, merchant or agent.

*Receiving of stolen property*

It is defined by *Section 410* as "property whose possession is transferred by theft or by robbery and it continues to be stolen property until it comes back into the possession of a person legally entitled to posses"

In industries, the company's property is stolen mostly by its own employees. This stolen property is either used by themselves or in most of the cases, this property is sold out to some shopkeeper or merchant, for monetary gain. Such person who purchases from anyone's stolen property as defined above is called the "Receiver of stolen property". *Section 411,413* and 414 deal with this offence of receiving stolen property. It would thus be remembered that not only the person who commits theft is an offender but the person who receives such stolen property also is an offender and is liable for punishment as receiver of stolen property.

*Cheating*

*Section 415* defines Cheating as follows:

Whoever by deceiving any person fraudulently or dishonestly induces the person so deceived to deliver any property to any person or to consent that any person shall retain any property or intentionally induces the person so deceived to do or omit to do anything which he would not do or omit if he were not so deceived and which act or omission causes or is likely to cause damage or harm to that person in body, mind, reputation or property is said to cheat.

This offence is also not of common occurrence in industries and hence it is not necessary to elaborate on this. *Sections 416, 417, 419* and *420* deals with these offences. 419 is a Penal Section whereas 420 deals with cheating and dishonesty inducing delivery of property.

*Mischief*

*Section 425* defines mischief as "whoever with intent cause wrongful loss or damage to the public or to any person, causes the destruction of any property or diminishes its value or utility is said to commit mischief".

Since this offence is not of very common occurrence but it is likely that in industries such an offence might take place, particularly the offence of mischief by fire. *Section 435* deals with this offence viz. Mischief by fire or explosion substance with intent cause damage to amount of Rs 100 or (in case of agricultural product Rs 10) mischief by fire of explosive substance is a serious offence under *Section 435* and is punishable with imprisonment upto 7 years and shall also be liable to fine.

***Criminal trespass***

*Section 441* defines criminal trespass as follows:

Whoever enters into property in the possession of another person with intent to commit an offence or to intimidate, insult or annoy any person in possession of such property or having lawfully entered into such property, unlawfully remains there with intent thereby to intimidate, insult or annoy any such person is said to commit criminal trespass.

*Section 442* defines house trespass: Whoever commits criminal trespass by entering into or remaining in any building tent or vessel used as a human dwelling or any building used as a place for worship or as a place for the custody of property, is said to commit house trespass.

***House breaking***

*Section 445* defines the offence of house breaking, the definition is given below:

A person is said to commit house breaking who commits house trespass if he effects his entrance into the house or any part of it in any of the six ways hereinafter described or if being in the house of any part of it for the purpose of committing an offence or having committed and offence therein he quits the house or any part of it in any of such six ways that is to say:

(i) If he enters or quits through a passage made by himself or by any abettor of the house trespass in order to the committing of the house trespass.

(ii) If he enters or quits through any passage not intended by any person other than himself or abettor of the offence for human entrance of, through any passage to which he had obtained access by scaling or climbing over any wall or building.

(iii) If he enters or quits through any passage which he or any abettor of the house trespass has opened in order to the committing of the house-trespass by any means by which that passage was not intended by the occupier of the house to be opened.

(iv) If he enters or quits by opening any lock in order to the committing of the house-trespass or in order to the quitting of the house after a house trespass

(v) If he effects his entrance or departure by using criminal force or committing an assault or by threatening any person with assault.

(vi) If he enters or quits by any passage which he knows to have been fastened against such entrance or departure and to have been unfastened by himself or by an abettor of the house-trespass.

*Section 454* is a **Penal Section** for committing house breaking by day. Whereas *Section 457* is a **Penal Section** for committing the offences of house breaking by night.

The offence of house breaking is also called as a burglary.

***Falsification of accounts***

*Section 463* defines forgery and *Section 464* defines making false documents. *Section 465* is the Penal Section for forgery. In fact all offences relating to documents are dealt with in the IPC from *Sections 463* to *477-A* which define falsification of accounts. These offences might be occurring in industries but the security officer can hardly do anything to investigate such offences. They will have to be referred to the police for investigation.

## Criminal Procedure Code (CrPC)

It is essential for the security officer and other senior staff of the security organization to have a fair knowledge about the crime handling procedures by the civil police. It is the basic duty of the police of the particular state to investigate and deal with the industrial crimes, maintenance of law and order in civil society. Criminal procedure code (CrPC) contains various procedures in respect of police investigation of crimes. Therefore, a security officer must be in complete know-how about the police procedures, which will assist him to a greater extent while dealing with industrial crimes in an industry office.

It must be borne in mind that all the offences defined and covered under Indian Penal Code (IPC) are not necessarily to be investigated and dealt by the police. In order to streamline the power and for the purpose of information and action *Section 2 (c)* of CrPC defines the offences as under,

- Cognizable offence.
- Non-cognizable offence.

### Cognizable Offence

This is an offence for which a police officer can arrest a person without a warrant from any court of law. Thus such offences have to be invariably dealt with by the police. How to deal with them will be discussed later in this chapter.

### Non-cognizable Offence

This is an offence in which a police officer cannot arrest anybody without a warrant from a court. Thus, if a complainant gives a complaint to the Police Station, the Station house officer will record it and if it is a non-cognizable, he will refer the complainant to lodge a complaint in the court of law, since he is not competent to investigate such an offence. The S H O will record such complaint in a register called "N.C.( Non-Cognizable)" offence register. If the complaint, however discloses a cognizable offence, then it is mandatory for a police officer to register the case and proceed immediately with its investigation.

We have stated above the two categories of offences viz. cognizable i.e. an offence in which a police officer has to take cognizance and investigate it and a non-cognizable offence in which the police are not require to take cognizance and investigate. But a complaint has to be recorded in the N.C. Register and the complaint has to be directed to lodge a private complaint in a criminal court.

Having understood the two broad categories of offences as cognizable and non-cognizable, it would also be necessary to understand also what are called "bailable offences and non-bailable offences".

### *Bailable offences*

This is defined by *Section 2 (a)* as an offence which is shown as bailable in the first schedule of this code and non-bailable offence means any other offence. The code of criminal procedure gives at the end the schedules showing bailable and non-bailable offences. By bailable offence meant that the offence concerned is cognizable and as such the accused is arrested by the police officer without warrant, but if such cognizable offence falls in the first schedule which shows bailable offences, the police officer can release the accused on bail. Whenever, a person is arrested by the police, it is mandatory that the arrested person is produced before the magistrate within 24 hours of the arrest. In certain cases of offences which are bailable, this obligation is waived, and the police can release the arrested person on a bail bond. The bail bond could be given by a respectable person who stands guarantee that the arrested person will be available for trial in the court. The bail bond could also be in the form of cash security.

*Non-bailable offences*

The arrested person will have to be produced before the magistrate within 24 hours as per mandatory provision, and the police have no powers to release him on bail.

The criminal procedure code has a large number of sections as many as 500 but only very important sections which a security officer should know will be dealt with in the following paras:

*Arrest*

*Section 43* lays down that any private person may be arrested or cause to be arrested by any person who in his presence commits a non-bailable and cognizable offence or is a proclaimed offender. After such arrest, the arrested man must be handed over to police officer or the nearest police station.

All major offences such as theft, robbery, mischief by fire with intent to destroy a house, etc. grievous hurt by dangerous weapons are cognizable and non-bailable.

*Sections 46, 54, 55, 59, 60 and 61* of the criminal procedure code deal with this subject. Police are empowered by law to arrest any person, who commits a cognizable offence. The law also empowers any citizen to arrest a person if he finds that a cognizable offence is being committed in his presence, as per *Section 43* mentioned above. Any arrest made by the security staff will be like a citizen's arrest only. The security staff has therefore, to make sure about the grounds whenever they arrest any plant employee for an offence. It must be remembered that if the arrest is not justified such detention amounts to "wrongful confinement" and the person responsible for it can be charged for a cognizable offence. Procedure for effecting an arrest and the circumstances and the extent to which it is to be used, has also been laid down. The person who is to be arrested should, be informed as to the reason of the arrest and the authority of the arresting officer.

*Section 46* states how arrests should be made by private persons according to it, in making an arrest the person making it shall actually touch or confine the body of the person to be arrested, unless here be a submission to the custody by word or action. If, however, the person to be arrested resists his arrest, the person making it may use all the means necessary to make the arrest. Nothing in this section, however, gives a right to cause.

The death of the person to be arrested unless he is accused of an offence punishable with death or with imprisonment for life.

*Section 52* lays down that the person making the arrest may take from the person arrested any offensive weapons which he has to the nearest police station.

*Issue of summons*

According to *Section 61*, court issues a summons in writing and in duplicate. Under *Section 62* such a summon is handed over to a police officer (among others) and the latter serves it personally as the person summoned. Every person on whom a summon is so served shall sign a receipt therefore on the back of the duplicate.

According to *Section 64*, if the person on whom the summon is to be served is not easily found, one copy of the summons can be served on some adult male member of his family residing with him and the latter will then sign receipt therefore on the back of the duplicate.

*Searches*

*Section 99, 100 and 101* of the criminal procedure code have laid down the procedure for conducting searches of premises. Ordinarily premises cannot be searched without a warrant from a magistrate but the police officers are empowered to conduct searches in a house in the course of an investigation of a crime, if they have reasonable suspicion that stolen property is concealed there except under these circumstances, even the police cannot conduct searches of the houses.

The security staff is required to conduct searches of the personnel and the vehicles, These searches could be (1) routine searches of the employees at the gate (2) searches of employees' lockers and (3) even searches of empoyess' house

*Searching of employees*

It will be essential that a rule will have to be introduced in the "standing orders" of the company that every employee will be subjected to a search at the gate or in the premises, to enable the security staff to conduct the searches. The employee will sign in token of his abiding by the rules.

*Routine search of employee*

The security staff normally conducts routine searches of the employees at the gates. While doing so extreme care should be taken to see that nothing is done or said to the employee, which would substantiate a charge of a false arrest.

*Searching employees lockers*

It should also be clearly stated in the company's rules and regulations that employees' lockers are subject to inspection at any time. Without previous notice being given. The purpose of such inspection may be ostensible for checking fire hazard, etc. Although many times, the most valuable reason from security point of view is that of searching the locker for stolen property which may be hidden there. If the lockers' searches are conducted in the absence of the employees, the security staff handling the searches may be accompanied by another person preferably the employee's supervisor or a member of the personnel department. The reason is obviously to overcome the charge that the stolen articles if found in the lockers are " planted " in the locker.

*Searching employees' houses*

The security officers are well advised not to conduct the searches of employees' houses on their own even if they have a suspicion that the employee has concealed the stolen property in his house. Because searching of any premises will need a warrant from a magistrate as mentioned above under *Section 100* of Cr.P.C. In absence of such a warrant the premises can be searched only by a police officer investigating any cognizable offence and he has reasonable suspicion that the stolen property is in that house. Even then he has to draw up proceedings under *Section 165* of Cr.P.C. recording there in the reasons in writing. It is only after drawing such a statement that he can search the premises in the presence of the security officer. Herein again he himself as the security officer must offer themselves for a search before beginning the searching of the house, so that the employee cannot make an allegation against the investigating officer that the property so suspected was planted. Thus in such cases the best thing for a security officer would be to register an offence of theft at the police station and the house concerned could be searched by the police in the course of investigations of the crime.

*Seizure*

Whenever searches are conducted at the gates or on the factory premises by security staff and stolen property is found either on the person or in the personal belonging or in the vehicles, the security staff will have to proceed to seize this stolen property from the employee. The seizure of such property will have to be effected by drawing up "*Panchnama*". Two independent witnesses will have to be called and the property recovered will have to be attached in their presence. A *panchnama* is a document which shows the circumstances under which the property was recovered, the description of the property and other details to establish the seizure. The *panchnama* will have to be signed by the *panchas*, The number of the *panchas* should be at least two. The person apprehended will then be taken into custody by the security staff and a formal complaint will have to be lodged in the police station having jurisdiction over the area and the property recovered and the accused will be handed over to the police for further action.

***Dispersal of unlawful assemblies***

According to *Section 129* an executive magistrate or a police officer not below the rank of a Sub-inspector, may command an unlawful assembly to disperse and it shall then be the duty of the members of such assembly to disperse. If it refuses to disperse, the executive magistrate or police officer may proceed to disperse it by force.

The force used by the police should be as possible consistent with the objective of dispersing the unlawful assembly as quickly as possible.

While so dispersing the unlawful assembly, the police officer or executive magistrate has the right to require the assistance of any male person for the purpose of dispersing the assembly.

***Section 238 to 249***

Describes the procedure for trial in warrant cases by magistrate. In brief, the magistrate first hears both the prosecution of accused and also goes through the papers of investigation prepared by the police. If he comes to the conclusion that there is no case against the accused person, he discharges him.

If on the other hand, the magistrate feels that there is ground for presuming that the accused has committed the offence, he (the magistrate) frames a charge against the accused and explains it to the latter. If the accused then pleads guilty and the magistrate feels that the accused has committed the offence, he convicts him and passes orders of punishment, (imprisonment and or fine as prescribed by the Sections of I.P.C. under which he is charged)

At the end of the criminal procedure code, there is the first schedule giving a list of all offences included in the Indian Penal Code and showing which are cognizable or non-cognizable, bailable or non-bailable. It should be referred to whenever such information is wanted about any offence.

*Another important section of the criminal*: Procedure code deals with urgent danger.

*Section 144*, the lone section in CrPC, is intended for temporary orders in cases of grave emergency irrespective of the fight of the parties concerned, provided there is sufficient ground for proceeding, and immediate prevention and speedy remedy is desirable

*Section 144*, of Cr.P.C. deals with power to issue orders in urgent cases of nuisance of apprehended dangers. This section provides,

(a) In cases where in the opinion of a District Magistrate, a Sub-Divisional Magistrate or any other Executive Magistrate specially empowered by the State Government in this behalf, there is sufficient ground for proceeding under this section and immediate prevention of speedy remedy is desirable such Magistrate may be a written order stating the material facts of the case and served in the manner provided by *Section 134*, direct any person to certain property in his possession is likely to prevent obstruction annoyance of injury to any person lawfully employed of danger to human life health or safety or disturbance of the public tranquility of riot or any affray.

(b) An order under this section may in cases of emergency or in cases where the circumstances do not admit of the serving in due time of a notice upon the person against whom the order is directed or passed ex-prate.

(c) In a district place or any other place in the district it is under this section that a District Magistrate or Sub-divisional Magistrate issues orders banning Assembly of five or more persons, carrying of lethal weapons, etc. with the intention of preventing apprehended dangers. In a district the powers of maintenance of law and orders are vested in a District Magistrate and it is he or his Sub-ordinate Magistrate who can issue these orders.

***Preventive measures to curb crimes***

It is an old and tried proverb—"Prevention is better than cure". It certainly fits well in the world of Industrial crimes. An experienced and foresighted security officer can always feel the nerve of employees and thus can appreciate the incoming problems pertaining to Industrial crimes. It is therefore, considered necessary for the security officer and also the management to visualize in depth the anatomy of the crimes related to mainly theft and pilferages. From various studies and survey of crime rates in different categories of industries, it is revealed that the figures given out are not correct. In most of the cases management does not like to involve themselves into legal implications. Thus cases are amicably sorted out by the security or labour officers. Mainly these cases fall into three broad categories:

(a) The thefts take which take place but not noticed.
(b) The thefts place, come under notice but not reported to police.
(c) The thefts take place, noticed, reported to police but no action is taken.

From the above categories, it is evident that volume or number of crimes, which is shown in the records or reported to police, are just the tip of the iceberg. However, to be more cautious and vigilant a security officer must study the following in detail to prevent crimes.

(a) The type of material and finished goods which are lucrative for thefts and pilferage.
(b) Mode of operations for carrying out theft and pilferage in an industry.
(c) Vulnerable areas, departments and shop floor, etc. for industrial crimes.
(d) Study the shift's time, when crimes are likely to take place.
(e) Keep an vigilant eye on the suspicious nature of employees.
(f) Carry out "surprise search" with the prior knowledge of management.

*Crime intelligence in industries*

An experienced Security Head will always try and collect valuable crime intelligence about the future trouble and crimes in and outside the industry. It is quite prevalent these days that a 'security/intelligence cell' is formed under the guidance of head of the security. It will mainly consist of 2–3 confident persons. They assist the security/labour officer in gaining vital information from employees about theft, pilferage, strike or any other unrest, etc. The security officer must create "positive sources" among employees who can give such vital and timely information about any impending crimes.

Security officer, based on information and previous reports/records about suspicious nature of employees possessing doubtful integrity, (crime) should prepare a detailed information register. This register must contain personal particulars of the notorious activities and details of crimes committed. A close watch inside as well as outside the industry must be kept on the activities of such persons. It will be prudent to keep a record of all shopkeepers in the area who is habitual purchaser of stolen goods. On getting sufficient evidence about their involvement in crimes, due warning must be issued by the management. In case the incidences are again repeated then these dealers/ contractors must be "Black Listed" to avoid any further dealing with them. If need be, security/vigilance officer must also inform local police along with adequate proof about such dealers whereabouts.

Legally a security officer, administration or labour officer in an industry has no power to deal with the industrial crimes. Primarily, by virtue of their appointment in an organization they are responsible to fore see and detect a crime. The local investigation can commence within the legal limits. Therefore, sufficient knowledge of IPC and CrPC is quite essential for dealing effectively with the industrial crimes.

# 10

# Investigation and Reporting of Offences

Crime investigation is one of the important charter of duties for the security manger/officer/security supervisor in any industrial organization. The primary aim of the security department is to prevent an act of theft inside the factory premises. Inspite of all the preventive measures it is found that thefts, whether petty or large do take place in an industry. It may be detected or at times may not be detected. However, nowadays there are number of occasions when cases of theft, assault and pilferage, etc. do come to the notice of security department.

*Theft*: The definition of "Theft" has been covered under Indian Penal Code *Sections 378, 381*. It is worthwhile to note that in order to constitute theft, the five basic factors as under are very essential:

(a) The dishonest intention to take property.
(b) The item/property must be movable.
(c) It must be taken out of the possession of another person.
(d) It should be taken without the consent of that person
(e) There must be some moving of property in order to accomplish the taking of it.

Right at the outset it must be known that legally no security manager or any other staff of an industry is empowered to investigate the crime. These powers are vested in the police on the authority of criminal procedure code *Sections 154–173*, however, the security officer can certainly investigate the crime inside the factory premises, apprehend the culprits and even recover the stolen property from his possession. These all acts are basically to establish the act of crime and if matter is reported to the police, this initial investigation will help police to a great extent in further proving of case. Therefore, adequate knowledge, of investigating a crime is very essential for the security officer and his subordinate. On the directives of management each case must be considered, whether it should be handed over to the police department or should only be investigated by the security department.

Security officer must only act once the written report, complaint is lodged by a department about the theft. On receipt of complaint the senior manager should be informed by the security officer about the inpending procedure. The management may like to analyze pros and cons of the incident i.e. the pressure from Labour Union functioning within or outside the organization.

Investigation should be handled at an appropriate level depending upon the employee/officer involved in the crime. It is not obligatory that every theft case is investigated by the security officer himself. If only a worker is involved then matter can be entrusted to an assistant security officer/security supervisor. If the involvement is of more than one person including an officer, than a committee can be appointed by the management to investigate the case.

In all such investigations the main task of the investigating officer/team should find out all the truth in the case by reaching to the bottom of the crime. Once all the facts are collected then matter should be reported in detail to the senior officer who had ordered the investigations. It will not be prudent for the security department to show undue interest into the puenitive part of the crime. This is basically the prerogative of the concerned officer ordering the investigations.

## OBLIGATION OF REPORTING THE CRIME TO POLICE

The decision, whether the case should be reported to the police or not should only be dealt by the concerned department, is entirely depend on the senior managers/management authorities. There are no laid down rules in this regard, however, various factors must be taken into consideration before arriving at such decision. If at any time, during the course of investigations it is revealed that any outsider, whether individual/more than one person are involved along with the company employee, then it is advisable to report the matter to police for action. In case if theft involves only item e.g. gas or chemical, which can cause accidents, firehazards or explosive, etc. then the case must be immediately reported to police to avoid damage and or injuries to other persons in the society. Other factors which will decide the merit of the theft and based on that the action as under may be taken:

(a) Once the report is made to the police they will arrive at the scene for investigation and may threaten the employees for various reasons. This act may force employee to be absent from the work thus adversely effect the shift/production.

(b) Some time it is mandatory to file an insurance claim from finance point of view, in this case reporting to police becomes obligatory since insurance company requires a copy of FIR for settling the claim.

(c) Some time management themselves would not allow security officer to proceed further in the case and direct him not to report to the police. Such instances are common when crime is of petty nature and senior managers do not want that case is given media coverage to avoid bad reputation of the organization.

## PROCEDURE FOR INVESTIGATING A CRIME

Once a written report has been received from a department regarding a theft/ crime, the security officer must plan the procedure for investigation within the premises. Following actions are to be taken by the security officer.

(a) *Arrive at the scene of crime*: Visiting the location of crime/theft, etc. and examining it in detail, is the most important function of investigation. It helps the investigator in observing all the evidences in total clarity leading towards the circumstances under which the crime have been committed. Examinations assist the investigator to decide on future courses of action and further methods of investigation in the correct direction.

(b) *Ascertain direction of the crime*: During investigation the direction of entry before crime and exit route after completion of crime must be found out. It will give out the weakness in access control including drawbacks in interior and exterior security system. Routes of entry/ exit will reveal whether any vehicle has also been used in the crime. These information will assist the investigator in identifying the routes used finally by the culprit/accused.

(c) *Modus-operandi of the crime*: While carrying out the investigations the methods of committing the crime should be observed carefully. It is generally found that some criminals are expert in executing a crime in a particular manner which may not be possible by others, Therefore, any fact leading to the modus-operandi of the crime can give vital clue in identifying the culprit.

(d) ***Identifying the witnesses***: The investigator must try and identify the persons who were the eyewitnesses to the act of crime. These persons can give valuable clues/information about the culprit and reason of crime, etc.

## TECHNIQUE OF EXAMINING THE WITNESSES

It is very essential that first hand and real time information about the crime is extracted from the witnesses without causing them any undue stress strain and compulsion. The following guidelines must be adhered to:

(a) Each witness should be examined separately in a office or room where there is no noise or disturbance.

(b) Examination must be conducted as early as possible so that firstly all the events are fresh in their mind about the crime and secondly there are no threats or pressure from the culprit side.

(c) When witness is being examined the other witnesses should not be in the hearing range. This will help the investigating officer/team to have an independent version of the crime.

(d) It is important that first of all trustworthy and honest witnesses are examined to get the correct sequence of the events leading to crime. This information will help him to arrive at correct decision and finding of the case. Witnesses who are not trustworthy or of doubtful integrity should be examined afterwards to match the findings.

(e) The witnesses should be put to ease and then ask them to give out the whole sequence of act of crime in their own manner. Then further questions to bring out facts must be asked to the witnesses.

(f) As far as possible avoid asking "Leading Questions " to the witness e.g. "Did you see the accused or not ". It must be ensured that no important details are missed out while questions are asked to the witnesses.

(g) The whole statement once narrated by the witness should be produced in writing and read over to the witness or he should be allowed to read himself and sign it as correct or put his thumb impression on it. A remark to that effect must be made below the statement that the entire statement has been read over to the witness in the language he/she understands and he/she signs it as correct. Investigator must sign this remark. Similar action must be taken while recording a statement, confession or an evidence of accused or suspected person.

During the process of examination of witnesses, generally there are three types of witnesses as under:

(i) ***Reliable witness***: There may be a person whose reputation or integrity may be at stake due to the crime. These persons will give an honest and reliable statement in order to bring out the complete facts in the case. These witnesses must be examined first with due care and thoroughly.

(ii) ***Unreliable and hostile witnesses***: Some people who are either directly connected with the crime or in some manner have undue sympathy for the suspect/accused. These people will try and give false and incorrect statement which may mislead the investigator. At times they change their statement/evidence to show that they have no vital information about the crime. Such person should be carefully examined with lots of tactful manners. Correct analysis of these statement can reveal the accused's line of self-defence and other foul measures he/she may adopt in due course.

(iii) ***Uninterested witnesses***: While investigating the crime there may be some witnesses who are neither to gain nor to loose anything out of this particular case. Therefore, he will not try to mislead the investigator and may come out with some vital information. In some cases he may not like to involve himself due to inconvenience. Therefore, one should handle these witnesses tactfully and with pursuance.

## INTERROGATION OF THE ACCUSED/SUSPECT

During investigation it is quite likely that suspect or accused may confess his/her crime.

The suspect's confessional statement will be of immense assistance for both the security officer and management to take adequate preventive measures to avoid reoccurrence of this nature. However, the interrogation should follow the following lines of action.

(a) *Aim*: What was the aim behind it, was it thrill, requirement/necessity, to gain some experience in field of crime or to take revenge, etc. from some company official.

(b) *Gaining access*: How did he manage to get an access for committing the crime.

(c) ***Assistance/Help***: How many other persons either from industry or some outsiders are there who provided some help in committing the crime.

(d) ***Property disposal***: After crime, how did he dispose the property and to whom, try and identify the purchaser of stolen property. May be that the accused has kept the item inside the premises or outside the premises awaiting disposal

(e) ***Weaknesses in security system***: While interrogating the suspect/ accused, it may be possible to find out the weaknesses in existing security system. This will help in removing the existing flaws.

## RECORDING OF STATEMENT

Once all the facts related to a crime has been collected by the investigating officer/security officer, these information must be recorded as a statement. The recorded statement can be subsequently used for further action, if management decides to dispose off the case in the form of departmental action. The following points must be borne in mind:

(i) Mention place and date of recording the statement

(ii) Write "statement of Shri/Smt. __________ Full name __________ Department, Designation, Residential Address, Age of the suspect/ witness."

(iii) Mention the connection of witness with the crime in detail.

(iv) Write down how, what and when he/she had seen about the crime. Put down only relevant details, avoid writting anything which is not connected with crime. Be specific with all the details.

(v) If witness desires to produce any evidence as the proof of crime, may be material or documentary. These must be attached as Exhibits with the statement.

(vi) Once statement is over, then relevant questions, to extract some more or specific information, can be asked and recorded with the answers below the statement.

(vii) The completed statement should be read over to the witness in the language he/she understands and his/her signature or thumb impression is obtained, this certificate must be signed by the investigating officer.

(viii) While recording the statement be precise and specific avoid using words like "opinion" or 'views, 'etc.

## INVESTIGATION OF CRIME BY POLICE

Once the senior officer of management has taken the decision of reporting the crime to the police, then the police procedure will commence for investigating the same. It will be the duty of the security officer to assist the police in investigations. Therefore, it is necessary for the security officer to have a fair knowledge of the entire procedure to be followed by the police which is mentioned in succeeding paras.

### First Information Report (FIR)

*Section 154* of Criminal Procedure Code deals in detail about the FIR this the first important report which is lodged at the police station under whose jurisdiction the crime has been committed. Person lodging a FIR must inform the police all the details related to crime. Because this is the first legal document which forms the basis of the entire course of action in future. If possible an important eyewitness should be taken along to the police station by the security officer for lodging an FIR. All information collected in connection with the case during factory's investigation must be given to the police records, a copy of the FIR duly signed and stamped by the police officer, should he collected by the security officer for future action.

The action on "Cognizable offences" and "non-cognizable offences" has already been discussed in chapter six along with their definitions.

### Crime Investigation

Once the report of the committed crime has been lodged with the police the officer will decide whether the crime is a cognizable offence or not. If it is cognizable offence then FIR will be lodged in the police register. The investigation of crime is the second step in dealing with the crime, the procedure for investigation will commence thereafter.

### Visit to the Scene of Crime

After the police have registered a FIR, the concerned police officer, at the earliest will proceed to the scene of offence to investigate all the events leading to the crime. Security officer must ensure that till the police arrives at the location, the evidences are not disturbed by any one. If need be adequate security guards must be posted at the scene of crime. They must ensure that no undue crowding of the place is permitted. If any public road passes near the scene, then one or more security guards should be posted to regulate the traffic. Once the police arrive at the scene they will observe all the clues and evidences which may assist finally in detection of crime. Once police have completed the investigation or necessary interrogations at the site then only, if allowed by the police, security guards can be removed from the scenes and normal routine may be allowed to continue.

## Recording of Evidences

After the investigations at the scene of offence are completed, the police officer will record the evidences/statements of all the people, who in his opinion are either connected or have some knowledge about the crime. The police is authorized under sec 162 of the CrPC to record all the necessary statements for further investigation of the crime. These statements are almost on the similar lines as recorded by the security officer during his local investigation, the police also records the same facts as given out by the witness and in the same language which the witness speaks and understands. The police officer will interrogate thoroughly all the facts related to the crime. The statement should read at the end e.g. "The statement is correctly written according to what I have stated" The police officer should sign at the end of the statement as "Before me".

## Interrogation by the Police

Interrogation is a technique which is to be used during the process of examining/interrogating. Police officer to ensure that all facts and evidences given out by the complainant, witness, suspect or accused are not misleading but assist him in tracking the culprit. The due impact of sympathetic and psychological pressure must be put to extract the needed information.

## Confession/Statement of the Accused/Suspect

Police officer has to exercise due precaution while writing a statement of the accused. Some criminals are so expert that they will try to misguide the police officer and give misleading statement. Therefore, police officer must use patience tact and psychological means to take out the truth about the crime. It may be remembered that even if "Confession" towards crime has been made, police must continue recording complete statements related to the crime. The confession made to the police officer, as per *Section 25* of the Indian Evidence Act, is not admissible as an evidence in the court of justice. Because it is a normal tendency on the part of criminals to turn hostile in front of the Magistrate in the court and they change their statement altogether from what he had given earlier in police station. In some cases whenever a Magistrate is present at the time of recording a statement or the confession made by an accused, under *Section 164* of CrPC, is valid. In this case even if the accused/suspect backs out from his/her confessional statement, the Magistrate concerned can be cited as one of the witness.

## Action on Stolen Property

During the course of investigation in theft cases, if the investigating officer gets suspicious about the stolen property that it may be hidden at some place, house or shop, etc. the police as per *Section 165* of the CrPC is empowered to search those premises without any search warrant. Any property, recovered during such searches will be confiscated by the police. A Panchnama called "seizure Panchnama" will be prepared in respect of the property. However, if an accused/suspect makes a 'confession' about the crime including disclosure of some place, house, shop, etc. where he/she has kept the property, the police will record the confession under *Section 27* of the Indian Evidence Act and will proceed to the place for recovering the property alongwith the accused. All recovered property in this case will be confiscated and a Panchnama called "Discovery Panchnama" will be prepared. In present situation the confessional statement about disclosure of the property is valid in the court of law under sec 27 of IEA. It will be ensured by the security officer that all information pertaining to disclosure of property, if known to him during the preliminary investigations, must be divulged to the police officer for assisting him in investigation.

## Acquiring of Evidences

The importance of good evidences occupy a predominant position in the investigating process, every police officer will try to pinpoint a culprit and establish his/her links/connections with the crime. Therefore, it is an essential task to collect all valuable evidences related to the crime. The evidences are of four types as under:

(i) Verbal evidence.

(ii) Documentary evidence

(iii) Circumstantial evidence
(iv) Expert's report/evidence

As mentioned above, verbal, documentary and circumstantial evidences are self explanatory and require no elaboration. However, expert report/ evidence can be categorized as under

(i) Hand writing expert report.
(ii) Finger print expert report
(iii) Forensic report about hair and blood, etc.
(iv) Ballistic expert report about weapon and ammunition used
(v) Chemical analyzer's report about blood and poison, etc.

During the investigation of theft cases police will try and obtain maximum evidences to prove that recovered property was stolen by the accused. To prove this point it is very important that a proper " identification" is carried out by a responsible person to confirm that this is the property or material which was stolen and belongs to a particular industry. Without proper identification the cases of theft, pilferage or burglary, etc. can not be proved in the court of law. Similarly if the accused has not been properly identified related to the crime, the police will arrange for an "Identification Parade" of the accused. Once the accused has been identified by some witness then court proceedings will proceed further in the case,

## Closure/Finalization of Cases

If during the course of investigation the police gathers enough evidence against the accused then police prepares proper charge sheet and files in the court. On receiving the charge sheet the Magistrate proceeds further with the proceedings. In case adequate evidence is not available for filling the charge sheet in such cases police will submit a final report to the court which is called "A Final" and on receipt of this Magistrate will grant "A" summary for closing the case. Besides "A" summary, following other procedures are also adopted by the police.

(i) ***"B" summery***: If the police finds that a false complaint is lodged, then magistrate grants "B" summery.
(ii) ***"C" summery***: During investigation if police finds that no offence is committed, then 'C' summery is granted by the magistrate on the request of the police.

(iii) At any stage of investigation if it is confirmed that the case is a 'Non-cognizable' offence, then it will be classified as Non-cognizable and not cognizable offence.

## Action in the Event of Unnatural Death

The security officer must be aware of as to how to deal with unnatural death cases. In an Industry generally accidents and suicides are the main causes of unnatural deaths. *Sections 175* and *176* of CrPC gives in detail the procedure to be followed in such cases. Once any report of unnatural death is received from any department security officer should move immediately to the scene On reaching there he must post security guards to ensure that no evidences are disturbed till the arrival of the police. Then a report must be made to the concerned police station. Once the police arrives, detail investigation will be carried out including taking photograph of the victim and scene. Later police will prepare "Inquest Report" and send the body for Postmortem examination. Till the disposal of the body, proper security guards must be posted near the dead body. Security officer must provide full cooperation in collecting of evidence and during witness examination.

### *Charter of Duties of a Security Officer*

As discussed earlier that a security officer's primary task in an Industry is to prevent crimes related to theft, pilferages, assault and affray, etc. Although under the authority of law he does not enjoy any legal authority to deal or dispose off any offence related to personnel and property. However, by virtue of his appointment and responsibility towards management he has to exercise various precautions to prevent and curb the crimes. Therefore, his charter of duties are as follows:

(i) Since he is an employee of the Industry his loyalty and integrity must be for the management.

(ii) His behaviour towards other officers and employees of the organization must be cordial, courteous and but firm.

(iii) He must keep his eyes and ears always open to get adequate advance information of the incidence/events to happen subsequently.

(iv) He must pay regular visits to all departments, meet the head of department to find out about any problem regarding security.

(v) In case of any report or advise/suggestion from any officer for improving security measures he must give these points due attention. If need be corrective measures should be taken immediately.

(vi) He should be accessable to each worker, employee for listening to any complaint, etc.

(vii) He must keep a vigilant eye on the activities of union employees. Must talk off and on with Union Leaders about any problem of workers. Necessary report must be made to the management in this regards.

(viii) He should ensure that all subordinate security staff is punctual, disciplined and well behaved with all employees and visitors.

(ix) Must keep complete information about regular visitors and their particulars and profession, etc.

(x) All employees of suspicious nature, must be kept under constant vigilance.

(xi) Proper 'information sources' must be created to get adequate news about any impending crime and labour unrest, etc. In case of such reports he must immediately report the matter to the management.

(xii) He must keep proper liaison with the Labour Office/Officer, Police Officer and other security officers of nearby units.

(xiii) Must prepare "Do's and Dont's" for his staff and must ensure its execution.

(xiv) Proper testing of all Fire Fighting equipments and mock-up fire drills must be conducted at regular intervals. Must have full record of all civil fire stations and hospitals.

(xv) Frequent testing and technical check-up's of electronic security equipments must be carried out to enhance life and efficiency.

(xvi) Security Officer must keep himself fully aware of IPC, CrPC, IEA and Labour Laws, etc. He must keep complete security staff fully informed about Right of Private Defence of Personnel and property which is governed under *Sections 96–106* of IPC.

## REPORT WRITING

### Importance of Report

Report writing is a major task for the security officer in an organization or official complex. All the unusual happenings in a day in the form of theft, pilferage, burglary, assault, riot, unnatural death and any type of accident, etc. must be noted down in the "occurrence register" and afterwards must be reported to the senior officer deputed or management. All violations of rules and procedure should also be observed, noted and subsequently reported. In medium and large size organizations a security officer will keep a close watch on the Labour activities, union intelligence, any impending strike or unrest and forward his report alongwith his recommendations of actions/suggestions to management.

The layout and contents of the security officer's report must be very clear, concise and should convey to the management the correct picture of the labour activities and other events inside the organization.

## Proforma for Incident Reporting

There will be number of occasions when a security officer has to report about an accident or incident to the top management. Therefore, it is advisable to prepare a detailed format/proforma on which such reports can be forwarded. Suggested layout is as under:

### *(a) Who*

(i) who was the first to inform about the incident.
(ii) who are the personnel involved in incident.
(iii) who are the victims.
(iv) who are the witnesses.
(v) who are the suspects.
(vi) who will initiate the complaint. (Note Name, Address and Telephone Number and other relevant information)

### *(b) What*

(i) what is the whole story of the incident.
(ii) what happened before, during and after the incident.
(iii) what actions were taken by those involved in it.
(iv) what was stated by each individual.
(v) what evidence has been collected.
(vi) what authorities were contacted after incident.

### *(c) Where*

(i) where did the incident occur.
(ii) where were all the individual before, during and after the incident.
(iii) where was evidence found.

### *(d) When*

(i) when did the incident occur.

(ii) when was it discovered.

(iii) when was it reported.

(iv) when did authorities arrive at the scene.

(v) when was any arrest made.

### *(e) How*

(i) how did the loss occur.

(ii) how was it discovered.

(iii) how did security department reacted to incident.

(iv) how expensive is the loss.

(v) how loss of this nature can be prevented in future.

### *(f) Why*

In this Para security officer must give out his comment/recommendations as under:

(i) why did the loss take place.

(ii) why was the crime/incident committed.

(iii) why did personnel involved in the incident committed the crime.

Based on the report forwarded by the security officer to the Head of Administration and further to the top management, the complete strategy of the counter action or preventive measures will be chalked out by the management. It must be noted that report of labour intelligence and union activities, which will effect the overall working of the organization in various disciplines, must be prepared by collecting information from different sources. For such information collection security officer will organize a "Intelligence Cell" consisting of 2–3 reliable and resourceful employees from security/ Admn./HRD department. Few dependable sources must be created among employees to give valuable and advance information about forthcoming events in the organization. The collection and collation of Labour Intelligence is a vital process in the efficient functioning of any organization and corporate offices.

# 11

# Labour Problems and Industrial Legislations

## Labour Problems in an Industry

Labour problems constitute a serious menace to the Industrial world and require a workable and acceptable solution, if not to eradicate them completely, at least to mitigate them right at the initial stage. In an Industry the security department operates either with Administration or under Personnel Department. Therefore, a security officer is not directly connected with the labour problems because these do not fall under his area of operations. But a security officer indirectly gets involved deep into all the labour problems arising in an Industry. In an Industry it is very difficult to specify or define a labour problem. Because in every case it has variable causes, impacts, disciplines and cannot be confined to any similarity. It is quite likely that without a visible impact on industrial growth and rift between employees and management or even between management and trade unions, the labour problems can be there in an Industry. There are no laid down areas or boundaries for labour problem to erupt in an industry. Thus it is very essential that security officials must know as to what is going on into the mind of employees and into what shape and size of labour problem it can finally develop, if necessary preventive measures are not taken in time.

*Definition*: A problem, irrespective of its size which relates to mutual relations between the employers/management and employees, will be termed as labour problem.

In order to analyze these problems, one can categorize these as under:

(a) Problems arising out of statutes.

(b) Problems arising from the rifts in relations between employers and employees/management.

### *Problems Arising Out of Statutes*

In India, the Tea Plantation Industry in Assam was the first to attract legislative control. A number of Acts were passed from 1863 onwards to regulate the recruitment and other labour problem. But the most important of the Acts, which was passed, was workman's compensation Act 1923. The main legislation concerning labour problems are enumerated in succeeding paragraphs.

(a) Workmen's Compensation Act, 1923.
(b) Trade Unions Act, 1926.
(c) Payment of Wages Act, 1936.
(d) Industrial Employment (Standing Orders) Act, 1946.
(e) Industrial Disputes Act, 1947.
(f) Minimum Wages Act, 1948.
(g) Factories Act, 1948.
(h) Employees State Insurance Act, 1948.
(i) Employees Provident Funds and Miscellaneous Provisions Act, 1952.
(j) Payment of Bonus Act, 1965.
(k) Payment of Gratuity Act 1972.

The above mentioned legislations are the main statutes out of which a labour problem will originate in an Industry. It is not obligatory on the part of a security head/officer to know in detail all these legislations. However, he must have a fair knowledge as to what are the tasks which security staff has to perform in addition to their daily routine in case of any labour problem, with the above mentioned acts, it is basically the Personnel/Administration Manager or Labour officer who are directly involved with labour problems, however, a security officer should have basic knowledge of the following important Acts.

## INDUSTRIAL DISPUTES ACT 1947

The Industrial Disputes Act 1947 extends to the whole of India and it came into operation on the first day of April 1947. The object of the Act as laid down in the preamble of the Act is to make provisions for the investigation and settlement of the Industrial Disputes.

### Main Features of the Act

Some of the distinguished features of the Industrial Disputes Act 1947 are as follows:

(1) Any Industrial Disputes may be referred to an industrial tribunal by an agreement of parties to the disputes or by the state government if it deems it expedient to do so.

(2) An award shall be binding on both the parties to the dispute for the specified period not exceeding one year, it shall be normally enforced by the government.

(3) Strikes and lock-outs are prohibited:

   (i) During the pendency of conciliation and adjudication proceedings.

   (ii) During the pendency of settlement reached in the course of conciliation proceedings.

   (iii) During the pendency of awards of Industrial Tribunal declared binding by the appropriate government.

(4) In public interest or emergency the appropriate government has power to declare the transport (other than railways) coal, cotton textiles, food stuffs, iron and steel industries to be a public utility service for the purpose of this Act for a maximum period of six months.

(5) In case of lay-off or retrenchment of workmen the employer is required to pay compensation to them.

(6) Provision has also been made for payment of compensation to workmen in case of transfer or closure of an undertaking.

(7) A number of authorities such as works committee, conciliation officers, courts of inquiry, labour court, tribunal and national tribunal are provided for settlement of industrial disputes. The nature of powers, functions and duties of these authorities differ from each other but each one of them plays an important role in ensuring industrial peace.

Now an endeavour is being made to illustrate the main definitions covered under this Act. These are mentioned below:

### *Industry*

Industry means any systematic activity carried on by cooperation between an employer and his workmen (employees) whether employed by himself or provided by some other agency, for the production, supply or distribution of goods/services with a view to satisfy human wants or wishes, whether or not:

(i) Any capital has been invested for the purpose of carrying on such activity.

(ii) Such activity is carried on with a motive to make any gain or profit and includes:

(a) Any activity of Dock Labour Board established under *Section 5-A* of Dock Workers Act 1948.

(b) Any activity relating to promotion of sales or business or both carried on by an establishment but does not include.

(iii) Any agricultural operations except where such "agricultural operation" is carried on in an integrated manner with any other activity and such other activity is the predominant one.

### *Closure*

Closure means the permanent closing down of a place of employment or part thereof.

### *Court*

'Court' means a court of inquiry constituted under this Act.

### *Industrial dispute*

There is no specific definition for an industrial dispute, however, following elements should exist to constitute an industrial dispute:

(a) A dispute or difference between (i) Employees and employers (ii) Employers and workmen (iii) Workmen and workmen.

(b) The dispute or difference should be connected with (i) Employment or non employment (ii) Terms of employment (iii) Conditions of labour of any person.

(c) The dispute may be in relation to any workman or workmen or any other person in whom they are interested as a body.

***Labour court***: Means a labour court constituted under *Section 7* of the Industrial Disputes Act 1947.

***Lay-off***: The following are the specific features of a lay-off.

(1) An employer, who is willing to employ, fails or refuses or is unable to provide employment for reasons beyond his control.

(2) Any such failure or refusal to employee or worker may be on account of:

(i) Shortage of coal, power or raw material

(ii) The accumulation of stock

(iii) The breakdown of machinery

(iv) Natural calamity

(v) Any other connected reasons.

(3) A workman who is so deprived of employment must be such whose name is borne on the muster rolls of his industrial establishment.

(4) The workman must not have been retrenched.

***Lockout***: "Lockout" means the closing of a place of employment or the suspension of the work or the refusal by an employer to continue to employ any number of persons employed by him.

Lockout is the action of keeping the labour away from the work by an employer with the view to resist their claim. There are four ingredients of lockout.

(1) It will include:

(i) Temporary closing of any place of employment by the employer

(ii) Suspension of work by the employer

(iii) Refusal by an employer to continue to employ any number of persons employed by him.

(2) The above mentioned acts of employer should be motivated by coercion.

(3) It should be an industry as defined in the Act.

(4) A dispute in such industry.

***Strike***: Strike can be defined as under:

(1) Cessation of work by a body of persons employed in any industry acting in combination

(2) A concerted refusal of any number of persons who are or have been employed in any industry to continue to work or to accept employment

(3) A refusal under a common understanding of any number of persons who are or have been employed in an industry to work or to accept employment.

***Types of strikes***: There are basically three types of strikes as under:

(1) ***General strike***: A general strike is one where workmen join together for a common cause and stay away from the work, depriving the employer of their labour needed to run the industry. Token strike is also a kind of general strike. Token strike is for a day or for few hours or for a short duration because its main object is to draw the attention

of the management by demonstrating the solidarity and cooperation of the employees whereas general strikes period will be longer. Token strike normally precedes a general strike.

(2) *Stay-in-strike*: A stay-in-strike is called as "tools-down-strike or pens-down-strike." In this type of strike, the employees report for their duties, occupy the premises but do not work. The employer is thus prevented from employing other labour to carry on the business. The presence of excited labour in the factory premises is a great threat and danger to the safety and security of the organization.

(3) *Go-slow-strike*: In "go-slow-strike" the employees do not stay away from the work or shop floors and offices, they report for their duties and work but with a slow speed in order to lower down the production of the factory, with the result cause loss to the employer. Go-slow is infect not a strike within the Act, but is a serious misconduct in its nature.

In addition to the above three types of strikes which is very commonly resorted to by the employees. The following other agitations are also considered as strikes by the employees but as per sub *Section 2* (q) of the Act these are not termed as strikes.

(i) Sympathetic strike
(ii) Hunger strike
(iii) Work to rule.

***Difference between lockout and lay-off***

(1) Lockout is an act, on the part of an employer taken to coerce or pressurise the labour, lay-off is for trade reasons beyond the control of the employer i.e. it is not an intentional act.

(2) Lockout is due to an industrial dispute and continues during the period of dispute; lay-off is not concerned with a dispute with the workmen.

***Difference between lockout and closure***

(1) Lockout may be temporary whereas closure is permanent.

(2) Lockout is a weapon of coercion in the hands of employer; closure is generally for trade reasons as discussed in the definition.

(3) Lockout is during an industrial dispute whereas in the case of closure there need not be any dispute.

## Role of Security Staff During Industrial Unrest

Having seen various definitions of industrial unrest which are basically responsible for most of the labour problems. Therefore, it is very essential for the security officer to understand in detail the implications of all these. As we are well aware that primary tasks of security department is to ensure safety and security of personnel, material and machinery during the periods of strikes, lockout, lay-off or closure, etc. All the actions of senior manager and management will depend upon the labour intelligence reports submitted by the security Head/Manager from time to time.

In order to remain alert and vigilant all the time, the security officer must adhere to the following.

### *Knowledge of past labour unrest*

It is very important for the head of security to know the part history, if any, of the industry. He must read in detail and also should get necessary update from personnel manager and labour officer. All types of strikes which had taken place in the organization alongwith their reasons, details of unions and their leaders what was the outcome, details of actions taken by the security staff and management must be studied. The nature of strike whether violent or peaceful, any arrest, etc. made or not, any interference by police. Whether management declared any lockout consequence to the strike. Various aspects related to the strikes must be known to the security officer. All these information will assist him in keeping a close watch on the anticipated moves of the employees and the labour unions.

### *Information of labour unions*

Security officer should have a comprehensive knowledge about the labour unions which are operating inside the premises or even supporting from outside. Some valuable points are as under:

(i) Union leaders are either from within the industry or they are from outside.

(ii) What are the political connections of the labour union. Which are the local state or the national level leaders supporting the union.

(iii) Whether the political leaders are hostile or sympathetic towards management.

(iv) Has there been some changes in the union leadership from the past, if so, what are the reasons.

(v) What is the attitude of present leaders towards the organizations.

(vi) What is the integrity and loyalty of union leaders.

### *Union rivalry*

In an industry where more than one trade unions operate, it is quite possible that their union rivalry will always persist. The employees will also be divided on the decisions taken by the union, of which they are not members. Security officer must keep a close watch on such rivalry and if possible, take advantage of it in the interest of the industry.

### *Miscellaneous causes of labour unrest*

Besides strikes and lockout there can be in numerable causes of labour unrest in an industry. Sometimes small rift between workers and management or between union and management can develop into a big unrest. These are as follows:

(i) Shop/Machine floor rifts between workers and supervisor/manager.

(ii) Managerial attitude towards redressal of grievances put up by the employees.

(iii) Fixation of wage/salary structures.

(iv) Dearness allowance or grant of bonus.

(v) Union rivalry in the initial stages.

(vi) Procedure followed in settling various employee's demands.

(vii) Procedure adopted for promotion concerning one or more employees.

### *Actions on impending labour unrest*

Constant vigil must be kept on all the employees with suspicious nature and security officer must collect maximum advanced information about any impending unrest. The security officer should take the following actions, if some information about strike/strike notice is received by the management.

(i) Activate all the sources to gather all the information about impending strike/unrest.

(ii) Plan and position at various important places adequate security guards inside the factory premises to ensure full protection for materials and machines, etc.

(iii) Depending upon the analysis of threat adequate protection should be provided for management and other senior officers/managers.

(iv) Proper information/report must be made to the concerned police station. Necessary information from time to time must be passed about the strike.

(v) Security officers must observe carefully the negotiations, if any, going on between the union leaders and management. If the demands are met then strike may not take place at all. Sometimes it is possible that "Lightening Strike" may be there in the industry without any proper notice. So a security officer must be very alert and keep a track of all the labour activities.

## Action by Security Officer During Strike

In case of a strike in the industry the following measures to be adopted by the security officer:

(i) The complete security department must be able to occupy their assigned duties as per industry's standing orders, in case of a strike. In case the strength of the guards is considered inadequate, then requisite number of security guards must be arranged from the local agency.

(ii) Constant police liaison must be kept with the police station and all the important information should be passed on to the police officer at regular intervals or on occurrence.

(iii) Security officer or Personnel Manager/Administration Manager must obtain injunction orders from the civil court or a labour court. Those orders should be enforced by the police as these are always essential for such actions. Injunction order's enforcement are very important in order to safeguard the organization's property.

(iv) In case some workers wish to join the work, then adequate protection must be given for them during the strike.

(v) The security officer is the only officer possibly during the strike whose report from time to time will matter a lot for the management to chalk out their future plans and strategy to resolve the labour problem.

## THE FACTORIES ACT 1948

There has been an enormous rise of large scale Industries/Factories in India in the latter half of the nineteenth century. Major Moore Inspector-in-chief of the Bombay Cotton Department in his report in 1872–73, first of all raised the question for the provision of a suitable legislation to regulate working conditions in the factories. The first Factory's Act was enacted in 1881. Since then, the Act has been amended on many occasions. The Factories Act 1948, consolidating and amending the law related to the Labour in the Factories/ Industries, was passed by the Constituent Assembly on 28 August 1948. The Act received the assent of Governor General of India on 23 September 1948 and came into force on 01 April 1949.

## Changes Introduced by the Factories Act 1948

Following important amendments were made by the Factory's Act 1948:

(a) The definition of the term "Factory" was widened to cover all industrial establishment employing ten or more workers where power was used and twenty or more workers in all other areas.

(b) The distinction between seasonal and non seasonal factories was abolished.

(c) Chapter III of the Act of 1934 was split into three parts dealing with health, safety and welfare of the workers. These privileges are extended to every work place irrespective of number of workers employed.

(d) The minimum age for the children for employment has been raised from 12 to 14 years. The minimum hours of work for children have been reduced from five hours to four and a half hours.

(e) Employment of women and children between 7 P.M. to 6 A.M. is prohibited. For overtime work the workers are entitled to twice of their normal rate of wages.

## Important Definitions

*Adult*: Means a person who has completed eighteenth years of age.

*Adolescent*: Means a person who has completed his fifteenth year of age but not completed his eighteenth year.

*Child*: Means who has not completed his fifteenth year of age.

*Young person*: Means a person who is either a child or a adolescent.

## Salient Features of Factory Act 1948

Chapter III of the Act has been divided into three separate portions as under:

1. ***Health***: Under health following aspects are covered:

(a) Cleanliness in all the work places will be maintained including machine floor, inside office or verandah, etc.

(b) Disposal of waste and effluents will be carried out under effective arrangements.

(c) Ventilations and temperature of all work place will be so kept that flow of fresh air is maintained regularly.

(d) *Dust and fumes*: Effective measures will be adopted to ensure that work places are free from dust and fumes, if any in the organization.

(e) *Overcrowding*: No room in the factory will be overcrowded to become injurious to the health of the workers.

(f) *Lighting*: All work places and passages will have adequate natural or artificial or both lights in adequate quantity.

(g) *Drinking water*: Adequate drinking water will be provided within reasonable reach of every worker. All water points will be legibly marked "Drinking Water". Whenever more than 250 workers are employed provisions will be there to provide "Cool Drinking Water."

(h) *Latrines and urinals*: Sufficient number of latrines and urinals will be provided separate for ladies and gents. All such places will have sufficient water, proper lights and ventilations.

(i) *Spittoons*: In every factory there will be sufficient number of spittoons in convenient place. These will ensure that workers do not spit in the factory premises except in spittoons.

2. *Safety*: Under safety, various measures are to be adopted by management to ensure that adequate safety is maintained for all the workers at their work places. These are as under:

(a) Fencing of machinery.

(b) Work on or near when machinery is in motion.

(c) Employment of young persons on dangerous machines.

(d) Striking gears and devices for cutting of power.

(e) Self-acting machine.

(f) Casing of new machinery.

(g) *Hoist and lifts*: In all factories all hoists and lifts will be in good mechanical condition, sound material and with adequate strength.

(h) All floors, staircase and means of access in a factory will be kept clean and clear of any material which may cause a slip to the worker while working or walking.

(i) *Protection to eyes*: Full protection to the eyes of all the workers will be provided from dangerous light and fume of glare, etc. suitable goggles will be issued to all such employees.

(j) Protection against explosive or inflammable dust and gas, etc.

(k) Adequate precautions in case of fire.

(l) Full safety of building and machinery.

(m) *Provision of safety officers*: In an industry where 1000 or more workers are employed a safety officer will be employed to look after the health and safety of the employees.

3. *Welfare*: As a measure of welfare for the employees, following facilities will be provided as per Act:

(a) *Washing facilities*: Adequate number of washing facilities separate for male and female workers will be provided.

(b) Facilities for storing and drying of clothes.

(c) *First-aid appliances*: Suitable first aid boxes with all permissible contents will be provided and kept at easily accessible points. One box must be catered for every 150 employees. Wherein more than 500 employees, one ambulance room with a qualified nursing assistant will be maintained.

(d) *Canteen*: Every factory, where more than 250 employees are there, will operate a well equipped canteen for the workers. It will be ensured that adequate space, furniture and food stuff are arranged by the management. The canteen will run on "No Profit No Loss Basis."

(e) Provision of shelters, rest rooms and lunch rooms will be made in a factory where more than 150 workers or more are employed.

(f) *Crèches*: In a factory where more than 30 women workers are employed a crèches will be provided by the management for the use of employee's children under the age of six years. These will be provided with:

(i) A woman incharge of the crèches.

(ii) Adequate space and toys for playing.

(iii) Free refreshment and milk, etc. will be provided for the children.

(iv) Facilities for washing and changing their clothes.

(v) Facilities for mothers to feed to their children at regular intervals.

(g) *Appointment of welfare officer*: A factory where 500 or more workers are employed, one or more welfare officer should be appointed to look after the welfare needs of the employees.

## THE INDUSTRIAL EMPLOYMENT (STANDING ORDERS) ACT 1946

The absence of standing orders in an establishment very often leads to avoidable friction between employees and the management of an industry. With the advent of Trade Unions and collective bargaining, the new labour problems in maintaining industrial peace and protection for the society were created. To give effect to the new ideology of defining a law precisely for each occasion to govern the conditions of employment, the Industrial Employment (Standing Orders) Act 1946 was enacted by the central government. It is obligatory upon all the employers covered by this act to define conditions of employment under them. The conditions of employment must also be known to the employees working in that organization.

### Application of the Act

The object of the standing orders is to make it understand and clear to both the parties on what terms and conditions the workmen are offering to work and the employer is offering to engage them. All these conditions must be reduced into writing in the form of standing orders. The act applies to every industrial establishment:

(i) Situated within the Indian Union except the state of Jammu and Kashmir.

(ii) Employing 100 or more workmen on any day of the preceding 12 months.

### Contents of the Standing Orders

All the standing orders must be certified by the Government certifying officer who is normally a Labour Commissioner. All standing orders are to be prepared on the lines of "Model Standing Orders" provided by the Labour Commissioner Office. Essentially the contents will include the following:

(a) Classification of all workers i.e., whether permanent, temporary, on probation or apprentice, etc.

(b) Timings of shift and offices.

(c) Method of recording attendance and late coming.

(d) Shift working and rest days.

(e) The procedures as to how the workers will be intimated about holidays, hours of work, pay days and wages rates, etc.

(f) Point of entry and exit for workers and orders/procedures for searches, if any, to be carried out by security staff.

(g) Conditions and authority to grant leave and holidays.

(h) Commencing and stopping of work at workplaces, the responsibility for stream lining any procedure, if need be.

(i) Termination procedure for service, notice, etc. to be given by employer and workmen to the management.

## The Payment of Wages Act, 1936

The need to protect the wages earned by the workers had been felt from the early years of the twentieth century, but it was as early as 1925 that a private Bill called "The Weekly Payment Bill" was for the first time introduced in the Legislative Assembly. The Royal Commission on labour in India made some valuable recommendations. The present Act is mostly based on those recommendations. A bill of Payment of Wages Act, based on the recommendations of the Royal Commission on Labour was introduced in the Legislative Assembly in 1933 but could not take the shape of the Act because of the dissolution of the Assembly. The present Payment of Wages Act was passed in 1936 and came into force on 21st March 1937. This Act extends to whole of India.

### *Application of the Act*

The Act applies in the first instance to the payment of wages to:

(a) Persons employed in any factory.

(b) Persons employed (otherwise than in factory) upon any railway by a railway administration or either directly or through a sub-contractor, by a person fulfilling a contract with the railway administration.

(c) Persons employed in an industrial or other establishment specified in sub clauses (a) to (g) of clause (ii) of *Section 2* of this Act.

### *Definitions*

(a) ***Employed person***: Employed person includes the legal representative of deceased employed person.

(b) ***Employer***: Employer includes the legal representative of a deceased employer.

(c) ***Wages***: The wages as defined in the Act includes any privilege or benefit, which is capable of being estimated in the money. The following are not wages:

(i) Travelling allowance or the value of any travelling concession.

(ii) Contribution paid by the employer of a workmen towards:

  (i) Any pension

  (ii) Any provident fund

  (iii) Any sum paid to a workman to cover any special expenses incurred on him by the nature of his employment

  (iv) Leave carried forward to the next year.

(d) ***Privileges or benefits***: The following privileges and benefits are included in the wages:

(i) Free accommodation

(ii) Monetary benefit to a women employee while delivering a child,

(iii) Dearness allowance

(iv) Overtime pay or allowance

(v) Benefit in the form of food and clothing

(vi) Gratuity payable to workmen at the time of retirement

(vii) Bonus.

(e) ***Difference between wage and salary***: To determine whether an employee's receiving wages or salary is based on the basis of the period for which the amount is agreed to be paid. Wages are generally paid to the workers and as per agreement could be daily, weekly, fortnightly or monthly. Whereas salary is for supervisors, officers and managers who are paid on monthly basis.

(f) ***Overtime***: Since duration of work is fixed for every worker as eight hours in a day or maximum of 40 hours in a week of six days. One day in a week will be given holiday for each worker. Therefore, any work in excess of that is done in a day or on a paid holiday, the worker will be given 'double' the wage than normally paid for that duration.

Wages must be paid within seven days for an establishment with less than 1000 persons and before the expiry of the tenth day after completion of the month where more than 1000 workers are employed.

(g) ***Wage deductions***: The permissible authorized deductions, which can be deducted from the wages, are given below:

(i) Deductions for absence from duty.

(ii) Any fine imposed.
(iii) Deductions for damage or loss of property.
(iv) Deductions towards accommodation, electricity.
(v) PF, Profession Tax and Income Tax, etc.
(vi) Any amount of loan installment, etc.

(h) *Minimum wages*: The government has fixed the rate of minimum wages for each category i.e., skilled, semi-skilled and non-skilled workers.

## THE PAYMENT OF BONUS ACT, 1965

The payment of Bonus Act 1965 is the outcome of the recommendations made by a Tripartite Commission, which was set up by the Government of India in 1961. The recommendations of the Commission were received by the Government on 24th January 1964. On 2nd September 1964 the Government implemented the recommendations subject to certain modifications. The Payment of Bonus Ordinance 1965 was promulgated on 26th May 1965.

### Scope and Application

This Act extends to whole of India and will apply to every factory and organization/establishment in which twenty or more persons are employed on any day during an accounting year. Every employee shall be entitled for the bonus to be paid by his employer in an accounting year, provided an employee has worked in the establishment for not less than thirty working days in that year.

### Disqualification for the Bonus

As per the Act an employee shall be disqualified from receiving the bonus if he/she is dismissed from the service for:

(a) Riotous or violent behaviour while on the premises of the establishment.
(b) Theft, misappropriation or sabotage of any property of the establishment.

## Amount of Bonus

As per the provision of the act where an employer has any allocable surplus in any accounting year, then he shall be bound to pay to every employee in respect of that accounting year, a minimum bonus which shall not be less than 8.1/3% (8.33% to 20%) of the salary or wage earned by the employee during the accounting year or one hundred rupees whichever is higher. In a case where allocable surplus exceeds the said amount of minimum bonus payable to the employees, an amount in proportion to the salary or wage earned by the employee during the accounting year subject to a maximum of twenty percent (20%) of the salary or wages.

## Procedure to Work Out Bonus

In an establishment the Gross Profit is initially worked out for that accounting year. The following deductions are made, as applicable from the gross profit to work out allocable bonus.

(a) Depreciation
(b) Taxes
(c) Development rebate
(d) Rehabilitation
(e) Returns on capital and reserves
(f) Remunerations for working partners
(g) Available and allocable surpluses

It must be understood that statutory bonus of eight and one third percent shall be payable whether there are profits in the accounting year or not. As per the provision of this act bonus has become an implied term of employment and not dependent upon the profits. Employees are entitled to festival bonus only if there is an implied agreement or it is paid as a customary bonus. The minimum bonus under this Act is a right which vests in the employee and no further adjudication of the right to the payment of minimum bonus is called for. It constitutes an existing statutory right. However, denial of this right by the employer does not render it an Industrial Dispute calling for an adjudication by way of reference to *Section 10* of Industrial Dispute Act read with *Section 22* of the Payment of Bonus Act.

# 12

# Fire Protection and Safety in Industries and Corporate Houses

## Aspects of Fire, Accidents and Safety

In an Industrial organization all safety precautions are observed to ensure that either no accident takes place or chances of accident gets minimized as far as possible. An accident in an industry or office can be defined as an "Unplanned and Unexpected event that may occur and thus results in damage to property, injury to personnel or both". Whereas safety can be defined as anticipated positive actions to prevent any damage to property, loss of life or injury to personnel.

If we visualize critically it can be seen that an accident generally results from a sequence of events and if there is a timely interruption in this sequence, an accident generally can be prevented. This is where a fire incident can be easily avoided if adequate and timely precautions are observed at various places. It will be interesting to know that losses caused due to fire in Industrial Houses, both in Public and Private sectors, have been much more severe than all crimes combined together. There can be nothing more devastating and injurious to lives than fire. A small spark due to short circuit or human carelessness falling on any inflammable material may become a raging trolly of flames and can transform the whole Industrial House or Office Complex into a towering inferno. In Petroleum and Oil Industries a small spark from a faulty electrical equipment may cause tremendous devastation with the entire storage tanks of oils and lubricants besides causing loss of machinery, buildings and even human lives.

In Industries/Factories there have always been a serious fire risk due to nature of various raw and finished goods, types of machinery and off course careless behaviour of employees. Serious damages to machine, material and loss of lives or injury to personnel have been the main outcome in the last two decade. It is interesting to note that all fire incidents are followed by various level inquiries and commissions, these enquiry commissions submit their reports, but very unfortunately-outcome and suggested measures are all left out in files for imaginations. The glaring examples are as under:

(a) New Delhi Fire in Gopala Towers 1983
(b) New Delhi Fire in Siddharth Palace Hotel 1986
(c) Uphar Cinema New Delhi 1996
(d) Fire in Ordanance Factories Bharatpur (Rajasthan) and J&K in 2000–2001 and in Army Vehicles lodged with ammunition near Bikaner in January 2002 respectively.

Unless government decides to enforce stringent preventive measures which have been suggested/ recommended by various inquiries, the devastation will continue to be caused by fire havocs in Industries, Factories and Public places.

When we study the anatomy of fire it is well known that there are three basic constituents of fire as under:

(a) Oxygen
(b) Heat
(c) Fuel in any shape

Fire will always require all these following three factors, in case one or more of these three factors are denied or removed, then there can be no fire accident. Fire always starts by voluntary or involuntary ignition. It may spark out of a electrical short circuit, any naked light i.e. unextingushed Cigarette/ Bidi, matchstick, localized heat arising out of rising temperature or friction of two objects, etc.

*Classification of fire*: All fires can be classified under the four following categories:

(i) *Class "A" fire*: In class 'A' fire the fuel normally consists of general wood or wooden material, textiles, paper garbage, plastic, rubber and such other commonly used materials.
(ii) *Class "B" fire*: This is the second category of fire which will require petroleum products, grease, paints, solvents, cleansing fluids and alcohol, etc. as its fuel.
(iii) *Class "C" fire*: In this class of fire the fuel will consist of gaseous substances under pressure. e.g.: LPG, etc.
(iv) *Class "D" fire*: This is the type of fire where fuel is of highly inflammable nature i.e. magnesium, titanium, sodium and potassium, etc.

*Electrical fire*: The electrical fire, generally can't be categorized in any class. Because a Electrical Short Circuit Fire can subsequently take place into a class A, B, C or D types of fire.

Security officer or fire officer as the case may be, depending upon the size of the Industry, should be able to classify correctly the type of fire, which can assist him in choosing the correct fire fighting appliances and extinguishers or safety measures. Wrong classifications may result in incorrect choice of fire fighting equipment which can be heavy on losses to property and personnel. One must exercise due caution in case of mixed types of fire i.e. class 'A' and class 'C', where extra precautions have to be taken to avoid undue losses and injury.

*Fire hazards and causes*: In modern Hi-Tech industries, where electricity is used for almost each function at machine shop and other technical process, the risks of electrical short circuits enhances manifold. Other Industries, which are producing items of petroleum, oil and lubricants, rubber, plastics, chemicals, solvents, LPG and explosives, etc. are highly vulnerable to accidents or fire incidents. Incidents of fire are largely related to the extent of awareness among workers/employees and levels at which various preventive measure are adopted. It is worthwhile to know that fire incidents are comparatively less in Industries which are producing highly inflammable products like petroleum, oil and lubricants and explosives, etc. than in those factories which are producing wooden, textiles or paper products, etc. The main reasons are that rigid enforcement of fire prevention rules and guidelines. It is said that-"as long as employees/workers regard the products as fire risk and take strict precautions, the fire incidents are much less than if employees become negligent/careless and ignore the fire preventive measures".

As it has been mentioned earlier that nature of fire hazards in an Industry will generally depend upon the types of products and the raw materials used. Fire can breakout in an Industry while handling of material, processing, storing and transporting of products. The common causes of fire are enumerated below:

*Common causes of fire*:

(i) Naked Flame
(ii) Smoking or unextinguished cigarette buds
(iii) Electrical sparks/short circuits and over heating
(iv) Hot works
(v) Static electricity discharge

(vi) Friction and overheating
(vii) Fire risks from neighbouring areas
(viii) Non adherence of explosive rules (Do's/Do'nts)
(ix) Poor house keeping i.e. Disposal of garbage and incinerator operations, etc.

## *Handling of Various Types of Fires*

(a) *Class "A" fire*: This type of fire where fuel supplied is not very inflammable but is normal combustible material. In such cases plain water jets, foams and soda water type extinguishers are used to control the fire. As a matter of fact the application of water prevents oxygen and heat from participating in the operation. Water initially extinguishes the flame and brings down the temperature which prevents further ignition to form the fire. In class 'A' fire Carbondioxide type extinguishers should not be used since the cooling effect by this equipment is very temporary and ignition may occur soon after that which can be more dangerous. It is advisable that following types of equipments are used for class 'A' fire:

(i) Water Jets from Hose Pipes
(ii) Water Buckets
(iii) Sand Buckets
(iv) Stirrup Pumps
(v) Soda Acid (Water) Extinguishers
(vi) Gas Water Extinguishers

(b) *Class "B" fire*: In this class, fuel element is of highly inflammable nature like petroleum, oil and lubricant products. To overcome such fires the foam, carbon dioxide and dry powder types of extinguishers are used. Foam serves as insulation and prevents oxygen supply for continuing the fire besides giving it a cooling effect to reduce the heat. Plain water must not be used under any circumstances as the volume of fuel or fire will spread to other areas very fast because petroleum products are lighter than water and will float over it into the surrounding areas. However, once the petroleum fuel has been burnt out completely, then water can be used to extinguish the fire when it becomes almost class 'A' fire.

(c) *Class "C" fire*: For this type of fire, the fire extinguishers containing dry chemical powder or even carbon dioxide should be utilized.

(d) *Class "D" fire*: The main fuel supply for this type of fire is through highly combustible materials like magnesium, sodium and titanium, etc. This type of fire does not take place very frequently. Extinguishers of dry chemical powders of various sizes and capacity are used to tackle such fires.

(e) *Electrical fires*: Fire breaking out in electrical equipments and machinery is quite common in modern industries. In such incidents carbon dioxide, dry powders and other vapourising liquids should be used to fight the fire breaking out of electrical leakage and short circuits, etc. All workers/employees must be trained to 'shut off' the main supply of electricity immediately. It must be remembered that water should never be used in the case of electric fire since water is a good conductor and will give shock to the person using water.

## AVAILABILITY OF FIRE EXTINGUISHING EQUIPMENTS

### *Portable and Water Type Fire Extinguishers*

It is very essential that selection of fire extinguishers is made by considering type of fire, building, layout, material or machinery involved in the fire and related hazards with the outcome of fire. Presently the availability of portable fire extinguishers are as under:

(i) *Chemical and dry powder extinguishers*: Baking soda is the primary ingredient involved in dry powder type extinguisher. It is a bad conductor of electricity and acts as a insulating sheet on the surface of the fire, because it prevents oxygen from joining the brokenout fire. Its main use is against 'D' class of fire. A new extinguishers known as ABC extinguisher is also available for use of all types of fire. The task of these extinguisher is to act as coolent and reduces the heat, an important factor in burning of fire.

(ii) *Soda acid type*: This extinguisher contains baking soda solution in the container and sulphuric acid vial in a chamber situated on top of the extinguisher's body. A pointed plunger is fitted over the vial to pierce it when needed for operation. To operate this extinguisher one has to lift it at waist height and shake it well to ensure baking soda mixes fully into the water, then by turning it upside down break the vial of sulphuric acid by hitting the plunger on the ground. The acid then gets mixed with soda water and with pressure water jet comes out of nozzle. This water jet is pointed on to the fire, once the extinguisher operates the entire quantity of water is drained out which acts as coolent at the broken out fire. This equipment is basically used against class 'A' fire.

(iii) *Carbondioxide extinguishers*: Carbondioxide extinguishers (called $CO_2$) are pressure filled and they act as coolant on the fire. This type of equipment is widely used in class 'B' and 'C' types of fire. $CO_2$ type of extinguishers are also useful in electrical and other combustible types of fire. It is generally not used in class 'A' fire. In an Industry the fire extinguishers must be stored at suitable places near to machine shops, office complex and store/ware houses. Appropriate markings e.g. "For Use," "Use in case of fire", etc. should be displayed for the benefit of the factory or office employees.

(iv) *Dry pipe sprinkler system*: This type of system is generally used in the cooler region where water normally freezes in the pipes. The pipes has air underpressure which keeps the water level below the valve fitted at the main riser. Heat sensitive sprinklers are suitably fitted at vulnerable places and these get ruptured when the present temperature limit is exceeded. The air underpressure in the pipes escapes and water rushes into the pipes and the process of sprinkling commences.

(v) *Water pipe sprinkler system*: In this, the water is always present in all the pipes underpressure. Due to the excessive heat the sprinkler's head gets ruptured and water rushes out of the pipes through nozzles and the quantity forms a water blanket over the fire. It acts as coolant and reduces heat from the fire.

(vi) *Hose system*: These hoses are generally made of woven jute and cotton fiber which is waterproof. The size of the hose is normally 2.5″ diameter and it has one side male coupling and on the other side a female coupling where nozzle is fitted for directing water under pressure on to the fire. Besides, water these hoses can also be utilized for directing foam on to the fire. The male coupling is fitted to the water tailors pump or to the water hydrant through pressurized water which can be made available for fire fighting. The water for usage with hoses can be made available from any of the following sources.

(a) Water tank/reservoirs
(b) Water towers
(c) Wells, rivers and ponds, etc.
(d) Pressurized water tanks with fire tenders
(e) Water tailors
(f) Water pipes from Municipal Corporations.

## MODES OF FIRE FIGHTING IN INDUSTRIES

### *Water as Main Source of Fire Fighting*

Water is the main sources for fire fighting as it either acts as coolant or used for extinguishing the fire. The distinct advantages of water in fire fighting process are enumerated below:

(a) Availability of water is almost everywhere and can easily be stored.
(b) Cost is almost negligible.
(c) It is also used in forming films of foam over petroleum, oil and lubricant fires.
(d) No special training is required to handle it and can be used from safe distances with high pressure pumps.
(e) It only reacts with few metals, hence is not harmful in use over metals. It does not give out any toxic gas after use.
(f) It is clean to use and also dries off easily.
(g) It absorbs maximum heat in comparison to other substances used for extinguishing fires.

### Impacts of Water on Fire

As explained earlier water has number of distinct advantages for using it in extinguishing most of the general fire. The main impact of water on fire is as under:

(i) ***Cooling action***: The water acts as a wonderful coolant on all general fires. The water reduces the temperature of the fire spot and area around the fire.
(ii) ***Extinguishing action***: The application of water sprinklers is normally undertaken to create a cool surroundings around the fire. It prevents the fire from spreading to neighbouring areas. In Industries water sprinklers are used on the following:

(a) On the outer portion of the oil tanks.
(b) Conveyor belts.
(c) Shop floors of wooden work.
(d) Jetties.
(e) Handling of petroleum products when oil fire becomes general fire.

### *Precautions for the Use of Water*

One should ensure that water is not used on:

(a) Materials which reacts violently with water e.g. Sodium, Calcium Carbide, etc.

(b) Non water proof electrical installations.

## Halogenated Hydrocarbon Extinguishers (HALON)

HALON is a hydrocarbon derivative in which the atoms of hydrogen are replaced by three fluorine and one bromine atoms, when this is used to extinguish the fire, it prevents the formation of three radical (short lived electrically charged chemical atoms) which inhibits the spread of fire and breaks the chain of combustion. This chemical action is known as "inhabitation" which takes place on contact with flame. Halon is odourless and non-conducting gas which is non-toxic for the human beings. It vapourises fast and dries off quickly after use, visibly it is as clean as water.

### *Uses of HALON in Industries*

(i) *For highly inflammable materials*:

(a) Oil tanks

(b) Inflammable and perishable products

(c) Solvent Stores

(ii) *Power installations*:

(a) Drilling platforms

(b) Turbines

(c) Electrical installations

(d) Hydrocarbon pumping stations

(e) Ship's engine rooms

(iii) *Miscellaneous fire*:

(a) Telephone exchanges

(b) Computer/Software installations

(c) Museums

Halon type extinguishers are normally advised for use in fully closed environment. The recommended concentration of Halon is 5–7 percent. It can be automatically actuated by the fire detection system.

### *Precautions for use of HALON*

It is advisable that halon should not be used in:

(a) Deep seated class 'A' fire (paper, textile and woods)
(b) Substances like sodium and magnesium which are highly reactive
(c) Self-oxygenating products like nitrates.

## Low, Medium and High Expansion Foam Systems

Low, Medium and High Expansion Foam can be produced through a foam generator by air blast agitation of a liquid foam compound with water. Generally, the proportion of foam compound is 3–6% while producing the foam with water.

### *Expansion Ratio of Foam*

Foam expansion is the 'ratio' between the volume of the foam obtained and the initial volume of the solution. The various expansion ratio are as under:

(a) Low Foam–Below 25, normally 5–10 ratio
(b) Medium Foam–Between 25–300 to 1 (Synthetic Foam Compound used)
(c) High Foam–Over 300–1 (Synthetic Foam Compound used)

*Drainage time*

(a) *Low expansion foam*

The drainage time for low foam expansion is defined as the time needed for the foam to dropout at least 25% of the solution from which it is formed into foam. This time must be more than 5 minutes for Protein types of foam and above 1½ minutes for aqueous film forming foams.

(b) *Medium and high expansion foam*

The drainage time will generally vary with the type of foam compound used but in any case it should be more than 1½ minutes.

### *Advantages of Low, Medium and High Expansion Foam System*

*Low foams*:

(a) It is non-toxic towards human beings.
(b) It can be used over a good distance.

(c) It does not stick to material.
(d) Penetrates places of difficult access.

*Medium and figh foams*:
(a) It is non-toxic for human beings.
(b) Less amount of water is consumed.
(c) Does not stick to materials.
(d) It can reach fire in difficult access areas.

### Uses of Foams in Industries

Foam is considered a good coolant and an insulating agent for oxygen. It forms a sheet over the surface of fire and thus prevents oxygen, one of the three important factors, with other two i.e. Heat and Fuel. Foams are generally used in sensitive industrial areas as under:

(a) Petroleum, oil and lubricants.
(b) Chemicals
(c) Paints and varnishes/solvents.
(d) Oil producing platforms.
(e) Drilling platforms.

*Uses in buildings*:
(a) Aircraft hangars.
(b) Machine shops/Shop floors.
(c) Warehouses/Godowns.

*In refineries and storage tanks*:
(a) Pumping stations.
(b) Refinery installations/storage tanks.
(c) Oil pipelines carrying petroleum products.

*Miscellaneous uses*:
(a) Merchant and Indian Navy ships.
(b) Engine test facilities.
(c) Other Naval units.

*Precautions for use*:
Low, medium and high expansions foams should not be used on the following types of fire:

(a) Materials which reacts violently with water e.g. Sodium, and Potassium, etc.

(b) Electrical equipments in circuits, till the fire is fully converted into a general class 'A' fire.

(c) Low foam should not be used on liquid gases with boiling points below ambient temperature. Medium expansion foam is used to protect small hazard volumes or surfaces exposed to wind. High expansion foam is generally used for the protection of large enclosed areas.

## Mobile Fire Fighting Equipments and Systems

In addition to the static fire fighting equipments and systems which are generally used in most of the Industrial Organizations and Factories, Large Industries, Fire Fighting Organizations and Civil Defence Organizations possess number of Mobile Fire Fighting systems and equipments to cater for the fire incidences in areas where adequate measures for static fire fightings are not available. These are as under:

(a) ***Powder vehicles***: Powder vehicles is a very potent fire fighting equipment. The vehicle can carry up to a maximum of 400 kg powder. However, vehicles which are polyvalent they are capable of discharging powder and also foam simultaneously or depending upon the type of fire, these can be sprayed separately. The vehicle generally uses nitrogen as propellant gas which is very effective in extinguishing liquid and hydrocarbon fire very quickly. For example in 30 seconds to 60 seconds it can put off a fire in an area of 30 sq. mts.

(b) ***Foam vehicles***: These vehicles are very effective in large fire of petroleum, oil and lubricant. These vehicles are made of glass reinforced polyester and contains a tank with the capacity of 10,000 liters water. Its output is 500 cu mts per hour ($m^3$/h). A semitailor is capable of carrying 10,000 liters of foam compound with a discharge rate of foam in 1200 cu mtrs per hour ($m^3$/h). The vehicle is fitted with the following compartments:

(i) Foam compound tank.

(ii) Water tank.

(iii) Water pump and foam compound pump.

(iv) Monitor and auto proportioning system.

(c) ***Fire tenders for civil defence***: These fire tenders are generally used by civil defence and civil fire stations for dealing with class 'A' fire. It has a water tank of the capacity of 3,000 liters with output rate of 120 cu mts per hour ($m^3$/h). A water bowser with capacity of 9,000 litres of water is also used by the Civil Fire Brigades. These firemen use Snorkels and turn table ladders to extinguish fire in high rise offices/buildings. The tallest ladder available in India is 61.5M high.

## Electronic Fire Alarm System

All security staff and other employees of the Industry/Offices must be trained to extinguish the fire as soon as it is detected in its infant stage. Later it becomes quite dangerous for both material and personnel. Therefore, Government by passing relevant legislation, have made it compulsory to install fire preventive measures in all industrial and residential accommodations. For all organizations under Factory Act 1948 have become obligatory to adopt adequate fire preventions and early detection measures. Some of the measures which are in use and available in the market are as under:

(a) ***Heat detector***: This system functions at a preset temperature level i.e. 77°C and gets electrically operated when temperature of the room/chamber exceeds. The increase in temperature causes rapid expansion of the air inside the chamber, which the bleed hole of the detector cannot accept the increased temperature and it raises electrically activated alarm as warning of fire.

(b) ***Smoke detector***: These electronic detectors consist of double chamber of ionization type with one chamber remaining closed and other open. The air in the chamber is ionized with the help of a tiny radioactive alpha source. Once the fire smoke enters the chamber the ionization current in the open chamber causes the difference in the voltage of the chamber and thus the smoke/fire alarm is activated. These detectors use radio active material for fire detection in the initial stages. The alarm indicator flashes LED signals with an interval of 5 seconds with a + 2 sec. The whole system operates on 12 volt DC.

(c) ***Flame detector***: These equipments are best suited for the places which are vulnerable to flash fires. These detectors operate by using infra-red sensors which respond to the presence of any flame. It possesses a cylindrical head which consists of an infra-red sensor and a solid state processing circuit. The sensor may be Lead-Sulphide photocell. The spectoral response of the sensor is infra-red rays between the wavelength of 1–3 microns. It is capable of detecting flame of a petroleum fire in a bowl 20 cm diameter and 1 cm deep at a distance of 30 meters in the direct axis of the detector.

## *Integrated Fire Alarm System*

With the advent of new inventions in the field of Industrial safety, most of the Industrial organizations and offices prefer to use integrated fire alarm system than using number of detectors for smoke, flame and heat, etc. In this system various electrical signals are received in case of any warning in the control unit. Here in control unit the signals are analyzed and a decision is arrived at as to which warning is to be activated. It has its power supply unit in case of an electric failure. The system is computer controlled and capable of performing number of preset functions simultaneously without the help of an operator. It can also activate the automatic fire extinguishing system, if required and fitted in the organization. It controls the power supply and shuts down to the place under fire. This system is latest in the family of fire detection and fire fighting which is fully controlled by the computer.

## *Precautionary Measures and Fire Safety*

(a) ***Periodic check of all equipments***: Security officer must ensure by way of promulgation in factory standing orders, the day or date in each month when all fire fighting equipments must be checked/tested for the serviceable condition. A iron nail of adequate size, tied with strong thread around the handle of all foam/soda water extinguishers must be inserted into the outlet of the nozzle. It will prevent the nozzles from getting blocked with mud or other dirty materials. Each extinguisher must be painted with white marking the date of testing e.g. "TESTED ON __________ 15 January", the testing date can be written with white chalk, etc. after the testing is over. If carbon dioxide gas is less then the extinguisher must be refilled again.

(b) ***Maintenance and marking on door's/windows***: In each building, shop, machine floors and offices, etc. few doors, depending upon the number of persons employed/working in it, must be specially earmarked as emergency/fire exits. So that in case of any accident or fire incident, all employees can move out safely from the affected area. These doors and windows must be painted in red colour "USE IN EMERGENCY" and "EXIT". At night also adequate light should be there to illuminate these markings. All employees must be briefed properly as to which door/window, they must use for escaping during any emergency and fire, etc.

(c) ***Fire drills***: Security officer, with prior permission from personnel/administration department, must conduct fire fighting exercise to test the effectiveness of equipment and knowledge of each staff. Mock fire drills should also be conducted at regular intervals (at least quarterly) to test the drills/actions of other staff in case of an emergency or fire, etc. Alongwith fire drills the training and use of first-aid must also be checked during fire drills. Security officer must ensure that all departments/office staff adhere to all the drills as laid down in Factory Standing Orders.

(d) ***Maintenance and updating of standing orders***: Security officer in consultation with Administration Manager must always review the Fire Fighting and Industrial safety parts of the Factory standing orders. In case of any amendments or addition/deletion, the standing orders must be kept up to date. The amendments must be duly informed in writing to all the departments for action, if considered necessary. Record of updating/inspection must be kept in the initial pages of the factory standing orders alongwith the remarks and signature of the officer with date.

(e) ***Close liaison with civil fire brigade officer***: Administration Manager/ Security officer must be in close touch with Civil Fire Brigade Officer. He must keep them informed about any special item's requirement in case of fire in the industry. Also must keep himself update regarding any new techniques or latest equipment's induction in Fire Fighting Department. Telephone Numbers of all Local Fire Brigades and Police Control Room, must be clearly displayed in Exchange, Security and other offices clearly.

(f) Any employee found, or in habit of, violating fire precautionary measures must be warned and in case of repeating the same, disciplinary action may be instated against him.

(g) ***Display of fire fighting standing orders***: All fire fighting standing orders must be clearly displayed on the notice boards of each department/office for the knowledge of each employee.

(h) ***Positioning of fire equipments***: It is very essential that during preventive stage various fire fighting equipments, depending upon the type of threat from fire, are kept at suitable places in the factory/office premises. As per the size of the organization the number of water tanks, fire points and fire hydrants, etc. must be planned and positioned to deal with any fire incident effectively. The list of fire equipments must be clearly displayed at each fire point and it must be checked by security officer at regular intervals. The records of these checks must also be maintained at the fire points properly.

(i) *Emergency lights*: Each department and office building/room must have adequate arrangements for emergency light, this will help the employees in escaping from fire affected areas safely through exit doors to safe places.

### *Fire Fighting Standing Orders*

In any factory, organization or office it is of paramount importance that every person, irrespective of appointment, must be assigned some responsibility in his own department/office in case of emergency or fire incident. These responsibilities, therefore must be laid down in factory fire fighting standing orders and should be known to concerned individual right from the beginning. It is very essential that all such responsibilities are comprehensively enumerated in the standing orders. Security officer or administration manager must ensure that a copy of these standing orders is forwarded to each department and office, etc. It is the responsibility of head of each department to ensure that all these standing orders are carefully read by each employee in their department. If necessary individual signature must be obtained to confirm that he/she has read these. Any amendment to these must be treated in the same way. Basically the following contents are suggested for inclusion in the fire fighting standing orders. Any other addition/deletion as for the industry's requirement can be made by the concerned officer formulating the standing orders.

(i) Must plan out a suitable fire fighting organization under administration manager/security head.

(ii) Identify the type of fire which can take place in the Industry and office so that selection of fire fighting equipment can be done as per the threat perception.

(iii) Identify the various fire risks areas in the premises of Industry i.e. high, medium and low risk areas.

(iv) Positioning of various fire fighting equipments at suitable places, ear marking of various fire points locations, etc.

(v) Earmarking of escape doors/windows in each departments and offices with proper red paint markings of "Use in Emergency", "Exit only", etc.

(vi) Assign various responsibilities to each employees in a group of 2–3 in all departments and offices in case of emergency or fire.

(vii) Security staff with the help of other employees from each department, (e.g. 2–3 persons to report to the security officer) will ear mark "Ambulance Party" and "Cordon Party" in case of emergency and fire. These party will work under the supervision of Security/Assistant Security Officer.

(viii) Receiving the civil fire brigades at the main gate and guiding them to the scene of fire.

(ix) Arrangements of adequate fire prevention methods and actions by way of suitable training to all employees for creating an awareness towards fire safety.

(x) Testing of the various fire equipments and rehearsals of fire fighting drills.

(xi) Training of all security staff in fire prevention, safety measures and fire fighting.

(xii) Operating and locations of fire alarm system must be known to each employee.

(xiii) Depending upon the size of the industry if need be, a separate fire fighting squad under a fire officer (especially in petroleum, explosives and chemical industries) must be employed otherwise they will operate under the security wing.

(xiv) Drills for evacuation of causalities must be properly laid down and rehearsed during fire drills.

(xv) Use of first aid equipment must be taught to all employees and it must be practiced during fire fighting practices.

(xvi) All classified documents almirahs must be properly marked with white paint -X- and written "Remove First In Case Of Fire." The evacuation drills must be clearly laid down with the responsibilities in standing orders.

(xvii) Security officers and staff at the main gate must ensure that no unauthorized person enters the premises. They should be very vigilant and alert to ensure that no property or product is taken out of the factory/offices without proper gatepass.

(xviii) A list of personnel must be made out and kept in exchange, who will be informed immediately in case of emergency and fire accident.

### *Actions to be Taken in Case of Fire*

(i) Any person who detects the fire in his area or office or anywhere in the factory premises must try to put off by using available fire fighting means e.g. Sand bucket, water bucket, extinguisher, etc. and if he feels that he may not be able to extinguish completely. He should shout "FIRE-FIRE", in Hindi "AAG-AAG" at the top of his voice to attract others.

(ii) If still the fire has not been under control by using local means, then inform Civil Fire Brigade by giving fire type, material under fire and location whether in open or inside building, etc.

(iii) As soon as security officer or his assistant arrives at the spot, he must take charge at scene and organize all the available means and personnel for fire fighting.

(iv) Ensure, if any, causality in the accident, that must be removed, First-aid provided and if required evacuated to the hospital.

(v) Arrange to receive all Civil Fire Brigade staff with Fire Tenders and guide them to scene of fire from the main gate.

(vi) Organize evacuation of valuable documents, material, which is not yet affected by fire, to safe place with utmost speed.

(vii) Ensure protection against theft and pilferage.

(viii) Carry out assessment of damage and losses to personnel and material.

(xi) After extinguishing the fire, ask for damage report and prepare Final Fire Report.

It has been observed and reported through media that most of the fires irrespective of the class of fire, except explosive fire, starts with small fire. But due to ignorance and unawareness of the employees the small fire takes the shape of devastating fire. The proverb of "A Stitch In Time Saves Nine," is perfect in case of fire control and industrial safety. Security officer must ensure the following:

(a) Up to date fire equipments and correct positioning in factory premises.

(b) Testing of equipments at regular intervals and ensuring full serviceability.

(c) Proper fire drills and training of staff in fire fighting and industrial safety.

(d) A sound and workable Fire Fighting standing orders and all employees must be aware about their responsibilities towards fire prevention and Industrial safety.

(e) Keep cool at the hour of emergency and fire incidents. Cool mind takes right decisions at the right time.

# 13

# Disaster Planning and Management

With the introduction of hi-tec equipments in the industries and offices, the ever growing competitions and the level of emerging challenges which these organizations have to confront within day to day survival, the industries are becoming more and more vulnerable to different kinds of disasters. The disaster could be of one or more type as mentioned below:

(a) *Natural*

(i) Floods and Cyclone
(ii) Earthquakes
(iii) Lightening Strike
(iv) Fire

(b) *Accidental*

(i) Chemical accidents e.g. union carbide gas leakage at Bhopal .
(ii) Liquefied Petroleum Gas (LPG) sphere or unexpended vapour cloud explosion.
(iii) Bursting of a boiler due to defective safety valve or other technical faults.
(iv) Bursting of pipe line carrying Petrochemical products

(c) *Man Made*

(i) Arson
(ii) Bomb explosion or other explosive attack
(iii) Sabotage
(iv) Civil riots
(v) Nuclear attack
(vi) Chemical or poisonous gas attack

It is very difficult or rather impossible to anticipate or forecast the time and type of disaster which may be encountered by any industry or organization. But as a foresighted manager/management one can analyze, chalk out various plans and take counter/preventive measures to minimize the loss of lives and damage to movable/immovable assets. Sound planning, to ward off the adverse and disastrous effects of natural, accidental or man made disasters, will assist, to a great extent, the management in evaluation of the strength of crisis in advance. Accordingly the management will be able to carry out meticulous planning for training of personnel in disaster management. If need be necessary rehearsals, at regular intervals and other drills to counter disasters should be conducted to undertake entire operations, at the time of need in flawless manner. Good rehearsals will considerably reduce the extent of loss/damage in an industry. The location of the plant, ecological layout and prevailing environment will play a major role in executing the complete plan with good speed, thereby affording an opportunity to management to commence the production/normal routine in the shortest possible time gap.

## Assessment of Disaster/Calamities

Before any step is taken towards planning, a team of senior managers should be deputed by the management to carry out a judicious and realistic assessment of the anticipated disaster.

It must be born in mind that all aspects relating to "most likely, likely and least likely" types of disaster/calamities are taken into consideration in this stage of assessment. The anticipated losses to personnel and material should be judged and then the procedures and drills should be adopted for each type of disaster. Assessment should be thorough and must include the requirements of various resources in terms of men, machinery and material. Basically following should be included in the assessment for any disaster:

(a) Nature and type of disaster which in case strikes the industry, the extent of damage it may cause to the men, material. Correct appreciation will be of vital importance.

(b) Location of resources i.e. men and machinery to counter the disaster.

(c) List of important personnel of industry with telephone number whom information must be passed immediately about crisis.

(d) Telephone numbers of various local organizations e.g. civil police, civil defence organization hospitals, fire brigades, neighbouring industries and institutions, etc.

(e) Extent of injury to men and evacuation procedures to be adopted. Whether any outside help from neighbouring units needed and, if so, to what extent in terms of man and material.

(f) The number of entry and exit points will be needed in case of each type of disaster.

(g) Whether plant/factory will be required to shut down partially or wholly. If so, approximately after how many hours/days the production/office routine can resume.

(h) Which all process can be used as safe alternatives, locations for man and material.

(i) In case the disaster can't be overcome single-handed, then joint appreciation of all available and required resources must be made in consultation with neighbouring units. This will require to formulate a Mutual-aid-scheme among all units/industries to assess the pooling up of all resources.

(j) The requirement of first aid centres with proper medical facilities in and around the industry.

(k) Immediate need for water and food, means/responsibilities for execution.

## Formulation of Disaster Plan

The arrival of disaster may give some warning or no warning at all. Therefore, once the realistic and meaningful assessment has been carried out, it will be comparatively much easier to formulate the disaster plan. The plan should be very simple, workable with minimum modifications and easy to understand for execution in the hour of crisis. Disaster plan can be defined as "a well planned strategy which is evolved, by considering various courses open, finally selected, rehearsed for optimum utilization of available resources with minimum delay and modifications for countering the disaster"

## PURPOSE OF PLAN

The basic purpose of the disaster plan is as under:

(a) Rescue and evacuation of all casualties to first aid centers and directly to hospitals depending upon the conditions of the personnel.

(b) To protect the lives of people who are not injured or directly affected.

(c) To contain loss of live and damage to property and environment.

(d) To ensure that almost complete situation is well under control within minimum possible time and factory is able to resume normal routine/ production.

(e) Ensure there are no further affects after the disaster.

(f) Waste no time in planning and consideration for the use of men and machinery.

(g) To inform all civic bodies with fastest means to ensure timely help in resources if provided.

(h) To activate the resources of neighbouring units in case any additional assistance is required.

(i) To avoid any theft and pilferage.

(j) To ensure that all officials and employees, who are not injured or trapped in the industry, are immediately taking on their assigned tasks as per planning.

(k) People/worker must not wait for the senior to arrive on the scene/ factory, they must commence their rescue/assigned work without wasting any time.

(l) To prevent any reoccurrence of such disaster.

(m) To review the plan after disaster is over for any rectification, modification as per the current experience.

*Essentials of the plan*: The contents of the plan will not be similar as each factory differs in it's location, size, products and extent of resources in terms of men and materials. However, certain things are generally common and considered essential for each plan and thus must be incorporated there in. These are:

(a) Methods to establish and identify the type of disaster i.e. explosion, fire, sabotage or any unlawful elements attack, etc. An effective "Disaster Management Cell" must be organized.

(b) Ability to communicate accurately with fastest means to all other officials, department, civil bodies and neighbouring units, etc.

(c) To activate immediately the means of fire fighting and evacuation of casualties, if any, without wasting any time.

(d) Shifting of material, machinery, if possible, and any other movable assets to safer places.

(e) Frequency of rehearsals and Mockup drills to ensure all employees are fully aware of their duties and responsibilities in case of disaster.

(f) Shut down procedures for machinery and other plant.

(g) In case single handed operation is not adequate then procedure for pooling of neighboring resources and their optimum utilization in addition to own resources.

(h) Proper security system to prevent spectators, which may cause hindrance in rescue operations.

(i) An organization's Public Relation officer must be authorized to brief media about disaster to avoid rumours.

(j) A "Follow-up Action Report" after debriefing to check the functional feasibility of the disaster plan.

(k) A final report should be prepared to include the actual losses and damage to men and material in terms of financial burden to the organization.

It is very important to organize a "Disaster Management Cell" consisting of senior managers and selected employees almost from each departments. Each individual must be assigned some duty and responsibility at the time of disaster. Frequent rehearsals/mockup drills must be organized to check-up whether each member is fully aware of his job. A suggested Disaster Management Cell's Organization is appended below.

## SUGGESTED DISASTER MANAGEMENT CELL'S ORGANIZATION

The disaster plan must contain a detailed location layout of the Industry. The layout should clearly indicate the location of each department, layout of main electric power line, hydrants locations/layout, telephone distribution box, etc.

***Disaster/emergency control room***: A room with central location must be earmarked as Disaster/Emergency Control Room. This room should act as a nerve centre of all the activities during disaster. Multiple communication system with direct lines to all senior managers, location plan of the Industry, Organizational chart of Disaster Management Cell and standing orders of the factory giving out detailed charter of duties of each employee must be available in control room. This room shall be activated immediately on occurrence of the disaster/emergency. Duty roster of responsible persons (Minimum two) should be worked out to operate the control rooms 24 hours a day. All information must be forwarded to control room from various departments on the progress of the rescue operations. All visitors and media persons must be directed by main gate security to the control room for any up to date briefing.

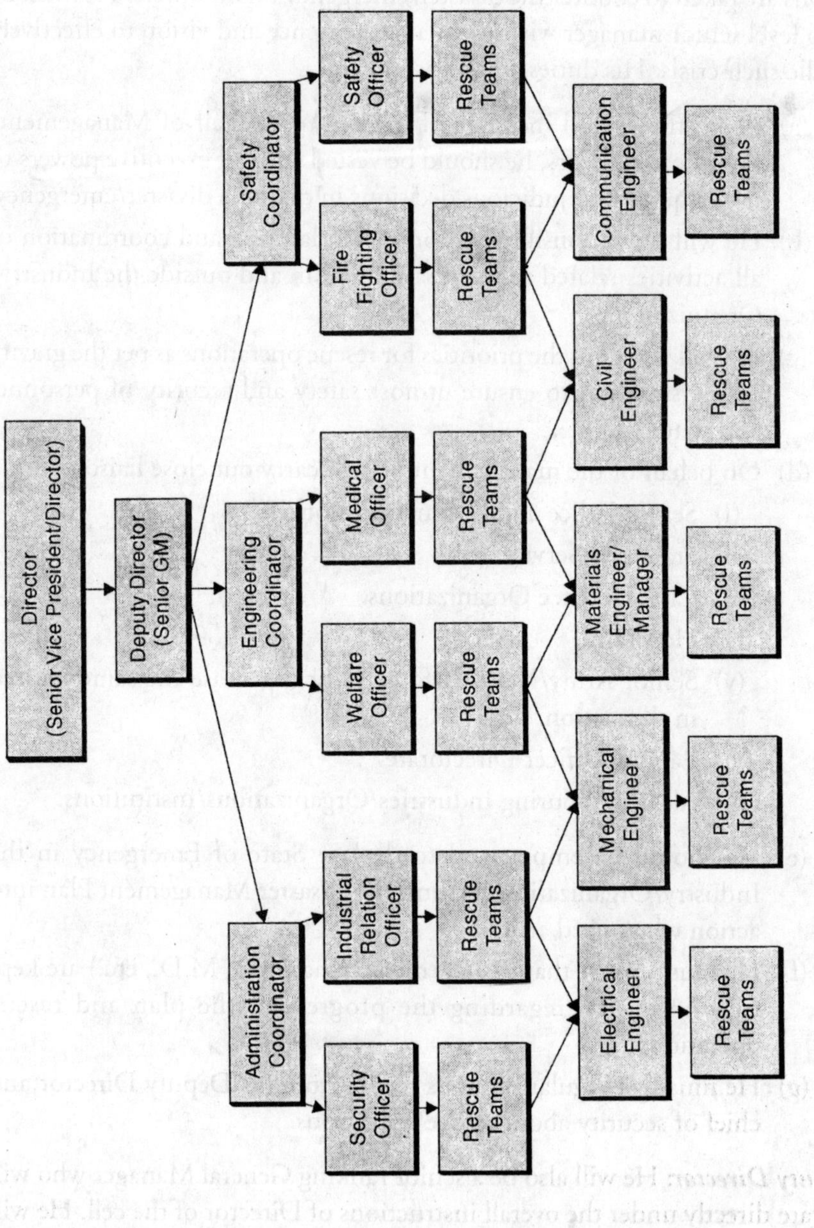


FIG. 13.1 SUGGESTED DISASTER MANAGEMENT CELL'S ORGANIZATION

## Tasks of Disaster Management Cell

***Director***: He is the overall incharge of the Disaster Management Cell and all actions are taken to counter the disaster/emergency on his orders. He must be a top level senior manager with adequate experience and vision to effectively handle such crisis. His duties will be as under:

(a) Being the overall incharge of the cell, on behalf of Management/ Board of Directors, he should be vested with all executive powers to take a quick and judicious decisions in case of a disaster/emergency.
(b) He will be responsible for complete planning and coordination of all activities related to the disaster within and outside the Industry/ Organization.
(c) He will work out the priorities for rescue operations as per the gravity of the situation to ensure utmost safety and security of personnel and material.
(d) On behalf of the management he will carry out close liaison with:
    (i) Senior Police and Distinct Authorities.
    (ii) State Fire Services.
    (iii) Civil Defence Organizations.
    (iv) Hospitals.
    (v) Senior Army/Navy/Airforce Official in case the same located in the station.
    (vi) Labour Officer Directorate.
    (vii) All neighbouring Industries/Organizations/Institutions.
(e) He should be empowered to declare State of Emergency in the Industry/Organization and enforce Disaster Management Plan into action when need arises.
(f) He must ensure that management (Chairman, M.D., etc.) are kept fully informed regarding the progress of the plan and rescue operations.
(g) He must get regular progress report from his Deputy Director and chief of security about rescue operations.

***Deputy Director***: He will also be a senior ranking General Manager who will operate directly under the overall instructions of Director of the cell. He will be responsible to ensure the execution of disaster plan, by each team operating under their respective coordinator, is carried out in flawless manner. His responsibilities will be as under:

(a) Ensure that disaster plan is put into operations without any doubt and delay.
(b) See that all emergency teams in each department operate under the orders of their respective co-coordinator.
(c) He will act as close co-coordinator between director and three main co-coordinators.
(d) He will plan and organize the training of special rescue teams in the factory/organization as per the disaster plan.
(e) He will be incharge of mustering all resources needed to counter the emergency. He will ensure procurement, deployment and operational maintenance of all plant and machinery.
(f) Keep director fully informed about progress of operation.
(g) Inform all employees and their families about facts of emergency to avoid rumours.
(h) Carry out liaison with police, civil defence and neighbouring units for additional assistance if required.
(i) Plan, if need arises for complete or partial shutdown of industry.
(j) Keep visiting the rescue operation site in case any special order/decision is required on the spot.
(k) Preparation and compiling of all After Action Reports including Final Report.
(l) Work out details of any compensation or grant to be paid to any employees and inform Director accordingly.
(m) Organize, as per situation, any specialist inquiry or technical inspection to find out the causes and prevention of any recurrence of such disaster.

***Main coordinators***: These officers will be operating directly under the Deputy Director of the Disaster cell as per the plan. Their duties will be as under:

(a) Directly responsible to Deputy Director for rescue operation as per the disaster plan.
(b) Responsible to plan, supervise and provide timely guidance to their each department officer for an efficient rescue work.
(c) They will keep Deputy Director fully informed about the progress of the rescue operations in all the departments.
(d) Keep a close watch on the entire rescue operation being conducted under the supervision of each officer.

(e) Ensure that all the employees of the department are kept in full picture of the entire operation in the Industry/Organization.
(f) Plan adequate rest and relief period for all employees involved in rescue operation in order to maintain optimum efficiency.
(g) Ensure that each employee is given a suitable task in disaster plan as per his capabilities.
(h) Prepare and maintain up to date list of telephone numbers and residential addresses of all the important appointments of the department.
(i) As per disaster plan, they must plan and arrange to organize the training of all teams personnel in various rescue work.
(j) Ensure that all employees are fully conversant with their team work, use of equipments and drills to be adopted at the time of emergency.
(k) Guard against spreading of rumours by employees.
(l) Lay special emphasis on training of first aid and evacuation of causalities.

*Officer-in-charge teams*: These officers will be operating under the orders of their department coordinators. They will ensure the following:

(a) They plan and organize their respective teams and arrange their rescue operations training as per overall disaster plan of the organization.
(b) Ensure that each team member is fully conversant with the tasks and responsibilities as per disaster plan.
(c) To see that employees, require to operate any equipment/machinery during emergency, are fully aware of its limitations and capabilities.
(d) Brief the department coordinator at regular intervals about the progress of the operation.
(e) Project initially during planning stage the requirement of any additional resources to achieve better results in rescue work.
(f) Pass on timely information to employee and families about emergency.
(g) Organize proper rest and relief as per shift to maintain better efficiency.
(h) Prepare and forward the detailed report about the disaster to the respective coordinator.

*Detailed report on disaster*: Based on the various feed back reports relating to disaster/emergency, the final report will be prepared in the organization, which will include the following:

(a) Type and causes (probable if not confirmed) of the disaster.

(b) Time and place of occurrence (details of eyewitnesses if any)

(c) Action taken.

(d) Number of department's involved including details of personnel.

(e) Detailed accounts of causalities i.e. dead, injured and missing, etc. (including hospitalization details)

(f) Losses and damages to be shown for materials, machines and immovable assets.

(g) Any destruction or loss of valuable documents.

(h) In case of any financial assistance needed from the government due to Government's policy on disaster/emergency.

## Tasks and Responsibilities of Security Department/Security Officer

The chief of the security and security department will be required to play a major role in ensuring that disaster plan is executed with minimum delay, disruption and interference. Their role and tasks will generally depend on the type of emergency the organization is being faced. Security officer must ensure that each security guard is fully aware of the gravity of situation and acts accordingly. Their duties will include:

(a) Ensure no unauthorized personnel are allowed to access into the factory as soon as the emergency has taken place. Special care to be taken to handle the families of employees who may try to force in the entry to get the inside information about their relatives/spouses.

(b) Immediately occupy their place of duty as per disaster plan to cordon the area/spot to prevent any theft, sabotage and pilferage.

(c) Ensure complete security and safety of personnel, material and machines, etc.

(d) Organize strict traffic control inside the premises. Do not allow any visitor's vehicle inside unless permission granted by Director/Deputy Director Disaster Cell.

(e) Protection of sensitive installations and security of valuable documents.

(f) Security officer must maintain close liaison at his levels with Police, Fire Brigade, Civil Defence and neighbouring units. Essential information "Need to Know Basis" must be passed after obtaining clearance from disaster cell.

(g) Regulate entry of outside resources at the main gate and direct them under escort to the disaster area.

(h) Control unruly mob and unwanted spectators at main gate and disperse them. If need be, request for police assistance.

(i) Organize complete fire fighting and safety measures inside the organization.

(j) Plan and train security personnel in Disaster Plan Management. Carry out rehearsals and mock up drills at regular intervals to ensure that all are fully conversant with the assigned tasks.

(k) Security officer must speak/brief the spectators and families of employees properly and firmly as and when they gather around at the main gate. Be polite and courteous.

***Formulation of mutual aid scheme***: It is quite likely that most of the natural disasters or even, men made emergencies cannot be fought single handed by any individual Industry or organization. In case the gravity of the disaster is so great that the impact of damages and losses may be spreading simultaneously to number of industries in that area. Therefore, it is essential that a workable plan must be formulated by pooling all available resources of the area to minimize the damages/losses in terms of men and material. The resources so pooled must operate under one "Head" who will plan the overall strategy to ensure optimum utilization of pooled resources for the benefit of all the industries in the area. Once the spread or threat of disaster is considerably under control, then pooled resources can be reverted back to their parents unit for rescue operations. Mutual aid scheme must be simple, easy to understand and execute with least amendments. The scheme should not be rigid but must be flexible which can be easily moulded to suit the type of disaster. Proper rehearsals must be carried out to judge the feasibility of the scheme.

***Strikes and large scale violence***: In an industry the rift between employees and workers, between employees and shopfloor supervisors, between employees and management and inter union is not an uncommon scene these days. At times small rift slowly takes a shape of big conflict, in such cases management gets adequate time to understand the actual causes of conflict and takes remedial measures. But some times small rift, conflict erupts abruptly and becomes beyond control with the result, sometimes it takes the shape of a sudden violence involving large number of people. During any large scale violence it becomes very difficult to provide safety and security to man and material by security department and management. During strikes, gherao and violence are innumerable incidents when senior managers and directors are subjected to assault and physical harassment. It is vital that suitable action plan must be formulated to counter the large scale violence including violent strikes and gherao, etc. The plan must include the actions as under:

(a) Comprehensive list of all suspicious personnel in each department must be prepared and keep a vigilant eye on them.
(b) All informations through "Intelligence Cell" must be continuously gathered regarding activities of such people and union activities.
(c) A detailed plan must be formulated giving out likely causes, actions at the time of violence and type of liaison needed with civil organizations e.g. Police and Fire Brigade, etc.
(d) Security officer must ensure that full protection to personnel and materials is provided till the police arrives at the scene.
(e) One must arrange for suitable photographs to be taken as an evidence of violence and loss/damage to personnel, property, and machinery, etc.
(f) Security officer to arrange adequate fire fighting and Industrial safety to provide maximum security.
(g) Proper first-aid and evacuations of causality should be organized in case it is required.
(h) Brief the Police on arrival about the details of activities leading to violence and personnel involved.
(i) Once the violence is under control a detailed report must be prepared by the chief of security and submitted to the Personnel/Administration Department for perusal and action.

Disasters/calamities will never arrive by giving adequate warning. It is such an unexpected and abrupt accident that it is rather impossible to ward it off totally. However, management with its foresight vision, intelligence from the factory sources and anticipated thought, can certainly minimize the losses and damages to personnel, machinery and immovable assets by formulating and developing a sound disaster plan. The plan so conceived must cater for various contingencies and courses open for disaster/calamity. Correct appreciation of resources in terms of men, equipments and material must be carried out for different types of disasters. Any additional requirement of resources, if considered necessary, must be arranged from neighbouring units/ public utility services located in the city. All employees must be assigned suitable duties and responsibilities during the hour of crisis. Rehearsals at regular intervals must be conducted to check the functional competance of the disaster plan. In case all these actions are taken in advance then management will never be caught in an awkward situation.

# 14

# Security and Safety of Airports and Aircrafts

## GENERAL

Every airport, whether operating civil flights, defence forces aircraft's or both, serves as a nerve centre for all types of air operations. All the aircraft's arrive and depart, from and to their respective destinations. Passengers travelling by National and International Flights arrive at the airports from far distances, complete their travel documentary formalities and depart for their destinations. Most of the airports, which operate night flight services for global destinations, keep humming with the passengers movements' throughout night. Modern airports, besides offering air travel facilities, have now been designed/renovated to house shopping arcades and facilities to cooperate conferences.

Therefore, in the present time, airports and aircraft's are becoming soft and lucrative targets for the terrorists and other unlawful elements. The hoax of bomb threat and physical attacks are the causes of serious concern for airport authorities and other security services operating there to protect and ensure safety of personnel, aircrafts and other infrastructure. Airport securities, besides providing safety to passengers, aircrafts and buildings, etc. have to cater for to counter the hijacking and sabotage activities. The airport security planning will encompass the protection and security of travellers, visitors, airport/airline's employees, passenger baggage runway, parking bay and air terminal buildings, etc. The recent example of most horrified and dastardly acts of four hijacked jet airlines, which were used as suicide bombers in New York and Washington on 11 September 2001, should provide us with enough reasons to enhance our existing airport security system with latest strategy and modern equipments. The planning has to be simple, effective which can inculcate confidence among air passengers and society. The effectiveness and confidence in the security system at airports will ensure smooth and safe air operations, which will give boost to national tourism and economic growth.

## Operations at Civil Airport

***Check in counter and boarding the aircraft***: All the persons, who plan to travel by air either within India or outside India, reach airport at a time which has been specified by the concerned airlines to complete their travel document formalities. On reaching the airport they get the complete baggage screened from the security point of view and then walk to the check-in-counter where the tickets are examined by airline staff for issue of "Boarding Pass". At the same time all the heavy baggage items, which a person is not entitled to carry with him/her inside the aircraft, will be deposited at check-in-counter. This baggage is called "check-in-baggage" and will be loaded into the aircraft by airline staff. The small bag or briefcase, etc. which can be carried into the aircraft is called "Cabin Baggage or Carry on Baggage." After obtaining Boarding Pass, a person can move into the "Departure Hold Area" for sometime, till the boarding announcement is carried out. Then finally all passengers alongwith their Hand baggage undergo security check and board the flight. Comparing to national flights, more time is required to undergo travel-related checks for international destinations.

All the aircrafts are parked on the tarmac parking bays. The security staff is adequately deployed to keep a close watch on all the parked aircrafts to ensure no unauthorized person gets an entry near or into the aircraft. The area of runway and taxi-tracks are also kept under proper surveillance by the security staff to prevent any unauthorized entry.

***Arrival of passengers by flights***: As soon as the aircrafts lands at the runway and finally arrive at the parking area, passengers alight from the aircraft and either walk or travel in airline bus to the arrival area which is little away from the departure hold. For national flight, normally there are no mandatory security checks at the arrival area. But passengers have to undergo various checks i.e. travel documents, passport, customs checks, any prohibitive item being carried, etc. After these formalities or even prior to these the heavy baggage can be collected from the baggage belt. Use of baggage trolley can be made to carry baggage up till car parking/taxi stand to proceed to their destinations.

Passengers, who are to travel further in the same flight after it is refueled or technical checks carried out, they are called "Transit Passengers" and can rest, till the aircraft is ready for onward journey, in the transit hold or transit hall. There may be some passengers, who are to take another flight from here to reach their destinations, they are called "Transfer Passengers". They wait at the airport for other connecting flight.

The above mentioned operations have been given out to project a general picture about the activities which take place at the airport involving arrival and departure of passengers and their flights. However, it is not obligatory for all the airports to have similar facilities. Only International airports will have custom clearance, money changers and duty free items shop, etc. some airports have different designs for arrival and departure halls depending upon the frequency and types of aircraft operating at that airport. But the common thing among all airports is the provision of adequate security arrangements for the safety of personnel, aircrafts, baggage and terminal building, etc. But the strength and equipment's for security and safety will depend upon the size of airport, passengers movement and frequency/types of flights.

***Identification of airside and landside***: At the airport areas where aircrafts are parked on tarmac, taxitracks, runways, and other places adjacent to these are called airside. The entry to these places are controlled and checked. Various access points are established to allow people/employees into the airside after proper security checks/controls. Landside is the area access to which is not controlled e.g. visitors car park. But entry from landside to airside has to be through security regulated access control points. No laxity will be observed in regulating the traffic from landside to airside i.e. runway, taxi tracks and parking bay, etc.

## Formulation and Concept of Airport Security

The concept of airport security is different in its formulation, planning and execution. It basically differs as it detects, controls and prevents dangerous acts not only in terms of physical threats to personnel, aircraft, equipment and materials but relating to the immigration, financial irregularities and carrying of prohibitive items into and from the aircrafts. Recent increase in the traffic volume of politicians, VVIP'S (Very Very Important Personalities), foreign dignitaries, eminent scientists and business corporate have enhanced the importance of Airport security and safety. The security staffs deployed at the Airport's in various capacities have to be very polite but firm, vigilant and a keen observer.

Airside protection measures must be well planned and executed to ensure that no unauthorized entry is permitted into Hangers, taxi tracks and runway, etc. To augment the airside resources perimeter fencing boundary wall must be constructed with suitably manned access point to regulate restricted entry. Adequate checking and screening of passengers, employees and other visitors arriving at the airport must be established at access point. Screened passengers fall into special category and it must be ensured by security personnel that they are segregated from other screened persons. These segregated areas used by passengers are called "Security Holds or Sterile Departure Lounge". Similarly adequate measures must be adopted to permit segregation all arriving and departing passengers. Similarly, adequate screening should be carried out of the "Transit and Transfer Passengers" before they are allowed into the Sterile Departure Lounge.

## Cargo Terminals

In most of the airports, keeping in view the security aspects, the location of cargo, hangers and terminals is so located that they provide a required barrier between airside and landside. Manned access control point must be used by all persons operating to handle, control and ensure delivery of the cargo. It must be ensured by the airport security officer that any person crossing over to airside is properly checked and screened. Besides personnel, the move of each cargo item irrespective of shape and size must be screened before it becomes a security risk.

## Parking Bays, Taxitracks and Runways

The entire area of parking bays, taxi tracks and runways play an important role in the overall conduct of air operations from an Airport. Therefore, it is an essential part of the security and safety measures at the airport security system. The complete area must be kept under close surveillance for unauthorized intruders. A vigilant watch must also be organized to ensure that no explosive/bomb, etc. are planted at any place. Security guards must be posted to the parking bays and mobile vehicle based patrolling should be organized for taxitracks and runways. Adequate lighting should be there at perimeter and boundary wall. In case perimeter area is very large then adequate numbers of guards/check posts must be planned in addition to mobile patrolling at regular intervals.

## Security Functions at Airports

The entire area of the terminal building, air traffic control centre, arrival/departure lounge and airside require proper security access control. However, the specific functions, of security department at the airport, are as under:

(a) ***Access control points/gates***: All the places whether in landside or airside, except vehicle parking areas, must be properly guarded at various access/entry points. In order to ensure a regulated and restricted entry into airside and selected places in landside as mentioned in Airport security standing orders/ programme, entry gates and access control points must be manned. Airport employees and airlines staff should possess valid Identity Card and other passengers/visitors should be in possession of aircraft journey ticket or an entry ticket valid only for landside, issued by airport authorities. The security guards at airside entry points must be very vigilant while checking for any unauthorized entry. In case of any anticipated threat to visiting VVIP'S or airside installations, the security guards could be posted in "Pairs" and with arms. The guards must be properly briefed by security officer to take necessary actions in self-defence when situations arise.

(b) ***Patrolling of airside***: It is another important task which security department has to perform. The mobile patrolling of airport perimeter/boundary wall, taxitracks and runway should be carried out at a regular interval. The mobile patrol should see that all access control points on airside are properly manned and no unauthorized or suspicious person is found over there. In case of any unauthorized or suspicious person is found, the patrol in charge must check the identification documents and investigate the reasons for being there. In case a person without any identification document, he should be interrogated by the security officer and take necessary action as per standing orders. Night vigilance must be proper and meaningful to ensure proper safety. In case of a VVIP flight the airside must be guarded and checked by both static guard and mobile patrol in addition to laid down security at landside.

(c) ***Screening of baggage and personnel***: All the people who arrive at the airport to board the flights for their destinations, must get their all luggage screened through screening machine fitted at most of the airports. After baggage has been screened, passenger collects their boarding passes from check in counter. They hand over their heavy baggage and carry with them only cabin baggage. Before entering the departure lounge each person and his/her cabin baggage must be checked/screened by proper equipment i.e. metal detector, etc. Security personnel assigned this task must be very tactful and trained to handle each case. Personnel operating at International Airports should have a very sharp observation power as foreign passengers departing may be carrying prohibitive items, explosive and weapon, etc. in a well concealed manner on person or in cabin baggage. Adequate Female Security guards are also needed to check and screen lady passengers. The incidence in America on 11 September 2001, where less than two dozen determined, highly motivated and well trained hijackers reportedly armed with nothing more sophisticated than Knives, accomplished with superb perfection the suicidal attacks with Jet Airlines at the very centre of the United States economic and military power. To ward off such dastardly acts, the screening staff must remember that no one is to be believed on face value irrespective of any officer, politician or eminent personality, etc. After due, check these passengers must be allowed an entry into the Departure Hold Area. They should not be permitted to mix around with arriving passengers and visitors, etc.

(d) ***Security of aircraft at parking bays***: Before departure and after landing at the airport, the aircrafts are parked in the parking bays for refueling and any other technical checks, etc. Passengers board the plane for their destinations by showing their boarding pass. Security guards should ensure that no unauthorized persons come near the aircraft thus endangering the security and the safety of passengers and aircraft. No visitors should be allowed near the aircraft. Besides, no vehicle of any airline, which may endanger the security and safety, should be permitted on the parking bay near the aircraft.

(e) ***Security of chartered aircraft/group tours***: In our country and also abroad many Travel Agents and Tourist corporation organize group tours from one place to another place or even different countries. These Tourist Corporation arrange for chartered flights to carry these group tours. At many airports special areas are provided to handle these groups tours and chartered flights are parked separate from the scheduled flights operating at the airports. Security officer must detail separate people to guard these aircrafts and handle these group tours so that security and safety is not Jeopardized.

## Problems in Using more than One Security Agency

The proverb—"Too many cooks spoil the curry", fits in well at any airport where more than one security agencies are employed to guard the airport. The airports authorities must be very careful to choose more than one agencies for assigning various tasks at the airport. Number of airport utilize one agency for perimeter/boundary duties and another agency for access control. With the result any intrusion in to the airside becomes no body's responsibility. They keep passing blame on each other. In such system, overlapping of duties is very essential and proper handing/taking over of duties must be carried out. Any lapse in the security must be reported immediately by the same agency and should not be passed on to the next person or agency. From the safe security point of view it is always advisable to employ only one security agency for entire airport security system. On number of airports now police, CISF are deployed to carry out security duties at airside and also landside. In case more than one agencies are deployed then Security Manager must laid down proper coordination and cooperations instructions which must be strictly adhered to for better security services. Adequate check up drills must be formulated to avoid any lapse in security.

## Provision of Security Barrier

In order to provide adequate security to airside, perimeter fencing/boundary walls have to be planned and constructed accordingly. Depending upon the anticipated threat of only cattles, intruders or both and the policy of airport authorities, it will be required. In case of fencing, choice of metal chain link, steel angle iron pickets or weldmesh coupled with barbed wire strings have to be made. Perimeter fencing of wooden logs are not recommended due to its short life and easy to penetrate. Fencing alone may not be sufficient, it must be augmented by an effective "Intrusion Detection System" on International airports where Instrument Landing system (ILS), as one of the landing navigation aid is deployed, then steel angle iron/steel rod fencing will not be advisable, instead wooden or plastic support will be organized for perimeter fencing. The height of the fencing should be as per the surrounding topography. However, the height on the landing and take off path can't be more than the laid down height in the Airport technical order based on the directions of Airports Authorities of India.

At the access control points besides a sentry post, a strong drop arm barrier should be put with suitable board "STOP" written in red colour on both the sides. It will prevent any intruding vehicle arriving as a gate crasher. The drop arm barrier can be further augmented by planting "Pop Up Barrier". This can be erected in case some vehicle has to be stopped which has crashed into as an unauthorized entry. The perimeter fencing should be straight as far as possible, it will assist in keeping a constant and clear watch.

Security fencing must be a reasonable physical and psychological deterrent for any intruder. Besides, adequate height it should have angle brackets on top of steel pillars with 3–4 strands of barbed wire. The angle bracket should always bend towards "Outerside" from where the intrusion is expected. The fencing should always be laid in conjunction with electronic detection system e.g. motion detectors, pressure detectors and vibration detectors, etc. to make it more effective. A close monitoring of warning signals/alarm signals should be done in security control room. Regular patrolling must be carried out to check any intrusion or temporary fault in the electronic equipments.

## Security of Airport Buildings

Various buildings at airports to include Air Traffic Control tower, departure, arrival lounge, VIP'S lounge, cargo terminal, check in counters, other security document check counters and other miscellaneous offices, etc. are all main hubs of the personnel activities. The design of the building should be such that in case of any explosion, attack or bomb emergency, etc. the extent of the damage in term of personnel and material should be bare minimum. It must incorporate all security norms and safety guidelines for providing optimum security at the time of crisis. Adequate access control/check points must be there to check every entry from landside to airside. As far as possible other commercial installations i.e. hotel, commercial shopping complex, airport employees union offices, etc. should be located at a reasonable distance. This will enable to enforce adequate and effective checks on entry points. Vehicles should not be parked within 30 meters from the frontage of the terminal.

The design and construction of the building must provide built in safety and security to the occupants. In case of any explosion or fire accident, the damages could be contained in the smallest possible area. The first floor balconies should not be overlooking the public area below in order to prevent any throwing of grenade or other explosive/fire devices.

Besides, physical posting of security guards the provision of electronic security system like mounting of close circuits television cameras will give better results by monitoring passengers/visitors movements inside and outside the airport buildings. The locations for mounting of CCTV cameras must be such so as to keep a detail and constant vigil on the movements of both arrivals and departures. The suggested locations for CCTV cameras are as under:

- (i) Entrance/access points.
- (ii) Kerb side.
- (iii) Check-in counters/areas.
- (iv) Exits.
- (v) VIP and other lounge.
- (vi) Security Holds/Sterile Departure Lounge.
- (vii) Baggages make up area.

(viii) Palletisation area.
(ix) Spectator terrace and galleries.

The mounting of CCTV cameras at conspicuous entry/exit points will prove as deterrent for a person with foul intentions. The ideal locations should be so selected by airport manager/security head that all the movements/activities of a person, from the time of his entry till exit or entry into an aircraft, are kept under proper surveillance.

## Security of Passenger Terminals

The basic aim of all the airport services is to provide swift and fastest processing system for passengers and their baggage. This is with a view to ensure that passengers are not put to any inconvenience during arrival and departure formalities. At the same time due safety precautions are to be observed to ensure security of passengers, baggage, aircrafts and other employees, etc. The main threats against which security at the airports have to be alert at all times, are attacks, seizers at airport area and hijack/subotage to aircrafts.

The main concern for security officer and staff is to ensure proper regulating systems for arrival/departure traffic. Passengers who are arriving from the landed flights should be guided towards arrival lounge for completing their customs clearance and travel document checks, etc. On the other hand passengers from the security hold must be guided towards aircraft awaiting at the parking bay. In no case these two types of passengers should be allowed to mix with each other. Where airports have arrival and departure on separate floors the problems are much less. But where aero bridges are used to carry passengers into the aircrafts, separate lanes are to be positioned. The arriving passengers must not mix with each other for handing over bag or any other items, etc. to departing passengers in the lanes.

## VIP Lounge's Security

Almost all the airports cater for the separate lounge where senior politicians, foreign dignitaries, senior diplomats and government officials and prominent business corporates can wait for some time till their flights or road journey arrangements are getting ready for destinations. These lounges are separate from normal arrival/departure lounges. Unlike other lounge, VIP lounge house both arriving and departing personalities, therefore, it is very difficult from security point of view to carry out required checks. These lounges have openings for airside and land side. Adequate Security measure must be established at airside access point. To enhance physical security measures CCTV camera can be installed to monitor movements of accompanying personnel with the VIPS. Even the entry to the VIP lounge must be regulated to keep a strict check on extra people moving into the lounge, this will assist security department to provide better security and safety measures. If need be, in case of a VIP movement the help of local police can be asked for to strengthen the security measures.

It will be prudent to emphasize that location of VIP lounge must be at a reasonable distance from the passengers arrival/departure lounge. This will ease out security problems and inconvenience to the normal passengers. In addition the quality of airport/airline services will considerably improve for normal flow of traffic.

## Cargo Terminal Security

The locations of cargo terminal differ from one airport to another. Normally cargo terminals are located between landside and airside and act as partition barrier between the two. All the cargo arrive at the reception area, here the staff arrange for unloading, inspection, weighing and then for storage in the terminals. Normally separate cargo terminal are provided as under:

(a) Departure cargo Terminal

(b) Arrival cargo Terminal.

### *(A) Departure Cargo Terminal*

Once the cargo, received for departure, is inspected, then it must be carried for X-ray machine screening and security clearance. After the security, checks are over then cargo is taken to airside for palletizing. Pallets of required sizes will then be shifted to the aircraft for loading. If possible to augment physical security CCTV cameras should be fitted to monitor all the activities. All the doors of airside opening must have proper locking.

### *(B) Arrival Cargo Terminal*

Once the cargo is off loaded from the cargo flights, it should be taken to depalletizing area inside the arrival cargo terminal. After all the pallets are opened, the cargo must be inspected and then stored separately, if it is to be shifted to another city by road. Vehicles for collection of arrived cargo should stay at landside and must be properly regulated at the entry points. CCTV cameras should also be installed in arrival cargo terminals to check the activities of handling.

In case if separate terminals are not provided for onward/inward, destinations, then care must be exercised by security staff to ensure that some sort of local partition is created and both cargo must not be mixed. The cargo which has been x-rayed and security clearance given should not mix with the cargo whose security clearance is awaited. At times there may be instances when large containers has to be carried directly to airside for x-ray/security clearance. For such cases, some entry point near cargo terminal must be large enough to such container traffic.

In case the cargo terminals are located far apart from the airport building, then care must be taken that proper entry points are established for security purposes. In such cases pedestrian on area must be earmarked properly and suitable access control be enforced.

## Security of Spectator's Gallery

The security measures at the spectator's gallery must be adequate to ensure that there are no threats/dangers to aircrafts at the parking bays and passengers moving in the arrival/departure lounge. The following security measure must be exercised:

(a) The location should be such that it provide a clear view of tarmac and both the lounge.

(b) The entry to the spectator gallery must be restricted by issuing of entry tickets.

(c) The area of gallery should not have any opening into the airside, if any doors are there those should be properly locked.

(d) Front view of the gallery must have shatter proof tuff glass to avoid any attempt of throwing a grenade or shooting at aircraft/passengers.

(e) Besides, having physical security one or more CCTV cameras could be installed to monitor the movements of spectators.

(f) In case some threats are anticipated then either proper screening at the entry gate or complete ban on the entry for sometime can be inforced. For screening, proper equipment and additional security staff will have to be posted.

## Car Park Security

Car park is a potential threat area for planting a bomb or an explosive to cause damage to parked vehicles, accompanying drivers and create panic among passengers. Therefore, the carpark must be at least 30 meters away from the front portion of the airport building. This will prevent any damage/injuries to passengers and aircraft in case of any explosion in carpark. Due to VIP movements, there is always a pressure that few car must be allowed up to the departing/alighting point near the aircraft. These facility can be provided by use of a suitable car hailer from the passenger terminal building to parking bay/VIP parking area. Care must be exercised by security staff to check if any unattended vehicle found near the terminal building, this must be removed immediately to a safer area before it causes any damages/injuries in case of any explosion, etc.

Car parking must be kept under proper check and observation by security guard. It must be ensured that no person/vehicle in suspicious manner is parked in the carpark. It must have adequate lighting to guard it at night. In case, where carparking is at more than one floor then movements should be thoroughly checked by security personnel. No entry or even view should be allowed of any airside including parking bay, etc.

## Access Control

Access control at the airport occupies a significant place from the security point of view. The following are the main access control points in an airport:

### *1. Departure Access Control*

All the passengers, who are to board flights for various destinations, enter the airport for check in counters and other formalities before they get into the aircraft. Proper security measures are to be adopted to regulate the entry to departure lounge, Care must be taken that accompanying persons should not create security problems and inconvenience to the passengers. In some small airports where there are no separate visitor's gallery, the visitors keep moving with the passengers and create unwanted rush in lounge. It may create potential threat for the security. Care should be taken to prevent any movement into airside of visitors/accompanying persons.

### *2. Arrival Access Control*

Arriving passengers should be regulated into the arrival lounge for collection of baggage, if any, and carry out custom and other travel formalities. They must not mix up with departure lounge passengers. Visitors/reception personnel must be kept at the entry point to avoid rush and security problems. Proper checking of luggage passes must be carried out.

Care has to be taken to ensure that no unlawful elements as visitors gain entry into terminals to carry out pickpocket or bag lifting activities. If possible "Meet and Greet Area" must be carefully earmarked for tourist and hotel representatives to receive/meet their clients/guests.

In order to ensure that no mixing up of passengers of arrival and departure lounge and of employees working in airside/landside, airport authorities must ensure that basic facilities like drinking water, toilets, and canteen for tea/snacks are available on both the sides. The normal commercial activities like bank, railway booking, tourist bookings, canteen, public call offices, post office and medical shop, etc. are suitably located at land side only. It will provide unwanted rush and pressure on security staff if these are at airside.

## Security Passes for Airport

The airport authorities and security department must jointly formulate the system of issue of proper photo identity card to the employees and similar permit for vehicles. The security staff must be properly trained to check and differentiate between a genuine and forged security pass. No one is to be taken on face value in case of security checks. There have been instances when unauthorized persons managed to gain entry with weapons and explosives into airside and attacked aircraft crews and passengers. No forcing of entry must be permitted unless proper identification has been established by security guards at entry/exit points.

The security passes/permit for entry into the landside and airside have to be issued specifically as per the employees work place need basis. The permits can be temporary, semipermanent basis or permanent. It should be categorized for a particular area or for entire airport area. Issuing authorities can select and decide different colours for each pass at large airports. Proper security screening must be done before employment and issuing of permit. At some airports if permit/pass authorities are more than one, then proper coordination has to be arranged to avoid any security lapses. It is always advisable that only one i.e. airport authorities issue the permits/identity cards to own and other airline employees.

In case of any repair/construction is to be carried out at airside or landside then bulk permit for workers can be issued to the contractor at his responsibility. Any security risk will be taken care of by holding contractor responsible and accountable.

The design of airport permit/identity card can be of suitable size and easy to carry. It should be attached to the chest on the pocket. Suggested contents are as under:

(a) Passport size latest photograph.
(b) Serial number of the card/permit.
(c) Full name and age.
(d) Employers seal and address (Airport or Airline employee).
(e) Date of issue.
(f) Visible identification mark on the body.
(g) Signature of issuing authority with office seal.

The permit/identity card should be laminated for long life and should be easily visible on the holder. If kept the pocket must be shown to security guard at the entry/exit point. A suitable permit must be designed for issuing to vehicles making use of airside.

## Strict Checks for Violations

Various security experts have opined that "No amount of security rules and regulations are adequate and effective unless proper checks are enforced to prevent violations". In the same scenario security officer and airport authorities must exercise adequate and strict checking of security rules and measures to avoid serious losses, damages to personnel and aircraft. If checks are, only of routine nature then these will be of no value. Therefore, checks and control measures should be monitored regularly as a surprise to find out the effectiveness of the security.

Security only becomes dangerous when it is taken lightly or in a friendly manner. Security staff must be firm but polite with the passengers, employees and also visitors. Any security violation must be immediately reported to the higher authorities. Strict action must be taken against the person violating or attempt to violate any security rule or measure. In case more than one security agencies are looking after the security at the airport then proper co-ordination must be carried out under the overall supervision of the airport security manager/officer. It is quite likely that in case of any security lapse one will try to blame the other, such attitude must be curbed with heavy hand. No unauthorized person will be allowed to entre into airside on friendly or intimacy basis. Similar rules must be observed with ex-employees who have left the service or services were terminated on discipline grounds.

## REGULATING MOVEMENTS OF VIPs

At all major airports, normally separate landing areas are allotted for the aircraft carrying a VIP. However, in some cases where there are no separate parking bay available, special arrangements might have to be made for VIP's arrival/departure. The following guidelines from security and safety point of view of the VIP's, aircraft and his entourage, must be adhered to by the airport authorities and security manager/staff.

(a) At arrival and departure, some VIPs insist that their vehicles should be permitted up till the aircraft at the parking bay. In such cases decisions has to be taken as to how many vehicles should be allowed to go to airside with the VIP in a very careful manner and security staff informed accordingly.

(b) At vehicle gate, in case of departure, VIP may be exempted from security checks but the driver, accompanying person, cabin baggage and hold baggage should be checked. Similarly, all other vehicles for Improvised Explosive Devices (IED), bombs and other passengers must be checked and their luggage screened as per rules.

(c) At the time of checking VIP, vehicles must be parked away from public view due to security reasons for avoiding any shoot out, etc.

(d) In case of arrival similar drills should be followed for customs and other travel-related checks, if need be.

(e) While VIP's luggage, at the time of arrival, may have to be collected from the aircraft bay itself, then this task must be done by the selected/ screened people belonging to department or organization who have invited the VIP. Security staff must not get involved in this.

(f) Security staff has to be very polite, courteous but firm in dealing with VIP and his entourage, such incidents of security checks may not be liked by the VIP or his personal staff.

(g) Sometimes the political party/other organizations wish to arrange some conference, meeting, refreshment and Dias/stage in honour of VIP, in such cases they will request security clearance/permission to organize all such functions, etc. One must consider all aspects of security before granting such permission inside airport premises.

(h) In case police protection is provided for VIP then proper liaison and co-ordination must be carried out by security head for dealing with gate entry, baggage, vehicles, and entourage security checks. The arrangements for frisking and baggage screening have to be made at the vehicle gate only.

(i) Number of times lot of people gather at the airport to receive/see off a VIP, in such cases security staff has to be very vigilant to ensure no unauthorized/unlawful element gets an entry into passenger's lounge or airside area.

(j) In case when VIP or entourage vehicles are allowed uptill aircraft in airside, then proper "Follow Me" arrangements must be made in airside to ensure security and safety.

### *Formulation of Contingency Plan*

Contingency planning is an essential aspect of all the planning strategies. No plan can be complete unless it has got a workable but different types of solution to the problem. Once Napoleon said—"You may have only Four courses open for a plan but enemy will invariably choose the Fifth one and you should be prepared for that". This is the contingency or alternate planning which will not allow you to lose the grip on the situation/crisis. Similarly, while planning airport security, one has to cater for various threats e.g. bomb, IED, any attack and hijacking, etc. The security contingency plan must cater for the following events:

I. The plan of action in case of an armed attack on an aircraft or premises by grenades, missiles, rockets or through armed invasion.

II. The action in case of any illegal/unlawful seizure of aircraft, control tower and airport premises. Plan should also cater for own aircraft being hijacked.

III. Action to be initiated in case of a hijacker from another country asking permission to land at the airport.

IV. Plan of action in case of sabotage to aircraft installation and airport premises.

The basic aim of making any plan and also contingency planning is to ensure that firstly enemy/intruders do not succeed in their plans and secondly minimize the damages/losses to aircraft, passengers and airterminal. All this will avoid inconvenience to the passengers and air operations can be resumed with minimum possible delay. The planning has to be within the framework of the directions as issued by Airport Authority of India from time to time. Certain modifications can be carried out by keeping in view the topography and location of the airports. These contingency plans must be finally approved by the appropriate authorities. Adequate liaison must be carried out with local police and other agencies if any additional assistance is anticipated in case of an emergency/threat.

To ensure that plan/contingency plan is successful, emphasis should be laid on the following:

(a) The plan must be 'COMPLETE' in all respect and must cover all contingencies, which can be thought off in a remote idea.

(b) It should have 'CLARITY' of action and must be understood by all people who are involved in putting it into action.

(c) All the 'CONTENTS' of each planning must be known to every participant.

(d) A detailed and meaningful "COORDINATION" must be carried out with all departments, airlines, and organizations who may participate in the planned action.

(e) The entire "CONTROL" must be entrusted to some senior and experienced person who is capable of handling the situation under all odds with cool mind.

(f) A flawless and an effective "COMMUNICATION" system must be thought off to execute all operations. More than one channel/type should be planned. Duplicate communication is advisable.

(g) A plan should also be visibly as "CONVINCING" and viable in execution. It should be a practical plan which may require minimum alterations and amendments.

(h) All modifications and amendments must be "INCORPORATED" immediately in the plan and should get approval from the appropriate authorities.

(i) Proper training and rehearsals at regular intervals are very necessary for any plan to be successful.

(j) A centrally located control room must be planned and established with adequate staff and means of communication to operate as nerve centre in case of emergency/threat.

(k) Detailed list of personnel and civil organization's telephone numbers must be maintained in control tower and other offices who will be informed immediately in the event of emergency/threat.

(l) Arrangements for shifting of passengers and other means needed to operate aircraft must also be included in the plan.

## EARMARKING OF BOMB DISPOSAL AREA/ISOLATED AREA

In the modern times one can read in newspapers on many occasions the instances of bomb/IED threats and hijacking of aircrafts. Therefore, it is obligatory for each airport authorities to plan for isolated parking bay and bomb/IED disposal area. Anytime when an information is received regarding an aircraft having a bomb/IED, it should be immediately towed away to the Isolated Parking Way, which should have the following,

(a) Airport must earmark a separate parking bay at a minimum of 100 meters away from other aircrafts parking bays.
(b) It should not have the view of other aircrafts landing/takeoff and airside, from inside the isolated aircraft.
(c) The location should not have any oil pipe/LPG line passing underground or powerline on top or below.
(d) The bay must not pose any hindrances in the air operations.
(e) It should have adequate lights for keeping a night watch.
(f) The parked aircraft should be kept under constant watch from a dug down sentry bunker, which should have proper communication means.

### Bomb Disposal Area

During the course of search operation the security staff may find some suspicious object in an aircraft. This must be immediately removed by an expert and taken in a vehicle to bomb disposal area for destruction. The area so selected must have the following ingredients:

(a) Should be an isolated area preferably a dug up trench or bunker where the vehicle could be driven directly for unloading the device.
(b) Route in and out must be well defined.
(c) Should be reasonably away from all air operation taxi tracks and runways.
(d) The isolated parking bay and bomb disposal area should be away from each other from operation point of view but may be in the vicinity.
(e) Bomb disposal area also must not have oil pipe line or power line/ water line underneath it.

(f) It should be away from public view and other air operations.

(g) Must have a proper bunker near to it, but at least 100 meter away, for waiting or watching by bomb experts. Even the security guard can make use of this bunker.

The entire system of airport security falls under the preview of specialized security. Security staff must be especially trained for their dealing with passengers politely but firmly, keeping a close watch on the regulated entry into airside and passenger lounge. The security system should be such that it does not pose problems and cause inconvenience to the passengers including VIPS, other politicians, diplomats, senior officials of government and private sectors. But at the same time proper security and safety measures must be enforced to safeguard passengers, aircrafts and airport terminal. No laxity or any carelessness have to be accepted in airport security system, as there are "No Second Chance" for a flying aircraft if all the safety and security norms are not followed rigidly. Security head and airport authorities must operate in close cooperation and carry out rehearsals of the emergency plans for achieving better security at the airports.

# 15

# Bomb Threats and Disposal

It is very common phenomenon these days that an airport official or any other important commercial organization getting a bomb threat call. But the basic difference, which makes it more critical and responsive in the case of an airport/flying aircraft, are the sense of urgency and threatened lives of many passengers/aircrew who pose helpless in the air. Therefore, the drills, procedures and speed of actions at various levels vary altogether at the airport/aircraft than any other static organization or institution where employees and other visitors can move to number of alternate places in the near by vicinity.

At each airport it is very essential that sound planning is carried out by considering various aspects of bomb threat calls, assessment and evasive actions to either ward off or minimize damages/losses. In case bomb is timely detected, it may minimize the damages and losses to personnel and property including aircraft. Well-conceived plan must be chalked out keeping in view the location of airport, topography and prevailing political environment. Once the plan is formulated, it must be forwarded to the appropriate authorities for approval. Approved plans must be told to all the effected employees about their duties they are expected to carry out. Proper rehearsals must be carried out at a regular interval to ensure that each contingency and part of the plan is workable and effective. During rehearsals if some modifications are warranted, those must be incorporated in the plan. The modified plan must be approved by the higher authorities.

Arrangements must be made to carry out liaison with police, firebrigade, hospitals, municipal corporations and district authorities. They should be informed about their role and needed assistance in case of bomb threats and action plan. Important telephone numbers must be displayed at exchange/control tower/offices, who will be immediately informed in bomb crisis.

## PREPARATORY ACTIONS

The security officer at the airport and the airport manager must take the following measure while finalizing the action plan.

(a) Find out the location and telephone number of the bomb disposal unit of military or police, which ever is located in the station.

(b) Carry out liaison and ask their availability for helping in search, defusing or removals/destruction.

(c) The search and screening of baggage and frisking must be strict to create a deterrent.

(d) Vehicle access control and security in carpark should be tightened up.

(e) Carry out surprise checks of hold baggage to ensure that staff is performing their duties well.

(f) An evaluation committee must be formed who will comprise of airport security manager/officer, airport authorities, concerned airline staff and should take appropriate decisions at the time of threat.

## SCRUTINIZING THE BOMB THREAT

In most of the cases the information of the bomb threat is received through a caller, who passes some information on the telephone to the authorities about the bomb threat. Once a threat call is received, there should be an effort by a responsible senior person to extract maximum information from the caller. A suggested set of questions/anticipation from the caller could be as under

(1) Question to be asked:

(a) Who are you, give your full identity if possible belong to which group, political party, etc.

(b) Calling from which place.

(c) Where (inside premises or in aircraft) what type and shape of bomb.

(d) How does it look like.

(e) Why did you plant it.

(f) When it will explode.

(2) Exact wording of the threat.

(3) Caller's identifying details.

(a) Age and sex.

(b) Accent of speech.

(c) Voice (loud, soft or whispering, etc.)

(d) Speech (slow, fast or excited, etc.)

(e) Manner (calm, emotional or vulgar, etc.)

(f) Any background noise (road, rail traffic, music, etc.)

(g) Any prompting from behind, etc.

(4) Was the voice familiar.

(5) Any other related information gathered from caller.

Once maximum information has been collected from the caller then it should be carefully collated to arrive at the types of actions to be taken.

Immediately the evaluation committee should discuss the pros and cons of the threat. All aspects of the threat depending upon whether suspected bomb/IED is in the terminal, aircraft parked, or aircraft in the air. All the important personnel/officials as per action plan must be informed about incoming threat calls. The evaluation committee must decide upon the threat perception whether it is "Specific" or "Non Specific". The result arrived at by the committee must be disseminated to all concerned i.e. police, fire brigade, district authorities and hospital, etc. so that they can gear up and activate their resources to meet the crisis.

## SEQUENCE OF ACTION

Once the committee has decided upon the type of threat, the action plan to counter the threat must be put into action. However, the action, procedure and other methods will depend on:

(a) Information about location.

(b) Type and lethality of the bomb/IED.

(c) How much times is available i.e. when the bomb/IED is likely to explode.

At an airport, the bomb threat can be categorized as per the urgency given below:

(a) Aircraft in the mid Air.

(b) Aircraft on the ground.

(c) Threat in terminal or airport premises.

## Aircraft in the Mid Air

Any call received at the airport about the bomb threat concerning an aircraft, which is in the mid air, must be immediately conveyed to the captain of the aircraft. The information about bomb/IED must contain all the details about type, shape, size and time of the explosion, if known. The captain of the aircraft is entitled to take all measures to ensure maximum security and safety of the passengers and crew-on board. The likely action to be taken by the captain and cabin crew will include the following:

(a) Captain of the aircraft will take various safety measure to search the bomb in the passenger compartment and flight deck.

(b) Ask all passengers to remove their cabin baggage from the overhead lockers and put the same in their lap. Thereafter crew to search all the lockers.

(c) Search the toilets, wardrobes, coat room area, galley and bar, empty seats and places under the seats.

(d) Check, if any suspicious looking like object, similar to the description given by caller, is found anywhere, then remove carefully to "least-risk-area" in the rear of the aircraft.

(e) Disconnect the electrical connection of the area to reduce the gravity of fire.

(f) While removing the device care should be taken to ensure that it is not tilted or moved, least it explodes accidentally.

(g) Captain of the aircraft will contact the nearest airport to descent and finally land at the airport.

(h) Once the aircraft lands at the airport, it should be guided to the isolated parking bay. All passengers must get down and move to safe places.

(i) All airport safety services must swing into action to guard against any explosion.

(j) If need be, depending upon the type of bomb/IED the bomb disposal squad must take necessary action.

## Aircraft on the Ground

The threat call for the aircraft on the ground is little simple than for an aircraft in the air. If a caller has informed about the bomb in the aircraft parked in the bay, following actions may be taken:

(a) Once the deliberation is going on of the evaluation committee, the staff must be ready to disembark passenger's (if on board), all baggage, food and mail, etc.

(b) Once decision is taken as specific threat then aircraft must be towed to the isolated parking bay immediately.

(c) Passengers should be asked to disembark from the plane with their cabin baggage and they must be moved to safe place or sterile lounge.

(d) Search of the aircraft, hold baggage and all other parts must be carried out by special teams trained in search/disposal of bomb.

(e) If required, help of aircrew of the aircraft must be taken to carry out search of all technical parts of the aircraft.

(f) If any suspicious item is found, then item should not be taken to the lounge for passenger's identification, but its description should be told to passengers to own up the item. Item should only be returned, once it has been cleared by the bomb disposal squad.

(g) If passengers are to be taken to lounge and later found that some passenger is missing without intimation, then it is a cause of worry and must be enquired in detail.

(h) If passengers are taken to the hotels for rest, then complete security check and screening of baggage must be done again before boarding the aircraft.

(i) If any bomb/IED is found it must be taken to Bomb Disposal Area and disposal squad must act accordingly.

## Building Threat

If the bomb threat is for any office, control tower or terminal building, then committee must decide whether:

(a) Evacuation of passengers/staff not required.

(b) Partial evacuation of staff is required.

(c) Complete evacuation of passengers and staff is required, this is a rare event.

In an airport building the announcement of bomb threat should not be done straightaway, it may cause serious panic among passengers. Running around here and there in search of a safe place may result in stampede, which must be avoided. Before any announcement is made for evacuation on Public Address System, the management and security staff must decide on safe exit routes and alternate locations where staff and passengers should be shifted till bomb search and disposal is over. The search of premises and lounge will be carried out by specialist persons or bomb disposal squad who are expert in this field. Security Manager/Officer should provide all the cooperation at the time of search. The search, besides lounge and premises must lay emphasis on the following likely places:

(a) Stairwell
(b) Elevator shaft access points.
(c) False ceiling areas.
(d) Rest rooms.
(e) Access doors.
(f) Unsecured points of access to plumbing and electrical fixtures.
(g) Air conditioning plant room.
(h) Main switches and valves.
(i) Record storage areas.
(j) Fire hose racks.
(k) Ceiling lights and removable fittings.
(l) Car parking area, hedges and big plants.
(m) Reception lounge.
(n) Pantry areas, toilets and bathrooms.

Once the search is carried out all the passengers if evacuated, must be screened and frisked with cabin baggage. After all search if any, suspicious looking item is found, bomb disposal squad must take proper action to carry it in a vehicle to bomb disposal area or consider destroying it in place depending upon the contents and lethality of the device.

## Process of Bomb Disposal

During the search if any suspected item or object is identified as a bomb or improvised explosive device, the following actions are recommended:

(a) No one should touch or attempt to remove the object as it may detonate and explode accidentally. Staff must wait for the arrival of bomb disposal squad and sniffer dogs, etc.
(b) On arrival of bomb disposal squad, they must decide on the gravity of threat and action for further disposal. They will ensure the type of device and use of detonator, etc.

(c) In case the device is found next to an aircraft then aircraft should be removed first to a safer place and remove device later, if required.

(d) In a building, sand bags must be placed around the device, but not on the device, to minimize the blast effect on doors and window glasses, etc.

(e) Removal, of the bomb/IED to a safe place for disposal, is very critical and must be done as a last resort and only by expert persons.

The bomb/IED threats are becoming quite common these days on the airports, important, commercial institutions, hotels and railways, etc. Proper action plan, in the form of standing orders, must be worked out to deal with all the contingencies. Proper liaison with Police and Military Headquarters should be carried out to avail the services of bomb disposal squad and sniffer dogs, etc. Suitable actions must be taken to ensure that there are no panic caused among passengers which is likely to result in more injury and damages. Air threat evaluation committee must decide on the type of threat i.e. specific or non-specific. Once decision is taken then all actions as per plan should be taken to deal with the threat.

# 16

# Security and Safety Management in Hotels

## GENERAL

The security management in hotels is some what different than what we have analyzed in normal industries and other corporate organizations. The hotel is considered as "Hospitality Industry" since it falls under the preview of Industrial Dispute Act. All the Industries have basically different type of regulated and restricted access control but hotels being a service industry vary to a great extent in access control. The production industry and other offices/ institutions have a controlled access where all employees, visitors, contractors, suppliers and all dealers and their vehicles are properly checked for the identification, theft and pilferage, etc. Once the security staff at the main entry point is satisfied, an entry is permitted. The hotels are basically open to welcome their customers as guests, therefore, no checking is carried out at the main entrance/exit. Therefore, the access control is as under:

### Access Control

#### *(a) Access Control for Guests/Customers*

The main gate entry and exit points are only manned for guests/customers in a hotel. The entry/exit point for hotel employees is normally separate from the main gate. The security staff is posted at the main access point to regulate car/vehicles and guide them into the hotel towards reception. No customer/ guests are checked for identity. However, the security staff has to be very vigilant. He must keep his eyes and ear open. They should be specially trained to recognize if the person is of any suspicious nature. Although the entry will not be stopped for him but other person posted inside can keep him under watch once he goes beyond reception. Similarly, access control for vehicle is altogether different than in any other industry. A proper watch has to be kept in the car park area or any vehicle left unattended next to main lobby or car park. The sentry of security staff in car park must ensure that all car drivers keep a vigil on their own car. They should not fiddle around with other cars.

The baggage of the guest/customers can't be checked for any security purposes as it will not be liked by the guests. All the baggage should be carefully carried by the "Bell Boys" to the room allotted to the guests. Since hotel industry is open for 24 hours, any guest can arrive at any time in any dress.

Similarly, the guest can't be checked while he is leaving the hotel at the main exit. It will bring very bad name for the hotel industry as such. His baggage have to be carried by the Bell Boys till exit and security staff posted at the exit gate is not allowed to carry out any check. Basically, no such system can be devised where guests/customers can be frisked or checked at the IN/OUT gates.

However, as a special case when some VIP/VVIP is occupying the hotel premises then some checks at the access points can be introduced for guests as a part of security instructions for the VVIP. This procedure is only followed in 5 Star Hotels as an exception than a rule.

### *(b) Access Control for Employees and Contractors, etc.*

Except the guests/customers, the access control system in all the hotels for employees, contractors, suppliers, vendors, etc. are followed almost in the same way as followed in any other production industry. As mentioned earlier there is a separate entry/exit for these people. All employees come as per the timings of their office or working shift into the hotel. Proper identity card is issued to each employee and their entry is regulated through time office. On arrival and departure they punch their cards in all the 3, 4 and 5 Star Hotels to put the timings of their arrival/departure. As per the standing orders each employee is checked at the exit gate to ensure that no hotel property is being taken by him/her.

All the contractors and his workforce are issued temporary permit to enter inside the premises. After finishing their job, all the workers go out from the exit gate. Security staff checks all the workers/labours for any theft and pilferage. Contractor is fully responsible for their conduct inside the hotel premises. Every supplier and vendor is also issued permit along with the item he is to supply and carry with him inside the hotel. Delivery chalan is checked at the exit gate for proper receipt by the storekeeper of the hotel. All outside vehicles are only allowed into the local carpark as such no vehicle can go inside the hotel. The procedure of search are laid down in the hotel's security standing orders and if necessary search of lunch boxes, newspapers/ magazines is carried out by the security department staff.

The security in a hotel basically revolves around prevention of theft and pilferage. Security staff must exercise all precautions so that all such cases can be prevented and no bad impression is given to any guest/customer. The security staff is responsible for the following aspects of thefts.

(a) Room Thefts (Guest baggage, cash, valuables and hotel's property)

(b) Property Thefts.

  (i) Linen

  (ii) Cutlery/crockery

  (iii) Liquor/wine

  (iv) Rations.

The security staff in any hotel, irrespective of its classification, which will depend on the facilities provided by the hotel to the guest, i.e. 3 star, 4 star, 5 star, is always confronted with the cases of theft and pilferages. However, management and security staff must plan for any disaster like fire accidents and bomb threat, etc. Here all the eventualities will be discussed in detail as under:

(a) ***Room thefts***: Once guest arrives at the hotel he/she will walk upto the reception for check in. After entering the particulars in the check in register, depending upon the availability of the accommodation, the guest will be requested to proceed to his/her room along with key. The baggage, if any, will be taken by the Bell Boys to the respective accommodation. When the guest proceeds for any job outside the hotel, the room key will be left at the reception. This will ensure that house keeping staff will arrange for cleaning of the room, change the linen and other items in the room. On number of occasions guest leave their cash, and valuables including jewellery inside the room. Although hotel management/security department insist that no valuable or jewellery, etc. is left in the room when it is not occupied

The housekeeping staff collects keys of all the concerned rooms or master key for doing-up the room. Here are the chances when the guests are not in the room, some suspicious nature of employee may be tempted to carry out a room theft. Although selection of all such employees is done by proper police verification and previous service records, but there are number of theft cases which take place in the hotels. Most of the time the hotel security staff resolve the issue by recovering the items. But at times the matter has to be reported to the police for investigation and action. Hotels generally avoid reporting cases to police, unless unavoidable, as it brings bad impression on the reputation of the hotel. Security officer must train their staff to keep an eye on all suspicious nature of employees to avoid such incidents of thefts and pilferage. Receptionist must always advise guests to keep their suitcase locked and leave valuables at the reception for safe custody.

(b) ***Property thefts***:

(i) *Linen*: In a hotel the housekeeper is in-charge of ensuring that all rooms are done-up daily including the cleaning of rooms and bathrooms, etc. Room boys and cleaners carry out the house keeping job along with housekeeper. Normally, all linen items like sheets, pillow covers, bed spread and towel, etc. are on clean exchange basis. But even then instances are reported when linen items especially bed sheets, pillow covers and towels are missing. Although hotel management agree that uptill 5% missing of items are there in the Industry. But if security staff and security officer are alert and vigilant these practice theft can be prevented to a great extent. Proper penalty in the form of pay cut must be imposed for a habitual offender.

(ii) *Cutlery and crockery*: In most of the star graded hotel, the items of crockery and cutlery are quite attractive. These items are issued to the room service, restaurants, dinning hall, etc. for the use of guests/customers. The items like spoons, forks and knives, etc. are the lucrative items for thefts. Generally crockery pieces are not taken away but only breakages are there due to careless handling. Security staff posted at various floors at exit gate must be very vigilant to check and prevent such instances of property theft.

(iii) *Liquors and wines*: In a hotel the theft and pilferage of liquor and wine is quite common from the bar and rooms. Although management ensures that bar men are of high integrity but on number of occasions waiters serving in the rooms and at the bar get involved in the theft of liquor. These items are very tempting, although issues are made to rooms on vouchers, which are signed by the guest. But even then theft and pilferage incidents are maximum for these items. Bar staff and security staff's alertness can put a curve on these habits.

(iv) *Rations*: This is another a very attractive area in hotel industry for carrying out thefts and pilferage. Kitchen stores are well stocked with the best available items of all verities of eatables to include fruits, dryfruits, butter, jams, cheese, eggs, etc. They are issued from the store to the kitchen on need basis for serving to the guest in various forms. It is very difficult to keep a strict check on these items in the kitchen. The kitchen and pantry are visited number of times by waiters, cooks and masalchis, etc. Therefore, proper checks by kitchen supervisors can minimize the cases of theft and pilferage pertaining to rations.

## Prevention of Fire Accidents

In all the hotels fire hazards are always a cause of worry for the management and security staff. The electrical gadgets and other equipments are always in action in large numbers and danger of short circuit can't be ruled out. It is very difficult to keep a strict control on the handling and use of electrical gadgetry by the guests. It is only that kitchen, air-conditioning plant/ equipments and other miscellaneous are used by the employees of the hotel that can be kept under vigil. The following points need special emphasis by Security Department/Administration Manager.

(a) A detailed, well thought out and easy to execute fire fighting standing orders must be prepared. And a copy, once approved by management, must be forwarded to all departments for necessary action.

(b) All employees and security staff/fire safety service personnel must know their duties and responsibilities in case of fire accidents.

(c) On each floor exit areas must be clearly marked for the information of all guests and employees.

(d) The training and rehearsals must be carried out at regular intervals to check the efficiency of fire standing orders. If any modification is needed, it should be done and get approved by the senior authorities.

(e) Periodical checks for serviceability of all fire fighting equipments must be carried out and if any replacement required, should be done.

(f) Frequent liaison must be carried out with local utility services i.e. police, fire brigade and hospitals by the security head.

(g) Electrical department must carry out periodical checks of all doubtful and likely fire hazard fittings and equipments.

## Intelligence/Vigilance Cell

In any hotel the main security problem is to guard against theft, pilferage and keep a check on the activities of employees trade union. These trade unions may be operating within the premises of the hotel or even from outside locations. Security manager has to form a reliable source of gaining information about suspicious nature of employees, trade union activities and extent of political interference in the working of these unions.

The rift between union leaders and management is not an uncommon phenomenon in hotels. Occasionally there are cases of theft, pilferage and misbehaviour with the guest. All these at times take a dirty turn and interference by union leaders become essential. Management does not like to report petty cases to police, since it brings bad reputation to the hotel. So unions play a major role in sorting out the cases. If the matter is not resolved then situation may develop into threat of a strike. Although there is always an understanding between management and employees union, which ensures the maintenance of essential services for looking after the guests. In such cases management will need first hand information about employees and union leaders' intentions. Security officer must create adequate sources among employees and security staff who should pass latest information to the security manager. A staff of 2–3 people must operate in the intelligence/vigilance cell to gain the information

Since hotel is also a part of industrial organizations and governed by the industrial dispute Act 1947, management must try and follow the rules of Labour Welfare Act, Factory Act and Minimum Wages Act so that good industrial relations are maintained between management and employees. The interference of unions must be to a very limited extent so that overall impression and welfare measures for the employees are in greater strength for curbing labour problems.

The hotel industry is a service and hospitality industry. Their security management is also different than in any other production unit. Security personnel must be specially selected and trained to keep a vigilant eye on the guests and employees, etc. The access control is quite different for guests and employees. The integrity and behaviour of all security staff must be very courteous, polite but firm while dealing with all hotel guests/customers.

# 17

# Organizing Security and Safety Management in Hospitals

## GENERAL

The security management in the hospitals is a specialized task, which is not similar to the normal industrial security. In production type industries security staff looks after the security aspects right from the time one enters the main gate and till he returns through the main exit. The access control is fully regulated by means of identity cards and security entry permit, etc. Although hospitals do fall under the preview of labour laws and are governed by the industrial dispute Act 1947. Therefore, all employees management are bound by labour laws.

The hospitals follow a peculiar type of service industry norms with daily visit of patients, their escort, relatives, friends, medical representatives and officials of pharmaceutical firms, contractors and suppliers, etc. Besides, all the employees and visiting doctors come to the hospitals for different jobs. Some of them go away after completing their various jobs and duties, but some patients get admitted for further treatment and their escorts relatives also stay with them in the ward or special rooms. It is not practically possible to issue pass or identity permit for such a large number of persons coming to the hospitals. At the same time it is not feasible and humanly possible to check each and every person's credentials by security staff at the time of entry/exit.

In hospitals depending upon the size, the security staff generally operates under Administration Manager. A security officer/manager is only employed in large hospital. Security guards and supervisors are either employed by the hospitals or they hire these services from a local security agency. In a hospital the basic requirement of security management is as follows:

(a) Prevention of theft:
   (i) Patient's, ward and rooms.
   (ii) Equipments and instruments.
   (iii) Medicines.
   (iv) Rations.
   (v) Linen.

(b) Access control of employees.

(c) Disaster management.

(d) Maintenance of discipline.

In hospitals there are no separate entry and exit for the staff members. All employees use the same entry/exit as for the patients and visitors, etc. The access control system thus occupies a significant place. This will be discussed in subsequent paragraphs.

## Prevention of Thefts

### *(i) Patient's Ward and Rooms*

Normally local patients do not carry large cash or valuable to the hospitals. Because all payments are generally done by their escorts/relatives. However, out city patients may bring cash and valuable like ring, watch and chain, etc. to the hospital at the time of admission. Once a patient leaves the room for investigation, checkup or operation, etc, he/she may leave behind cash or valuables in the room or near the bed. In such cases there are chances of theft taking place of these items. It is, therefore, duty of staff to brief the patients and relatives, not to keep/leave any such lucrative items behind. However, security guards must keep a watch that a staff who is not on duty in that ward/room does not enter into the room. Close eye on suspicious nature of employee must be kept to watch their movements.

### *(ii) Theft of Equipment and Instruments*

All the equipments and instruments are issued to a ward nursing staff or operation theatre staff. They are responsible for its security and maintenance. However, all the time it is not possible to guard all these equipments. Entry to ward can't be checked during visiting hours. Therefore, small items which are useful for a layman and easy to carry inside the pocket or carry-bag get lost. It is not possible to steal any big items. In such case it is the intelligence and observation power of the security staff, which can prevent such theft of equipments and instruments.

### *(iii) Medicines*

In government hospitals well-maintained medicine stores are there and all medicines are issued from there on vouchers to ward. In store all the medicines are taken on ledger charge and receipt vouchers are cleared. Issue of the medicine is regulated by making proper entries into the issue register. The issue vouchers are prepared and concerned nursing staff signs for the receipt. If the procedure is followed correctly and rigidly the theft and pilferage of medicines will not take place. But normally it is found and also management accepts that 5–10% of the medicines from government hospitals find their way to civil market or for personal use. In civil private hospitals there are no such medical store but all the medicines prescribed by the doctors have to be brought by the patient's escort/relation for use. So chances of any theft of medicine are remote in civil hospitals. It is the competence of security staff to trace the people who indulge in theft and take necessary action.

### *(iv) Theft of Rations*

Rations are issued from ration store to cook houses/pantries for cooking and further issue to the authorized patients in wards. Theft of ration is of two types. Firstly, the uncooked ration can be stolen, misused and carried homes by staff. Secondly, the cooked ration is eaten up/taken homes by employees. This is a very lucrative item and security staff must keep strict visual check at the entry and exit of lower class employees.

### *(v) Theft of Linen*

In all the hospital bedsheets, blankets, pillow covers and towels are given to the wards and special rooms for the use by the patients. These are issued by the house keeping in-charge to the ward nursing staff on vouchers. Later on, these items are issued on clean exchange basis i.e. whatever number of items are returned the same number are issued. The chances of theft are only from the ward or stores. The management accepts that small items like pillow covers and towels are stolen on number of occasions, however, report of such theft is very rare to the police due to the danger of bringing bad name to the hospital. Again it becomes the responsibility of the security staff to trace and prevent such incidents of thefts.

## Access Control of Employees

In hospitals the duty of access control of all the employees becomes a very difficult and a specialized task. Security staff employed at the main entry/exit points has to be adequately trained for this task. Very few large hospitals have separate entry and exit point for the exclusive use of employees, contractor and vendor, etc. In such cases access control becomes very easy and all suspicious nature of employees can be kept under close vigilance. As per the management orders or on receiving specific information from the intelligence sources the search of such doubtful personnel can be conducted. If there are no separate access points and employees use the same entry and exit like patients and visitors, etc. then the problem of security check and screening enhances. This is only the training and experience of the security officer and his staff, which can prevent theft and pilferage in the hospitals.

## Disaster Management

As already discussed in the earlier chapter about disaster management in detail, the same types of disaster can affect the hospital whether a natural, man made or accidental. However, it is not advisable to repeat all those problems and their counter measures. Everything pertains and relates in a similar way to a hospital also. However, security staff and administration should be well versed in dealing with fire accidents to avoid any large damages/losses to personnel and property of the hospital. It is the duty of every employee and security guard to take prompt action to extinguish any fire noticed in the hospital premises, one should never wait for the arrival of fire brigade tender or municipal fire services staff. Because it may take a shape which will require much more time and resources to extinguish or control it.

Hospital must have fire fighting standing orders, which must give out duties and responsibilities to all departments and employees. Fire preventive measures must be taken to ensure no electrical short circuit takes place. Employees looking after the electrical services must carry out periodical checks for loose and naked wiring. Security Officer/Administration Manager must earmark sufficient number of 'Exit' points in case of fire as per the likely strength of patients and employees. Sufficient number and types of fire extinguishers must be available on each floor along with fire hydrant for use of water. Security officer must carry out regular periodical serviceability test of all the equipments. Lastly, suitable rehearsals and training of security staff must be undertaken to ensure that they are well versed with the use of equipments. Important telephone numbers of persons and civil services, who should be immediately informed in the event of fire must be available with telephone operator and other offices.

### Maintenance of Discipline

In the hospitals one of the important tasks for the security department is to maintain discipline. On number of occasions patient or patients escort/ relatives, due to sentimental outburst lose temper on staff/nursing staff and at time situation takes an ugly turn. To prevent such situation security staff is posted at each floor. Management should advise nursing staff and other staff at reception and accounts branch, etc. to be more courteous and polite with patients. Some time patients and their relatives seek some information but they do not get a satisfying response from the staff. The anxiety and frustration at times leads to exchange of unpleasantary. Security staff should understand the mental anxiety of patients/relatives and behave in a polite manner. At times some of the visitors misbehave with nursing staff without any valid reasons, security staff must be firm with such persons and report the matter to security/Administration manager.

## MAINTENANCE OF INDUSTRIAL RELATIONS

In small hospitals basically there is no problem of industrial relations, but in large hospitals doctors, staff and nursing staff form their union or join some outside labour union. Nowadays it is not very uncommon to read in paper and watch on TV, the news of Resident Doctor's Strike, and the staff strike, etc. These activities are all indicatives of poor industrial relations and labour welfare. The strikes by doctors and nursing staff paralyze the complete operations in a hospital and causes extreme inconvenience.

Management must keep undercheck all the problems of Doctors and staff. Security officer must operate an "Intelligence Cell" Consisting of 2–3 reliable persons who will keep providing valuable information about impoending strike or any labour/employee's unrest. There should be close liaison with the hospital Labour union/Employee's union so that advance information is received and necessary preventive measures can be taken to prevent such ugly incidents. Such events bring very bad name for the management and also to the hospital as a whole.

The security management in a hospital is a peculiar and specialized task. The security personnel must be trained adequately to handle the instances of theft, pilferage and in case of disaster keep the situation under control. Security officer must exercise due caution in handling of patients and employees to keep a good name and reputation of the hospital.

# 18

# Security in Banking Operations

The importance of security management in banking operations occupies a significant place. All the banks whether schedule or cooperative carry out transactions of cash and lucrative documents like fixed deposit certificates, demand drafts, money transfer orders, lease and transfer deeds, government securities, various type of cheques and chequebooks. These all are termed as financial transactions which are very attractive for robbery, theft, pilferage and misappropriation. The planning and execution of security measures to prevent any misuse of cash and related documents call for a specialized security management in which knowledge, intelligence and initiative play a predominant role.

Before proceeding any further it will be prudent to analyze the general organizational structure of a nationalized bank, the standard organization is as under.

## HEADQUARTERS/CENTRAL OFFICE

The Central office or the Headquarters of a bank is generally located at one of the Metro city. Normally, it is the nerve centre of all the directing and controlling activities. The basic guidelines are issued by the Reserve Bank of India (RBI). Based on the directives of RBI all other policies and banking strategies are formulated and further issued to the circle and Zonal Headquarters. At central office following senior officers are located:

(a) Chairman/Chairperson.

(b) Managing Director.

(c) Executive Director.

(d) Chief General Manager.

(e) Other Senior Managers/Executives.

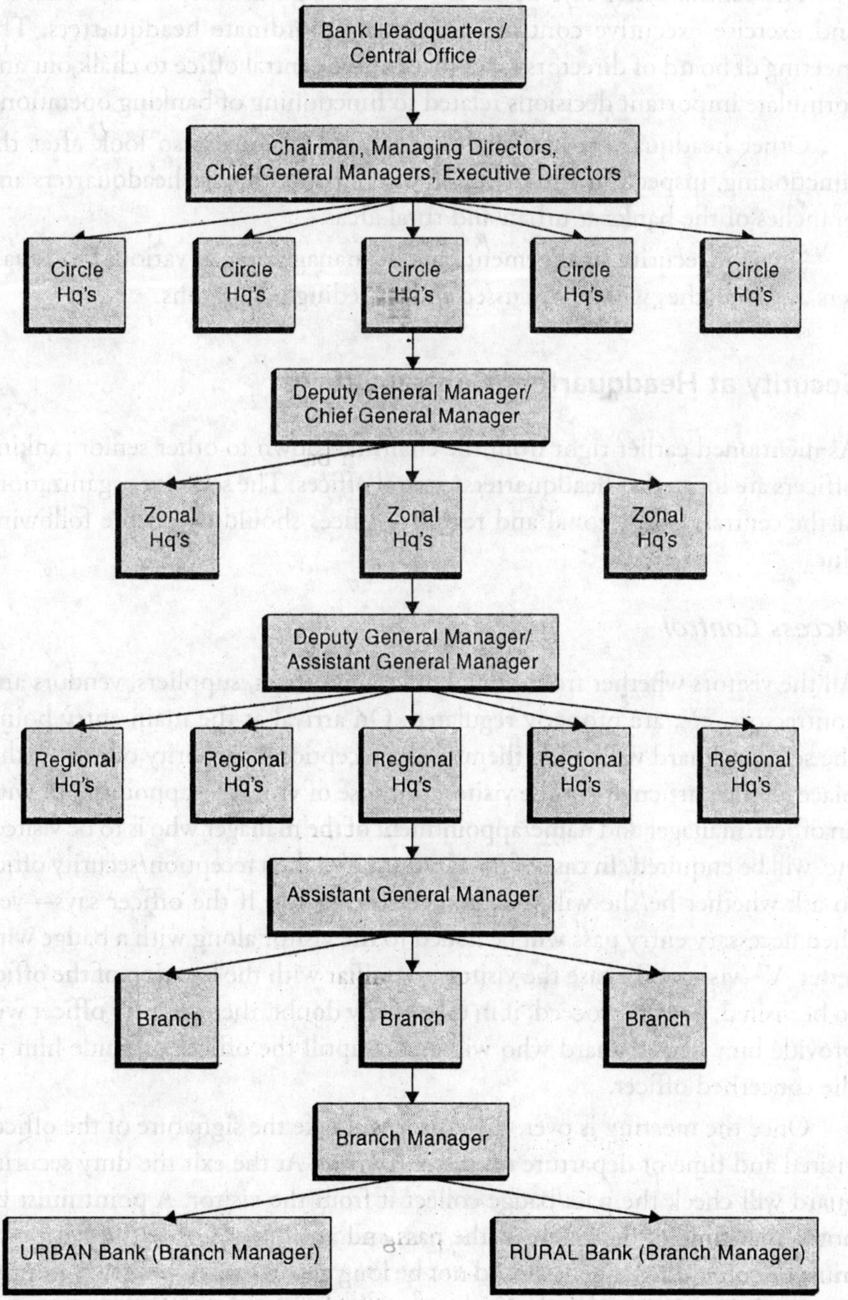


FIG. 18.1 GENERAL ORGANIZATIONAL STRUCTURE OF A NATIONALIZED BANK

The central office lays down all the policy guidelines, various directive and exercise executive control over other subordinate headquarters. The meeting of board of directors takes place at the central office to chalk out and formulate important decisions related to functioning of banking operations.

Other headquarters like circle, zonal and regional also look after the functioning, inspection and direction of their subordinate headquarters and branches of the banks at urban and rural areas.

Now the security arrangements and its management at various headquarters and branches will be discussed in succeeding paragraphs.

## Security at Headquarters/Central Offices

As mentioned earlier right from the chairman down to other senior ranking officers are located at headquarters/central offices. The security organizations at the central, circle, zonal and regional offices should be on the following lines.

### *Access Control*

All the visitors whether from other banks and offices, suppliers, vendors and contractors, etc. are properly regulated. On arrival at the main entry point, the security guard will guide them to the reception or security office. At this place all the particulars of the visitor, purpose of visit, any appointment with an officer/manager and name/appointment of the manager who is to be visited, etc. will be enquired. In case of no appointment, then reception/security office to ask whether he/she will like to meet the visitor. If the officer says—yes, then necessary entry pass will be issued to the visitor along with a badge with letter 'V' (visitor). In case the visitor is familiar with the location of the office to be visited, he will proceed, if in case of any doubt, then security officer will provide him with a guard who will escort uptill the offices or guide him to the concerned officer.

Once the meeting is over, the visitor will take the signature of the officer visited and time of departure on the entry pass. At the exit the duty security guard will check the pass/badge collect it from the visitor. A point must be noted that time of departure at the pass and visitors arrival at the exit point must be coinciding. There should not be long gap between these two-timing. Any undue gap must be clarified as to whether he/she visited some other officer to confirm the time gap. It must be ensured that unauthorized person is not allowed an entry into the office without enquiring all particulars by Security Manager/officer only, since all the policies and Directives are formulated and issued to subordinate headquarters, it is quite likely that some people with bad intentions may try to gain access to classified information.

In case of VIP visit to the central office then access control regulation are to be more strict and rigid. Hand metal detector or door type metal detector can be installed at the entry point for frisking purposes. Explosives/bomb detector should be used in case any threat from bomb or improvised explosive device is expected.

All employees including senior management must be provided with photo identity card duly laminated. They must be displayed at the chest during the working hours. Besides identification, it will inculcate a sense of security in the mind of all officers and other employees. No one should feel offended if any point of time the security personnel requests anyone to produce his/her identity card.

### *Security of Information and Documents*

Detailed instructions have already been written about normal security management of information and documents in an industrial organization. However, there are some specific measures which must be adopted in banking operations in dealing with security management of documents. It is pertinent to note that a central office will have important classified policy directives, valuable agreements involving large scale financial dealings, letters of credit, memorandum-of-understandings, loan and credit policies directives, etc. Besides these classified documents, central office stores fixed deposit receipts/ certificates, demand draft books, cheque books of different accounts and mail transfer orders, etc. whose security is of a special nature. Any fraud person getting an access to any of these documents might be able to cause heavy financial losses to some branch of the concerned bank

As per the normal security instructions all these documents are graded as TOP SECRET, CONFIDENTIAL, RESTRICTED and NOT-FOR PRESS, etc. the custody of these documents are the responsibility of various senior managers and are to be kept under lock and key in a safe cupboard or steel almirah, etc. However, from security point of view the following emphasis must be laid while handling these documents:

(a) Proper records of all INCOMING/OUTGOING Dak must be maintained in separate register on daily basis.

(b) Classified mail/correspondence marked "TOP SECRET" must always be addressed to an officer by name, who is authorized to know the contents of the letter. A separate mail register must be maintained for TOP SECRET documents.

(c) TOP SECRET correspondence must only be handled by authorized officer. It should be typed either by officer himself or by a steno in the presence of the officer. It should be despatched in "Double envelope" with sealed inner envelope.

(d) All classified files must be given page numbers and a docket sheet with the particulars of all content of letters i.e. number, date, original or and number of total pages must be maintained in the beginning of the file.

(e) Proper handing/taking over between officers must be done of all classified mail and documents.

(f) On the computer the code number of 'file' must be known to officers handling the correspondence.

(g) No classified correspondence/files should be carried to the officer's residence.

(h) All rough pages and carbon, etc. of classified mail must be destroyed by burning.

(i) Any classified correspondence, when made public or published in media, then the classification must be lowered and marked on it. All other recipients of the letter must also be informed.

(j) Destruction of classified documents/letters must be done by burning in the presence of an officer and destruction record to be maintained.

### *Disaster Management Planning*

Disaster Management in industry has been well covered in earlier chapter. In banking sector, basically the disaster are almost of similar nature as discussed in previous chapters. However, fire incidents must be adequately prevented, proper precautions observed and planning must be carried out in detail at all the circle, zonal and regional offices including at headquarters/central office. The under mentioned point will merit special considerations:

(a) In all Bank Headquarters, financial documents, government securities, MOU, letters of credit, important documents, fixed deposits receipts, demand drafts, cheque books and money transfer orders, etc. are handled in bulk quantity. Therefore, the fire risk becomes much more dangerous as paper catches small spark of fire very fast and also spreads quickly.

(b) All Head of security/Administration must ensure the following:

 (i) Workable and sound plan to counter any type of disaster/calamity.

(ii) All types of fire fighting equipments and extinguishers must be placed at each floor of the office building.

(iii) Employees must be conversant and security staff must be fully capable of operating these equipments and extinguishers

(iv) Security officer must organize rehearsal for fire exercise and serviceability tests for all fire fighting equipments.

## *Organization of Vigilance/Intelligence Cell*

Since all banking operations fall into the categories of industry, all the labour laws, industry dispute act, etc. are applicable to the employer and the employees. Bank officers and employees have formed their separate unions. These unions keep organizing various strikes in the banks thus interrupting and paralyzing the entire banking operations. Therefore, there is need that security head must organize a vigilance cell/intelligence cell in each Headquarters consisting of 2–3 people of deep loyalty towards organization. This cell must keep a watch on all the visitors and employees to gain all the information useful for security and safety of personnel and banking operations.

In bank branches, which operate next to all headquarters, primarily to cater the financial requirements of administration and employees, the collection of information should be more and timely. Vigilance cell must ensure that no unlawful elements move around in this branch as it will be different than the type followed in headquarters. The functions of vigilance cell may be different depending upon the type of headquarters, location and strength of employees, etc.

## *Categories of Bank Branches*

All the bank branches are basically categorized in 'A', 'B', 'C' and 'D' category. The following are criterion on which the category is awarded to a particular branch:

(a) Location (type of city, industries, etc.)

(b) Strength of employees sanctioned.

(c) Amount of fixed deposits, loans and other transactions.

(d) Amount of cash transactions (daily/monthly average of deposit/ withdrawals.)

Banks have two types of Branches, which operate, under a Regional Headquarters i.e. urban branch and rural branch. Normally all urban branches fall under categories from 'A'–'C', whereas rural branches under 'D' categories.

## *Security at Bank Branches*

All the branches functions under the supervision and control of Branch Manager. The staff and operations at each branch will be as per the category awarded to it. The access control at branch of the bank will be different than followed at the headquarters. Since branch will be visited by customers for discussions, advise, deposit and withdrawal of money, etc. the security guard posted at main gate will only keep an eye on all the customers. The guard posted inside the branch must keep a vigilant eye on the movements of all customers. Ensure that no pick pockets, and other unlawful elements operate inside the bank premises. The cash chest/locker in branch have double lock and jointly operated by Branch Manager and Accountant both having one key each. All branches must have "Special Security Instructions for customer" boldly displayed in the premises, the suggested contents are as under:

(a) Be aware of the pickpockets and bag lifters.
(b) Do not take out all money from the bag for counting, etc. except on the deposit counter.
(c) Do not believe any person for the safety of your cash.
(d) Count complete money of withdrawal at the counter before moving out.
(e) Do not accept any exchange of currency notes from unknown person in the bank that may be fake currency.
(f) Do not touch/lift an unescorted bag/briefcase in the bank, it may have bomb/IED. Inform bank officials immediately.
(g) In case of any discrepancy in records or currency payments in respect of withdrawals, inform bank employee on the respective counter.
(h) In case of bank robbery, etc. customers to 'stand' at their respective places, do not try and run here and there. Any stray bullet may hit and cause injury.

## *Security of Cash in Transit*

In all the Bank Branches whether urban or rural, the security of cash in transit is a major responsibility of security officer/staff and Branch Manager. Each day cash is drawn as per daily need from the central treasury chest, vehicle with armed guards (minimum two security guards) and bank accountant proceed with a chest, collect the cash and return to bank branch. In side the branch complete money is kept in the cash chest/locker which have a double lock's system. This is jointly operated by Branch Manager and Accountant.

Cash is issued to the cash counter clerk daily in the morning on cash voucher. After the banking operations are over, the complete transactions are tallied and balance of money is deposited in bank cash chest. Branch Manager must get the insurance arranged for the average amount of maximum cost kept in the bank branch. The following measures are suggested for bank branch to deal with the security and safety of cash in transit:

(a) Vehicle, going for collection/deposit in central treasury chest, must be mechanically in sound conditions.

(b) Minimum two armed security guards and a bank employee should accompany the vehicle.

(c) Average amount of cash being withdrawn or deposited must have adequate insurance cover for "Cash in Transit".

(d) The cash chest must have double lock system for safety purposes.

(e) Arrangements must be made for the cash chest to secure with vehicle by means of iron chain and lock for additional safety.

(f) Once the cash is withdrawn, the vehicle must not halt enroute for tea, water, etc.

(g) The route selected must be such so that vehicle does not have to stop at railway crossing, etc.

(h) Armed guards must be briefed by Branch Manager to take necessary action in case of robbery attempt, etc., enroute.

(i) In case of armed robbery attempt the bank employee must try to note down the BA No. Colour, make of the vehicle being used by the robbers whereas security guards should try to overpower the robber and handover to the police.

### *Action in case of Bank Robbery*

On number of occasions one gets a news of bank robbery/robbery attempt either in a urban or rural branch. Bank robbery is a very critical situation which security officer and bank employees including customers have to face. The gravity of threat will depend upon the number of robbers, types and quantity of weapons/bombs/grenades being carried by them. There can be no hard and fast rules or rigid instructions to counter/foil a robbery attempt. Basically No-two attempts will be similar in nature. Therefore, Branch Manager, security officer and staff must analyze the situation in a cool manner to handle it. Anxiety and confusion may add problem and increase gravity of threat to all present personnel, suggested actions are as under:

(a) The main door security guard should act very cool and try to save the situation by closing main entry into promises, if possible.

(b) If entry is forced he should raise an alarm in loud voice–Robbers–Robbers or in Hindi "DAKU–DAKU", if any electronic alarm or emergency hooter/siren is provided then activate the siren alarm.

(c) Note down or remember BA NO. colour and make of vehicle used by robbers.

(d) Try and identity driver and robbers, if possible.

(e) Once robbers are inside the premises, all customers be advised to stand where ever they are and not to run here and there. A stray bullet may hit them in case of shoot out.

(f) Branch manager or any employee must try to ring up police about robbery.

(g) Depending upon the number of robbers, if possible, security guard on duty in the premises must try to over power the robbers with the help of employees.

(h) Branch manager must try and negotiate with the robbers during conversation try and identify the robbers by their speech, language and tone, etc.

(i) If only cash is required, see if shootout can be avoided, because safety of employees and customers must be at the highest priority. As cash kept in the bank is always insured.

(j) As far as possible employees/customers must not provoke the robbers to start shooting it may cause avoidable injuries.

(k) Try and keep robbers engaged in negotiations till the arrival of police or any other military or para military assistance.

(l) Main gate security guard must try to immobilize the vehicle by some means, so as to avoid the use by robbers, shooting at tyres is considered best.

Bank security Management is a specialized task as it deals with cash and other lucrative documents. Personnel employed on security duties must be properly trained to handle various contingencies. They should be always vigilant and alert to prevent any grave situation or crisis management.

# 19

# Civil Defence Management

## GENERAL

All the industries in a country form part of civil society. All employees are the law abiding citizens living in the societies. The credit of progress and growth of the industries always goes to the sincere employees of the organizations. Any adverse effect on the production level of the industry, either due to external aggression on the nation or due to the internal riots and disturbances, shows on the economic growth of the country, which directly imposes its evil signs on to the society. Therefore, it is of paramount importance that every member of the society does his bit to ensure that any foul attempt on our national integrity or to disturb the peace in society is dealt boldly, firmly and bravely.

### Definition of Civil Defence

All active and passive measures adopted by the civil administration and members of the civil society to guard against and minimize the impact of external aggression in the form of land, air and sea attacks before, during and after the operations or due to civil riots and disturbances.

As it is imperative that all the three defence forces will be involved in fighting with the enemy. Therefore, it is only the civil administration and civil society which has to look after their own security and safety. Thus, the area of civil defence will be widened to include all the industries in the periphery of the operations of civil defence. The security, safety and ensuring optimum level of production in the industries will be one of the primary tasks in the busy set up of civil defence. The final aim of an enemy will always be to force own will on the other nation and degrade the fighting capability of the defence forces, lower the morale of the population by destroying will survive in the event of enemy operations by crippling the economic growth and industrial production. Enemy will always endeavour to inflict heavy losses and damages in terms of civil personnel and property so that the "will" of the entire nation is defeated to fight on the borders, in the skies or at sea. In order to ensure that the nation fights the enemy on all the three fronts with laurels, civil administration and society must join hands and resources together firstly to enhance the fighting ability of defence forces and secondly to ensure that the production level of all the industries are maintained against all odds of war.

## Importance of Civil Defence

As mentioned earlier, civil defence implies to plan, organize and execute, at the time of need, all possible measures for enhancing the country's capability to sustain the entire operations with ease and maintain the morale of civil population in the society so that damages and losses are minimum in terms of personnel and property. It is the defence, by the people of the society, of all the members of the society by gathering and mobilizing all available resources. These are the measures and precautions taken before, during and after the particular land, air or sea operations in civil. The basic tasks, as given in the charter of duties, for civil defence are as follows:

(a) Adopt all possible measures to save lives and minimize injuries.
(b) Ensure no damages/minimum damage, is caused to public, property and industries.
(c) Ensure high level of production with quality is maintained.
(d) Avoid rumours, panic and confusion among public and ensure build up of high morale.
(e) Try and maintain all essential services for the society.

# SUGGESTED CIVIL DEFENCE ORGANIZATION

Warden services are the vital links between the civil administration and Civil Defence Organization. Chief warden of the city is the eminent person of the town who has knowledge, patience and will to work for the cause of the society. Similarly, entire city is divided into Divisions, Sectors and Areas as per the size and population of the city. Accordingly the person, who is detailed as warden in the respective Divisions, Sectors and Areas must be a respected and of good repute in social service. Warden post is the smallest part of the civil defence organization which operates as an individual or group of posts to counter the threats of all attacks and disasters.

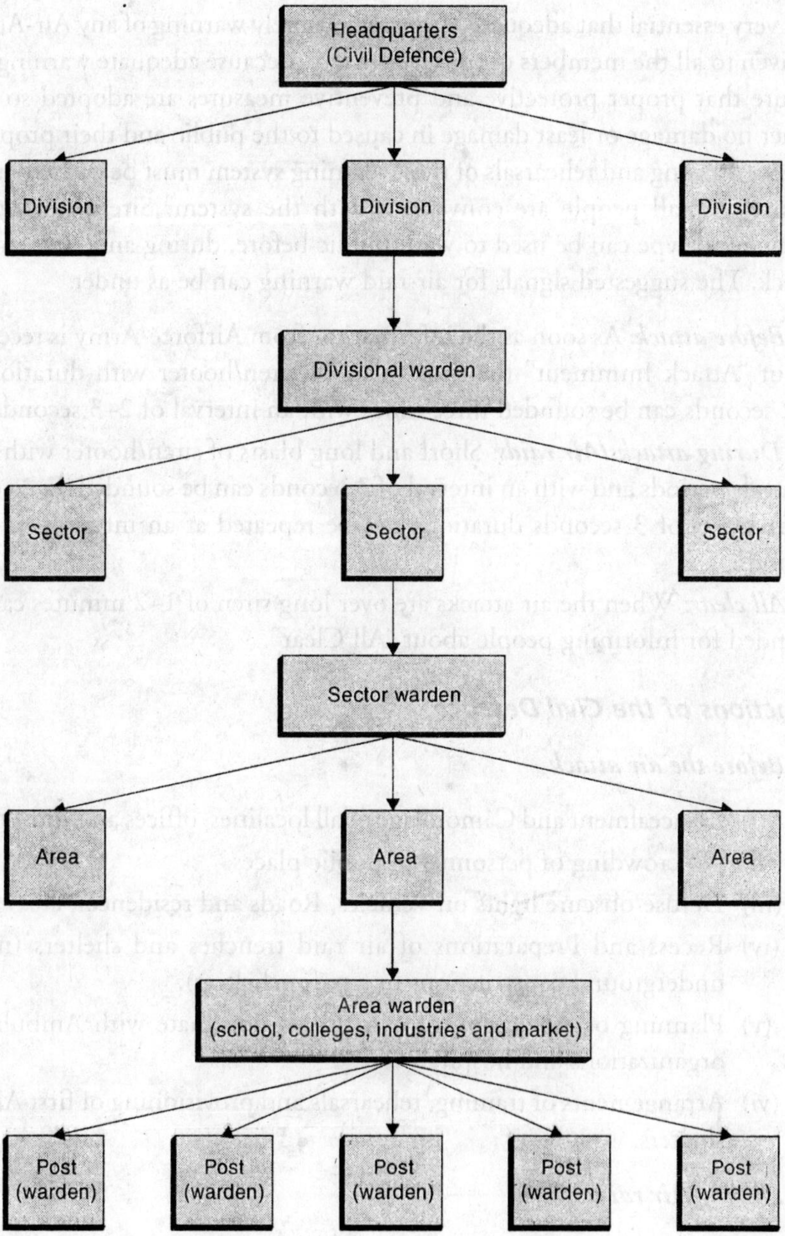


FIG. 19.1 SUGGESTED CIVIL DEFENCE ORGANIZATION

## Civil Warning Procedures

It is very essential that adequate, proper and timely warning of any Air-Attack is given to all the members of the civil society. Because adequate warning can ensure that proper protective and preventive measures are adopted so that either no damage or least damage in caused to the public and their property. Proper training and rehearsals of these warning system must be carried out to ensure that all people are conversant with the system. Sirens/hooters of mechanical type can be used to warn public before, during and after the air attack. The suggested signals for air-raid warning can be as under.

(a) ***Before attack***: As soon as the information from Airforce/Army is received about "Attack Imminent" the short blast of siren/hooter with duration of 1–2 seconds can be sounded three times with an interval of 2–3 seconds.

(b) ***During attacks/Air raids***: Short and long blasts of siren/hooter with 3–5 Seconds periods and with an interval of 3 seconds can be sounded. Even only short blasts of 3 seconds durations can be repeated at an intervals of 4–5 seconds.

(c) ***All clear***: When the air attacks are over long siren of 1–2 minutes can be sounded for informing people about "All Clear".

### *Functions of the Civil Defence*

(a) ***Before the air attack***

(i) Concealment and Camouflage of all localities, offices and Industries.
(ii) No crowding of personnel in public places.
(iii) Defuse/obscure lights on Vehicles, Roads and residences, etc.
(iv) Recess and Preparations of air raid trenches and shelters (mark underground constructions in city for shelters).
(v) Planning of evacuation of casualties-Coordinate with Ambulance organizations and hospitals.
(vi) Arrangements of training, rehearsals and provisioning of first Aid in shelters.

(b) ***During Air raid/attacks***

(i) Reporting of air raids and bomb attacks, etc.
(ii) Arrange evacuation after first aid.
(iii) Rescue casualties who are not able to walk.
(iv) Arrange transport for mass evacuation, if required.

(v) Adequate control of accident/attack sites, no over crowding with spectators.

(vi) Fire fighting.

(c) ***Actions after air raid/attack***

(i) Evaluation and disposal of dead.

(ii) Arrangement for distribution of food, clothing and shelters for all affected areas.

(iii) Salvage of property and assessment of damage.

(iv) Disposal of unexploded Shell/Bombs.

(v) Restoration of road, rail and air traffic.

(vi) Measures of hygene and sanitation.

(vii) Avoid spread of rumours through media.

## Responsibilities of Civil Defence

The basic responsibility of civil defence organizations is to prevent losses, damages and ensure maintenance of public morale at the time of war or civil riots. The main responsibilities can be categorized as under:

(a) ***Control and command, maintenance of communication***: For the success of any operation, there are basic requirements of some command, effective control and an efficient system of communications. Headquarters of civil Defence organization and other subordinate Headquarters are fully dependent on these important means.

(b) ***Rescue organization***: This will consist of various teams living in each part of area of responsibility. Their main tasks will be to locate and extricate different types of air-raid casualties from offices, industries, residential buildings and earmarked trenches/shelters, offer them first aid and evacuate to hospital. The dead bodies will be disposed off as per normal procedures.

(c) ***Casualty services***: These will be divided and located at various safe distances and these teams will provide and establish the following.

(i) First Aid

(ii) First Aid posts.

(iii) Mobile First Aid/surgical units.

(iv) Ambulance parties for evacuations.

(d) ***Fire fighting services***: Due to the air/bomb attacks there are number of instances when fire breaks out in various areas. These services will work in close coordination with normal fire service personnel for better results.

(e) ***Public utility services***: During attacks there are many chances when electricity supply, telephone service, water supply and sewage service, etc. may get disrupted due to heavy damages. These services will try and restore all these at the earliest.

(f) ***Repair and demolition services***: After the attack number of roads and buildings may have to be repaired or demolished for extricating persons and property.

(g) ***Salvage organization***: This is a very important and time consuming task for the personnel of salvage system. Once a residential building, office or Shopping complex is destroyed in attack, various valuable items of property are to be salvaged and kept in the safe custody till the owner arrives and claims it.

(h) ***Avoidance of rumours and panic***: There are number of people who will try and spread rumour to create panic and state of confusion among civil society, Civil Defence personnel must ensure that people are properly briefed about all the activities and their morale is not lowered. But complete civil population must join together to fight together with the enemy indirectly.

## Responsibility of Media

During war or internal disturbances media in every country has to play a very vital and positive role in maintaining the morale of people thus increase the 'will' to fight and defeat the country's enemy at border, skies and at sea. Radio and TV, etc. must give mature and confirm news to the public and no rumours or guess news, etc. At times enemy may try to infiltrate into our radio and TV and broadcast rumours to lower the morale of defence forces and civil populations. At times leaflets containing incorrect pictures/information about actions of our defence forces may be distributed by enemy's agents for spreading panic and confusion among public. These actions must be controlled by media and civil defence organizations. Therefore, there will be a need of morale boosting TV and radio programming and correct news items.

Needless to say civil defence organizations have to play an important role in building up of public morale to fight the enemy and ensure maximum safety and security of personnel and property. Another vital role will be to ensure complete industrial safety and optimum production in the event of crisis.

# 20

# Security Services as—Profession

## GENERAL

In the modern times, security has become an important part of every industry, office and institution, etc. At the same time organizing of security services for any private and or official jobs has taken a shape of a lucrative business. Because all residential societies, offices, commercial complexes, airports, hotels, hospitals, banks and all industrial houses, etc. need some security service in one form or other. With the result innumerable security agencies are coming up in the market in a tuff competition with each other. But the fact remains, that how many are able to provide satisfactory and quality services to their customer by following labour laws and observing government rules in respect of their employees. Most of these agencies take undue advantage of unemployed youth in the society and operate security services by flouting all norms and conditions as laid down by the government.

Many retired Para Military, Police and Defence Services personnel, etc. are also getting lured by this seemingly lucrative business but due to ignorance of rules and regulations get into lots of problem at a later stage. Keeping this in view, an endeavour is being made to provide some "Consolidated Know How" for organizing a better quality and competitive security services/agency.

To start with, a person who plans to organize a security services, must have his own building or office complex, as this is an important and obligatory requirement when the organizer applies for the code number with commissioner of Provident Funds. Before starting any security agency or within two months of business following license/permission must be obtained from the government.

### Sanctions and Permission for Security Agency

(a) Shop Act license for the security agency.

(b) Employees Provident Fund and Miscellaneous Provision Act 1952 code number.

(c) Permission from the office of contract labour (Regulation and Abolition Act 1970).

(d) Code number from the office of "Employees State Insurance Act 1948".

### (a) Shop Act License

Shop Act License is one of the very important requirements for commencing any business, industry or office, etc. Any business/factory employing 'Ten' or more workers have to obtain Shop Act License at least 15 days before starting the business. The organizer must forward the following details to the "Chief Inspector" of the factory at least 15 days before he begins to occupy or use any premises as a factory or office, etc.

(i) The name and situation of the office/Industry.
(ii) The name and address of the occupier.
(iii) The name and address of the owner of the premises or building.
(iv) Permanent address for communications.
(v) The nature of business to be organized.
(vi) Total rated horse power installed in the office/industry.
(vii) The name of the manager for the business.
(viii) The number of workers likely to be employed.
(ix) The average number of workers per day employed during the last twelve months.
(x) Any other miscellaneous information.

### (b) Employees Provident Fund and Miscellaneous Provision Act 1952

The organizer of the security agency has to obtain a " Code Number" from the commissioner of Provident Fund office for all the employees who are employed on wages for any kind of work. Every month the employer has to deduct 8.33% of the monthly pay/wages as Provident Fund and an equal amount will be contributed by the employer in employees wages/salary. The whole amount is deposited as per the code number allotted to the owner of the Industry/Business. The organizer must have office in his/her name.

### (c) Contract Labour (Regulation and Abolition ) Act 1970

As per this law any Business/Industry, employing twenty or more workers, has to obtain license about contract labour employment. The number of twenty is applicable to any contractor who employed on any day of the preceding twelve months twenty or more workmen.

### (d) Code Number From Employee's State Insurance Act 1948

The organizer of the security Agency/Industry has to obtain "Code Number" from the office of employee's state Insurance Act 1948 in respect of all the employees who are working in the Agency. Under this act all amount of insurance for each employee has to be deducted from his salary/wages every month and deposited as monthly premium towards insurance under the allotted code number. Normally all the security Agencies are planned and run on proprietary basis. There fore, it is obligatory to obtain/apply in advance for the above-mentioned licenses and code numbers, etc.

Once the formalities of licenses and permissions are over, the next step is to plan the strategy of the impending security organization. In this, another important is this, that whether the organizer is planning to provide security services to only private sector business/industrial houses or to the Public sectors undertakings as well. In case the security services are to be provided to Government organizations/Industries, then the organizer has to register his Agency with the "Director General of Resettlement at Army Headquarters New Delhi" (DGR).

*The Director General of Resettlement (DGR) requirements*

For registering, the security Agency the DGR'S requirements are as follows:

(a) Must be a retired defence services officer.
(b) Must have undergone a recognized diploma in Industrial security.
(c) Must have obtained all necessary sanctions and licenses from the government offices.
(d) Employees must be retired defence force, para military and police personnel.

## Organization Recruitment and Training

Once the organizer has planned to operate a security service, he must also think of a workable, efficient and an effective organization. On the basis of such organizational plan, the entire recruitment and training will commence. There is no laid down organization for a security agency, however, a suggested organization depending upon the requirement of security guards the whole organizational chart can be formulated as under:

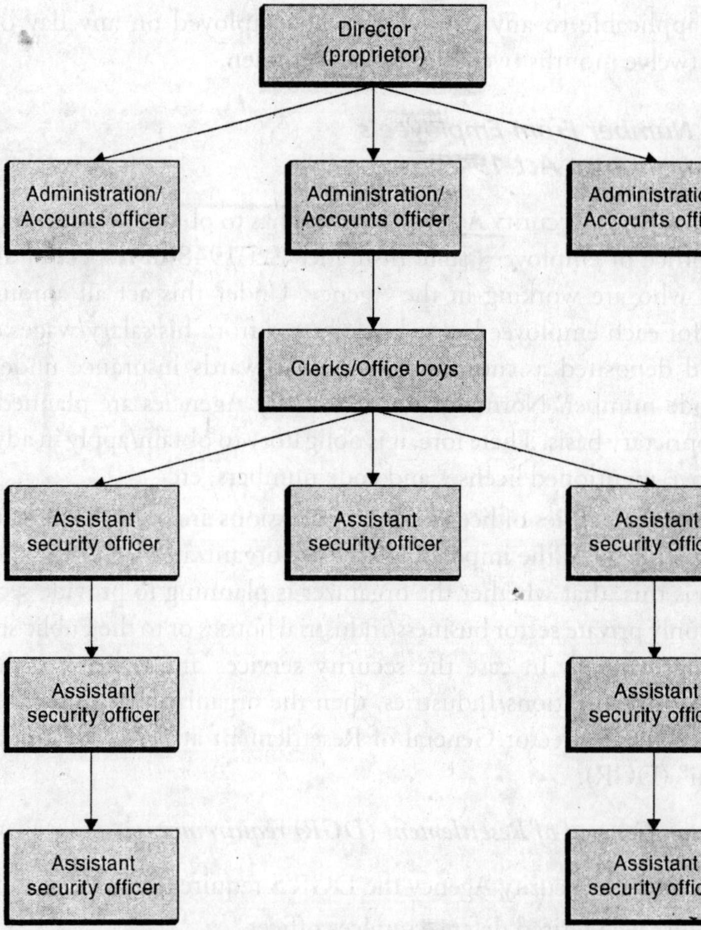


FIG. 20.1 SUGGESTED—ORGANIZATION

The organization must be flexible and workable. The director can employ one or more security officers for supervision and a suitable number of staff to deal with administration and accounts, etc. Under the security officer, one or two Assitt. Security Officers to supervise and check turnout, punctuality and discipline of the security guards. Assitt. Security Officer can be assisted, depending on the size and number of units where the services are provided by adequate number of security supervisors. Each supervisor will be fully responsible for suitable number of security guards, The number of Assitt. Security Officers and security supervisors are directly related to the demands made by various industries and other organizations.

### Recruitment

The recruitment of the officers, supervisor and security guards must be rigid and of quality. Otherwise the reputation of the security Agency will be spoiled with in no time. Preferably, organizer must recruit all the personnel who are ex-defence forces; para military and police personnel. Because generally these will be having basic security training, disciplined, physically fit and dedicated to the assigned duties. However, educated, physically fit and disciplined youth from the civil may also be recruited for the job. Personnel, who have been discharged from the services on disciplinary grounds, must not be recruited for the job. Organizer must get all the people verified from the police from security point of view. Female security guards should also be recruited for various industries/complexes.

### Training

Basically all the ex-defence forces, Para military and police personnel are trained for carrying out security guard duties. But still adequate training in Industrial security, handling of modern electronic gadgets and fire fighting equipments must be arranged at various levels for running an efficient and effective security Agency.

## Turn Out and Discipline

All the security supervisors and guards must be well turned out in smart uniform which can be as under:

(a) Peak cap/Baret/Pagri.
(b) Shirt and Trouser (must be of different colour than uniform of Defence Services).
(c) Belt (Leather/Web).
(d) Laneyard.
(e) Agency's arm badge and shoulder titles.
(f) Boot/Shoes with socks.
(g) Whistle.
(h) Cane (on need basis).

At least two pair of uniform should be issued to each person. It must be ensured that they are well dressed, have good haircut and daily shave (excluding 'SIKHS') for a smart and disciplined appearance. All security personnel must be briefed to be vigilant, alert, polite but firm while on duty and dealing with employees of the Industry/Organization and visitors, etc. Security personnel must have their eyes and ears open all the times on duty.

## Checks and Liaison

Security officer and Assitt. Security officer must carry out periodical checks of the security personnel on duty during day and also at night. They must meet the factories/Office Administration Manager and security officer frequently to get the feedback and efficiency/drawbacks of the services provided. Any disciplinary case must be dealt forthwith by investigating in details and action taken accordingly. Occasional visits and liaison will provide the inside report about functional ability of the security of the Security Agency. Proprietor/Director of the Agency must carry out proper liaison with the Head of Administration/Security of the Industry/Organization to get the proper feedback on the overall efficiency of the Agency.

## Administration and Documentation

The organizer of the security must follow all the rules of Provident Fund and state Insurance Act. Besides, the agency should adhere to the following labour laws for efficient administration.

(a) Factory's Act 1948.
(b) Industrial Dispute Act 1947.
(c) Minimum wages Act 1948.
(d) Payment of Bonus Act 1965.
(e) Payment of Gratuity Act 1972.
(f) Payment of Wages Act 1936.
(g) Workmen's Compensation Act 1923.

The organizing of a security Agency is a very challenging task in the modern competitive scenario. However, if one plans in a systematic way and then proceeds as per all norms of the profession, chances are bright that it will bring laurels. One should not get involved in illegal activities to avoid various government formalities as terms and conditions of organizing a security service.

# Bibliography


1. "Analyzing Arson After the Fact", *Security World*, 17(03), 1980.
2. Arnold M. Zais, "Safeguard your Conversations", *Security Management*, 26(02), 1982.
3. Belden Menkus, "Protecting Information Assets", *Security Management*, 20(03), 1976.
4. Carrol John M, "3 Missions for CCTV in Physical Security Detection, Surveillance and Access Control", *Security World*, 16(02), 1979.
5. "Changing Need in Security Communications", *Security Gazette*, 21(05), 1979.
6. Chris David, "False Alarms, Finding the Answers", *Security Gazette*, September 1984.
7. Dey Sc and Sc Kaushal, *Industrial Security Management*, Ashish Publishing House, New Delhi, 1993.
8. Egesdal SE.PE, "The Basis of Fire Alarm Systems", *Security Management*, July 1980.
9. *Fiber Optics for Fences Security Gazette*, December 1984.
10. Fisher A. James, *Security for Business and Industry*, Prentice Hall Inc., Englewood Cliffs, New Jersey, 07 632.
11. Frances J. D'addario, "Development of Security Self-efficiency", *Security Management*, 21 (01), 1977.
12. Frederick E. Hernon, "Management Rules on White Collar Crime", *Security World*, 13 (01), 1976.
13. William C. Garrett, *Infra-red Motion Sensor Evaluation Report*, 2237 Meras com, Fort Belvoir, VA, March 1978.
14. *Growing Markets for Security Monitors and Alarm Services*, Business Communication Co. Inc. Stanford, CT, 06906.

15. Harrison R. Cooper, Bill H. Lane and Francis E. Rutherford, "Metal Detectors, Come of Age", *Security Management*, 20(05), 1976.
16. Gregg E. Powell, "Identification Cards How to Select Them, Part-II", *Security World*, 12 (04), 1975.
17. James D. Kloss and Edward R. Christopherson, "A Behavioural Approach to Supervision", *Security Management*, 20(01),1976.
18. John Strauchs, "Getting Active About Passive Infra-red", *Security Management*, 26(06), 1982.
19. John V. Pulcini, "Cost Effectiveness in Access Control, *Security Management*, 20(05), 1976.
20. J. White House, "The Future of CCTV", *Security Gazette*, September 1984.
21. S.K. Kulkarni, *Industrial Security Management*, Everest Publishing House, Pune, 1988.
22. Lawrance M. Yaggi Jr., "CCTV as a Multi-building Access Control System", *Security Management*, 21(05), 1977.
23. Michael A. Agranogg, "An Evolution of Perimeter Protection Systems Available", *Security Management*, 21(05), 1977.
24. W.E. Oaborne, "Passive Infra-red Comes of Age", *Security World*, 14(05), 1977.
25. "Photo Infra Red Devices Inevitable for Schools", *Security Management*, 21(01), 1977.
26. "Reaping Protection Rewards from Audio Alarms and Invisible Beams", *Security World*, 16(01), 1979.
27. Sally A. Matleson, "Smoke Detectors Complete Industrial Fire Protection Cycle", *Security World*, 16(03), 1979.
28. San Luis Ed., "Office and Office Building Security", *Security World*, Publishing Co. Inc.
29. Stanley H. Leberstein, "How to Keep Trade Secret, A Secret", *Security Management*, 23(07), 1979.
30. Wayne Siatt, "Adding Access Control, To Control Station Monitoring, *Security World*, 19(03), 1982.
31. Wayne Siatt, "Risk Management, Balancing Threats and Protection", *Security World*, 18(04), 1981.
32. Weber Thad L., "Alarm System and Theft Prevention", *Security World*, 1981.